St. Laurence
The Holy Grail

St. Laurence & The Holy Grail

The Story of The Holy Chalice of Valencia

Janice Bennett

IGNATIUS PRESS   SAN FRANCISCO

" For my husband, *Jim*, our children *Scott* and *Anne*, and in memory of *St. Laurence* and the *Martyrs of the Spanish Civil War* "

Original edition published in 2002 by
Libri de Hispania, Littleton, Colorado
Publications about Spain
Copyright © 2002 by Janice Bennett
All rights reserved, including the right of
reproduction in whole or in part in any form.
Design by Scott Wilson

New edition published in 2004 by Ignatius Press, San Francisco
Printed by permission of Janice Bennett
Copyright © 2004 by Janice Bennett
ISBN 1-58617-075-9
Library of Congress control number 2004111616
Printed in Hong Kong

Contents

Contents

Illustrations

Cover: The Holy Chalice of Valencia as it appears today in the Cathedral.

Back cover: The first-century agate cup of the Holy Chalice, believed to be that used by Jesus to consecrate the wine into his blood. Courtesy of the Spanish Center for Sindonology.

Dust Cover Background: Getty Images/Photodisc.

exposed for the veneration of the monks during the Middle Ages.

11. The Eucharistic miracle of Daroca, associated with the Spanish Reconquest and impetus for the Corpus Christi celebration.

12. The Cathedral of Valencia, now gloriously restored after the desecration and burning of the Spanish Civil War.

13. *a.* The Cathedral of Valencia with the Chapel of the Holy Grail to the right of the entrance. *b.* The Door of the Apostles.

14. Interior of the Chapel of the Holy Grail.

15. *a.* Close-up of the Tabernacle of the Holy Grail. *b.* First Communicants listen as a priest narrates how St. Laurence saved the Holy Grail from the Romans.

16. Painting of the Last Supper by Juan de Juanes, depicting the Holy Chalice of Valencia. Museo del Prado, Madrid.

17. The Roca del Santo Grial and a photograph of Pope John Paul II blessing it in Rome in 1996. The Holy Father said Mass with the Holy Chalice during his visit to Spain in 1982.

18. Floral display of the Holy Chalice for the Corpus Christi procession of June 2001, and a detail of the Roca del Santo Grial.

19. The Corpus Christi procession in Madrid, June of 2000, and Valencia, June of 2001.

20. *a.* Roman cups in the British Museum, dated 1-50 AD, made of chalcedony and sardonyx, similar in style to the original agate cup of the Holy Chalice. *b.* Roman fine-ware cup with a sanded surface, from Tharros, Sardinia, about 10 BC to 50 AD. British Museum, London.

21. *a.* Roman fine-ware cups made in Italy about 1-70 AD. *b.* 'The Crawford Cup" of fluorspar, Roman, made about 50-100 AD. The emperor Nero (54-68 AD) is said to have paid a million sesterces for a fluorspar cup. *c.* Roman kotyle (drinking cup), made in Asia Minor in the 1st century AD. *d.* A pair of Roman silver cups from Asia Minor, about 1-30 AD.

22. The Cathedral of Huesca, entryway and details of Sts. Laurence and Vincent, cousins martyred nearly fifty years apart, the first in Rome and the second in Spain.

23. Representations of Sts. Laurence and Vincent in the Cathedral of Huesca.

24. The Hermitage of Loreto and detail of the façade depicting St. Laurence, constructed on the family farm of Sts. Orencio and Paciencia, his parents.

25. *a.* Cross at the site of the family farm. *b.* Road sign marking the spot

where, according to Huesca's tradition, the parents of St. Laurence would greet their twin sons Laurence and Orencio as they returned home from school.

Percival and Galahad with the Holy Grail.

Preface

The quest for the Holy Grail is a subject that usually provokes interest and discussion, often evoking images of medieval knights, archaeological digs, and a countless number of chalices with claims of authenticity, as portrayed in the film *The Last Crusade*. Most Americans imagine that this most sacred relic of Christianity, speaking of it in the most widely accepted meaning of the term,[1] as the cup used by Jesus of Nazareth to institute the Eucharist at the Last Supper, was taken by Joseph of Arimathea to England soon after the crucifixion. Knowledge of its whereabouts was soon lost, which instigated an exhaustive, but unsuccessful, quest for the Holy Grail during the Middle Ages that was carried out by valiant knights in shining armour. In recent times, when someone claims to have unearthed the sacred relic in some unlikely location, the vast majority will follow the story with avid interest, hoping that the elusive cup has finally been found. The same is true for most other relics, such as the recently claimed discovery of the entire crown of thorns that was supposedly buried in Syria with the body of one of the Knights Templar, or the "discovery" of Jesus' garden tomb by British archaeologists. The fact that the article concerning the crown of thorns appeared in *The National Enquirer* did not deter many otherwise intelligent people from accepting its validity, in spite of the fact that its thorns have been in the cathedrals and churches of Europe for centuries. Concerning the popular garden tomb in Jerusalem, a British guide remarked to me at the site that St. Helen could not possibly have discovered the tomb of Jesus in the fourth century, simply because

---

[1] Many people believe that the grail was not necessarily a cup. For example, Graham Hancock believes that the Grail is the Ark of the Covenant, and Dr. Daniel Scavone, Shroud scholar, is convinced that it is the Shroud of Turin.

she was *not* a British archaeologist. The veneration in the Church of the Holy Sepulcher from the time of Constantine the Great is dismissed as insignificant, in spite of the fact that so many prominent archaeologists have extensively studied the site, and remain convinced that it is the *Golgotha* of the crucifixion.

The reality is, however, that Christians did not bury the relics of Christ. From the first moments of Christianity, the objects used and worn by Jesus were thought to be sacred and were employed, first by Mary and the Apostles, as part of the Mass and other prayer rituals, and later deposited in the bosom of the Church as its priceless treasures. When necessary for security reasons, relics were hidden, but they were always painstakingly safeguarded by those responsible for their care. Often security demanded the absence of written documentation, but tradition kept alive the knowledge of their whereabouts in the Christian communities. When political dangers passed, the relics would resurface, to be venerated once again by the faithful as part of the depository of their faith. A relic without a history rich in tradition and veneration would have to pass especially strict criteria to be considered authentic, given the nature of Christianity.

Typical American beliefs about the Holy Grail are not the case, however, in Spain, a country that because of its geographical isolation and staunch Catholicism has become the final resting place for more than its share of relics. Although it may be true that Spaniards have become more skeptical and indifferent in recent years, perhaps due to the overabundance of relics in their churches and cathedrals, many of them trivial and rather dubious, as well as the modern belief that such objects are of no importance whatsoever, certain things are taken for granted, one of them being the presence of the Holy Grail in the Cathedral of Valencia. It is venerated daily in a small chapel to the right of the front entrance, called the *Capilla del Santo Grial*, or Chapel of the Holy Grail. Many visitors seem unimpressed when they view the small agate cup mounted on a medieval base of gold, pearls, and precious stones, perhaps because they do not

---

[2] St. Helen is the mother of Constantine the Great, who was proclaimed the first western emperor in 312 AD. After Constantine became sole emperor of East and West in 324, his mother went to Palestine to venerate the holy places. She is credited with removing the terrace and temple of Venus that the Emperor Hadrian had built over Golgotha and the holy sepulcher. Constantine ordered a church to be built, and St. Helen took charge of the execution of this work. The Church of the Holy Sepulcher in Jerusalem is today considered one of the holiest places of Christianity.

comprehend exactly what they are seeing, and because the reality of its presence can never quite measure up to the mystical Grail visions of Percival and Lancelot, nor to the idealized notion of the quest, glorified in the legends and films. A concrete object being venerated in a cathedral lacks that indefinable, elusive quality that has turned the Grail into a transcendental symbol of eternal life.

Nevertheless, the Holy Chalice of Valencia possesses a history rich in tradition, complete with tales of greed, bribery and murder, miracles, veneration, and enough historical material to make a Hollywood film capable of surpassing all known classical epics. Its story deserves to be written in English, because although it has been studied in depth by a Spanish archaeologist and its custodians from the Cathedral of Valencia have carefully recorded its history, it has not yet captured the interest of Americans, who are generally unaware of its existence. I discovered the Holy Chalice during my extensive travels in Spain. The first time I saw it, I must admit that I was a bit like the typical American visitor described above, thinking something along the lines of, "Why haven't I heard of it before?" After subsequent visits, reading the published material in Spanish, and researching the original sources in the Biblioteca Nacional of Madrid, I am convinced that it is without doubt one of the most interesting, priceless relics of the Catholic Church, along with the Shroud of Turin and the Sudarium of Oviedo, the companion cloth believed to have covered the head of Jesus after the crucifixion. I am a member of the Spanish Center of Sindonology (CES), the association responsible for the scientific studies done on the latter cloth and wrote and published a book about their findings, called *Sacred Blood, Sacred Image: The Sudarium of Oviedo, New Evidence for the Authenticity of the Shroud of Turin*. The Spanish Sindonologists have also professed an interest in the Holy Chalice, having published several articles in their publication, *LINTEUM*.

While researching this book, my husband and I travelled to three of the traditional hiding places of the Holy Grail: San Pedro de Siresa, San Adrián de Sasabe, and San Juan de la Peña, all secluded monasteries in the Pyrenees. The voyage to San Pedro is absolutely breathtaking, along narrow mountain roads over deep gorges that would make an inexperienced driver cringe with terror. The church is one of the oldest in Spain, but has been beautifully restored to its former glory. San Adrián, on the other hand, is a tiny church built over its predecessor, Santa María, in a location that makes one wonder why anyone would ever build a temple at that site. After inching up a pebble road in the rental car to a site high in the mountains, only a small sign next to the road is evidence that a church lies nestled somewhere in the area, because it is invisible from a distance of twenty feet. Constructed at the point where two brooks converge, the monastery is practically inaccessible, except by crossing the rapidly flowing water balancing oneself on the rocks, hoping and praying not to stumble. The monastery is surrounded by a deep trench, the reason why it is nearly invisible to passersby, not that there are many, or ever were. The inside is flooded, at least in the springtime, and its dark interior evokes a deep sense of mystery. The camera flash later revealed mysterious shadows on the walls, strangely reminiscent of human forms, that with a bit of imagination could be perceived as the ancient Knights Templar in procession. San Juan de la Peña, on the other hand, is truly a marvel of architecture, a monastery built into a cave under a massive rock at the top of a mountain that has always been shrouded in legend, tradition, and history. Entering into its sacred enclosure, the visitor is immediately transported back in time, reminded of its former inhabitants by the mounds of skulls and bones, as well as the replica of the Holy Grail that adorns a long table under the central arched vault.

The histories of the Holy Chalice of Valencia, published in Spanish, claim that a letter, written by St. Laurence himself, accompanied the relic to Spain, but that it was lost. Reference to the original, however, is made in an existing manuscript found at the monastery of San Juan de la Peña. This is supposedly the only written documentation of the tradition that St. Laurence, days before his martyrdom in Rome in 258 AD, sent the Holy Grail to Spain. I have found another manuscript, however, in the Biblioteca Nacional of Madrid, which contains a direct reference to the fact that St. Laurence was entrusted with the relic by Pope Sixtus II, and that very shortly before his martyrdom, Laurence in turn surrendered it to Precelius, a Spaniard who was in Rome at the time. The manuscript was first written in Latin by St. Donato, an African monk from the second half of the sixth century, who lived in the area of Valencia and founded a monastery on the promontory near Jávea. It was translated in 1636 by a priest from Salamanca, using the pseudonym of Fr. Buenaventura Ausina. Because this document contains many details of the life of St. Laurence that have never been published, it is completely translated into English. I have made the same attempt to preserve the flavor and tone of the original as was made by its seventeenth-century translator, who declared that he changed only what was absolutely necessary for comprehension from the Latin original.

Donato's manuscript will be compared with other versions of the life of St. Laurence, such as the Prudentius' poem and the *Passio Polychronii*, long considered as two of the major biographical sources for St. Laurence. They differ markedly, especially in style, but also in the sense that Donato's account contains unknown details of the life of St. Laurence, from the period before his family left Spain, to their life in Italy. It clarifies many of the contradictions and mistakes that are still being published, such as the notion that Laurence was born and raised in Huesca, left for Italy with his cousin Vincent as a young adult, and sent the Grail back to his parents. I have been able to verify the facts of this manuscript with information from the early seventeenth-century manuscript, *Anales del Reyno de Valencia*, written by Francisco Diago, which confirms that Laurence was born in Valencia, not Huesca, and also records the historically significant surrender of the Holy Cup of the Last Supper to St. Laurence.

Because the St. Laurence tradition is central to the story of the Holy Chalice of Valencia, I will dedicate the final chapter to veneration of the saint in Huesca, the city in Spain where Laurence's family originated. Huesca has many churches dedicated to St. Laurence, among them the sanctuary of Loreto, built on the site believed to be the former farm of his parents; the Basilica of St. Laurence, where special veneration takes place every year on August 10, the feast day of the saint; and San Pedro el Viejo, which tradition maintains was where the family worshiped so long ago. Huesca has developed their own tradition concerning the martyr that conflicts somewhat with historical reality, but it is interesting nonetheless.

The Corpus Christi procession in Valencia is perhaps one of the most impressive in Spain, with its countless floats and costumed participants that flow from the Cathedral's Door of the Apostles into the streets, where the entire city, visitors and inhabitants alike, gathers to welcome them. It culminates with the priceless Monstrance of the Blessed Sacrament, which is greeted with prayers, applause, and genuflections. Central to the procession is the *Roca del Grial*, a float depicting the Holy Chalice of Valencia, which was taken to Rome in 1996 to be blessed by Pope John Paul II. Every year the Holy Chalice is also represented in a unique floral display. Many of these images of the priceless relic will also be discussed, which form an important part of its patrimony, as well as the relationship between the Eucharistic Miracle of Daroca and the Holy Chalice of Valencia, and their connection to the Corpus Christi celebration.

Drawing of the Holy Chalice

This book does not attempt to narrate the story of the Holy Cup in the form of a novel, but is instead a documentation of its traditions and history in English, with references to historical sources. I will present the information in a manner that is as interesting as possible to the non-scholarly reader, with the hope that the human mind and imagination will be capable of providing the rest □

Janice Bennett

Littleton, Colorado, January 2002

16

Part 1

THE RELIC PAR EXCELLENCE

In like manner, after He had supped, taking also this excellent chalice into His holy and venerable hands, and giving Thee thanks, He blessed, and gave to His disciples, saying: Take and drink ye all of this, For this is the Chalice of My Blood of the new and eternal Testament, the Mystery of Faith; which shall be shed for you and for many unto the remission of sins.

The Canon of the Mass

Chapter 1

IN SEARCH OF THE HOLY GRAIL

I ndiana Jones in *The Last Crusade* is a modern personification of Percival and the Knights of the Round Table in the legends of the medieval grail cycle. Jones is an archaeologist who sets out in search of the Holy Grail, conquering numerous obstacles along the way just as did the legendary knights, until he finally finds the grail in Jordan's ancient city of Petra. But, alas, it is mixed in with a collection of chalices, and only the wise man can discern which one is authentic. Indiana reasons that the cup of a carpenter would have been very simple and humble, and instead of reaching for one of the more elaborate chalices encrusted with jewels, he takes the wooden one. This, of course, is one of the fallacies of the film, because wood was never used for drinking vessels in ancient Israel. It was too porous, and considered to be impure, especially for the very religious and holy ceremonies of Passover. In fact, even clay cups, the most common first-century drinking vessel, were not generally used for the special Seder meal for this reason, at least by those families rich enough to afford the more expensive stone cups in vogue at that time.

The Holy Chalice of Valencia is an ancient agate cup that fits this description perfectly. In the 1960s, the Spanish archaeologist from Zaragoza, Antonio Beltrán, determined that the upper cup, but not the golden chalice on which it rests, dates to the first century. The golden chalice, encrusted with jewels and pearls, on which the agate cup is mounted, was joined to the original relic in the Middle Ages, from the time when the Holy Chalice was in San Juan de la Peña, added in order to make the original agate cup seem more worthy of what it really is: the cup used by Jesus to consecrate his blood at the Last Supper. In fact, this agate cup also perfectly matches the description of two first century Roman cups in the British Museum, dated from 1-50 AD and made of chalcedony and sardonyx, similar stones.

The Holy Chalice of Valencia, as already mentioned, is a relic rich in tradition, history, legend, archaeological interest, and art. Tradition affirms that St. Peter, the first Pope, used it to say Mass, and that after the death of the Virgin Mary, he took it to Rome where the first Popes continued the tradition for more than two hundred years. During the Roman persecution of Valerian, the Church was no longer permitted to have property and possessions of its own. So when the Romans demanded the goods of the Church from Pope Sixtus II in the year 258 AD, he entrusted his deacon and treasurer, Laurence, with all of the ecclesiastical money and possessions, including the Grail. When the Romans arrested Laurence and demanded that he turn over the goods, Laurence devised a plan: he asked for a period of three days to collect everything, and used the time instead to disperse it, knowing that he would be martyred just as the Pope had been. He entrusted the Holy Cup of the Last Supper to a compatriot in Rome at the time, with orders to send it immediately to Spain, their homeland. The Romans were so angry at their loss that they did not martyr Laurence in the same way they had killed the Pope, by beheading him. Instead, they devised a torture that was the most hideous and painful ever employed until that time: they tortured him in every way possible, and then condemned him to a slow death over hot coals. The martyrdom of Laurence was so special that it was later immortalized in poems, stories, architecture and art, and the same can be said for his surrender of the Grail to the Spaniard, a most heroic action that cost the saint his life.

In Spain the relic is just as rich in tradition and history. Although there is no extant written documentation of the Holy Chalice until 1399, when it was turned over to King Martín el Humano (the Humane) from its home in San Juan de la Peña, tradition strongly maintains that it was in many locales prior to being safeguarded by the monks in their monastery, built into a natural cave in the mountains. There is evidence of it having been at Huesca, Jaca, the cave of Yebra, San Pedro de Siresa and San Adrián de Sasabe, where it was venerated and kept free from danger before and after the Moorish invasion of Spain in 711 AD. Even after the Holy Chalice was surrendered to the Cathedral of Valencia, it was still not safe from greed and plots to steal it. During the Spanish Civil War (1936–1939) the precious relic was protected from the riotous crowds of revolutionaries only moments before they burst into the sacred enclosure of the Cathedral. A woman carried it in her arms, wrapped in a newspaper, through the throngs of Communists, and hid it in a secret compartment that was built into a wardrobe.

The Marxists later ransacked her apartment trying to find it. Although they were only inches from its hiding place, the relic remained undiscovered, and the merciless revolutionaries would have killed her if it were not for the kindness of one of them, who risked his own life by urging his companions to spare hers. The chalice was then hidden in other unlikely places, including a trash cupboard in the kitchen of the home of this woman's brother, under the cushions of a sofa, and finally in a niche hollowed out in the stone wall of another home, whose owner had no idea of what it contained until the end of the war when it was removed and restored to the Cathedral.

The stories are amazing tales of saintly courage versus ruthless, satanic greed and hatred, and all point to the authenticity of that simple agate cup. It is not very likely that Romans, Moors, Crusaders and Marxists would all have so much interest in a fake relic of Christianity, because they destroyed so many religious objects of much greater material value. It is even reported that a group of Jews from Holland offered large sums of money to obtain the cup, with the threat of death for non-compliance to their wishes, but all to no avail because those responsible for its safekeeping, like St. Laurence, would have rather suffered martyrdom than surrender their precious relic.

Veneration of the Holy Chalice is another important and moving testimony to authenticity, with devotions, Masses, processions and other rituals that have been carried out through the centuries, without interruption save for the brief periods when the relic was hidden during the War of Independence and the Spanish Civil War. In 1959 the Holy Chalice embarked on a very special journey to the cities and monasteries of its past, greeted by all with inspiring displays of affection and reverence. Aside from the solemn and majestic Corpus Christi procession, the Holy Cup has its own special feast day in October when it is once again paraded through the streets of its beautiful city to be venerated by nearly every resident and visitor capable of standing in the crowds.

The Holy Chalice of Valencia has also had its share of archaeological interest, similar to that shown in the Grail by the world famous archaeologist Indiana Jones in *The Last Crusade*, but without the pitfalls. Antonio Beltrán from the University of Zaragoza was granted permission in the 1960s to conduct an exhaustive study of the relic, which led to the publication of his findings. He emphatically affirms that the upper cup could have been on the table of the Last Supper, and that even if someone were to question some of his affirmations and hypotheses, the likelihood that the upper cup of the Holy Chalice is that of the

Last Supper would still remain on firm ground. Even today, the Cathedral receives many proposals for study from scientists all over the world, who like Beltrán, would love the opportunity to examine the cup. As the Spanish writer Salvador Antuñano Alea humourously remarks, "If Indiana Jones had visited Valencia instead of paying attention to ancient medieval legends, he would have avoided all of the dangers of *The Last Crusade*.[3]"

As this same writer has pointed out, the Catholic Church has always venerated relics, from the very first days of Christianity, but this veneration is now criticized by many people, especially since the Protestant Reformation. Today some Catholics scorn the veneration of relics as a medieval and passé practice that should be abandoned in favour of a faith that they believe must be limited to pure spirituality, free from dependence on material objects for inspiration. As a member of a Spanish organisation that is dedicated to studying the relics of Christ, I am sometimes asked why we are wasting our time, and what our studies have to do with belief in Jesus. "Isn't faith enough?" they ask.

The answer is, "Of course." But as someone who has spent a great deal of time during the past five years investigating and writing about relics, I would add that although faith is sufficient when speaking about salvation, studying the history of relics has been one of the most enlightening, fascinating, spiritual, and faith-filled experiences of my entire life. From a historical perspective, through the study of relics I have penetrated into the mindset of the early Christian Church, beginning from the time of the Apostles. Relics for the early Church were a concrete link to Jesus, and a reminder of what he had suffered. As such, they were used in worship as a way of keeping his memory alive. When we understand the heroism of a saint like Laurence, who died a very slow and painful death in order to protect the Church's possessions, it is impossible to say that relics are not important. Today, the relic he saved with his life reminds us of the value of his martyrdom, and of that of so many other saints who died rather than compromise with the forces of evil. The Roman persecution of Christians ended shortly after Laurence's death, which strengthened the Catholic Church all over the world. Meditating on his life and on what he and his family considered important has been a deeply spiritual experience for me. It has taught me that we all too easily blend in with the anti-Christian values of modern society, instead of

---

[3] *El Misterio del Santo Grial* (Valencia: Kairos Media and EDICEP, 1999), p.17.

being willing to face the consequences of standing up for our beliefs and values with courage and conviction. I don't know any Christians who are quite like Laurence, his parents, and his cousin Vincent, all martyred for what many would claim today was not important enough to merit the sacrifice of their lives. The heroism of the twentieth-century Spanish martyrs, killed during the Civil War of 1936-1939, is generally ignored, in spite of the fact that many are now being canonized.

In the case of the Sudarium of Oviedo, another impressive relic believed to have covered the head of Jesus after the crucifixion, the scientific investigation of the bloodstains has revealed so much information about the pain that Jesus suffered for our salvation: the wounds he suffered, the nature of crucifixion, and the manner of death. It corroborates the Gospel of John 20:5-8, which has never been completely understood, offering a very concrete explanation for what John was talking about when he mentioned the "cloth that had been on the head of Jesus." I cannot believe that this is useless. On the contrary, studying this relic has strengthened my faith considerably, enabling me to understand the value and importance of the Crucifixion to a much greater extent, and contributing to a deeper appreciation for the care and veneration this linen has received in the Catholic Church throughout the ages, in spite of the fact that its caretakers didn't really understand what it was. The Sudarium of Oviedo also authenticates the Shroud of Turin, with its incredible image of the face of Jesus, because the stains and their position are so identical that the possibility that they did not cover the same person, Jesus, is perhaps two million to one. The painting done from the image that appears on the Shroud is now the first thing I see when I wake up in the morning, a vivid reminder of Jesus and his great love for all of us. When I look at it, I remember the great pain he suffered, and know that he is still alive. It is a beautiful gift for mankind, the only sign we should ever need to survive life's challenges to our faith. Relics can be a wonderful means of leading Christians to prayer and a greater love for Christ.

Concerning the veneration of relics, the Church maintains that it is a form of piety for the religious sense of the Christian people, which has always found expression in various forms of devotion surrounding the Church's sacramental life, such as the veneration of relics, visits to sanctuaries, pilgrimages, processions, the stations of the cross, religious dances, the rosary, medals, etc. They extend the liturgical life of the Church, but do not replace it.[4] We can understand the Church's esteem for relics in the Canon Law that prohibits selling them under any circumstances, or transferring without permission from the Holy See those being widely venerated, as well as asking that the ancient tradition of placing relics of the saints under the altar of churches be preserved.[5] No one would argue the value of a pilgrimage, the rosary, or the Stations of the Cross, because they are all popular forms of piety in the Church today. Likewise, the Christian community has always felt great esteem for relics and has used them as a means of catechesis and worship.

The word "relic," *reliquia* in Latin, originally meant "what had been," as Salvador Antuñano Alea explains.[6] The first Christians collected the remains of "what had been" of their brothers and sisters who were thrown to the lions, or burned as Laurence, just as Nicodemus and Joseph of Arimathea took the body of Jesus, in order to bury the mortal remains, but not in the sense of a normal burial. A martyr was a *witness* to Christ – the meaning of the word in Greek – and the bodies of those who had sealed their faith with their blood and who had been faithful to the end, like Jesus, were a symbol of faith in the Resurrection for the early Christians. For that reason they began to celebrate Mass over the tombs of the early martyrs, as a sign of communion and veneration, and of the inspiration that their example, or their testimony, gave them in those times of turbulence. The catacombs of Rome are filled with small chapels and altars that were placed over the tombs of the martyrs.

Later, during times of peace, churches were built over the tombs of the saints. This veneration of relics was always joined to its catechetical meaning, to remind us of the testimony of faith given by the saints, and the mysteries of our redemption. When the Church exposed relics for veneration, it was always so that, as Christians on a journey to our homeland, we would unite ourselves with those who have gone before us and who have already arrived safely in Heaven. Veneration of the relics of the saints was above all done on the feast day of the saint's death to this life and rebirth in the next, accompanied by a meditation on the example that was left to us of his or her heroic love for Jesus, asking the saint's intercession in the liturgy of the Mass, and commenting in the homily of the virtues that were shown

---

[4] *Catechism of the Catholic Church*, no. 1674 and 1675.

[5] *Canon Law Code*, no. 1190 and 1237.

[6] *El Misterio del Santo Grial: Tradición y leyenda del Santo Cáliz* (Valencia: Edicep, 1999).

during life. Veneration of relics was never meant to be an exposition of mortal remains as in a museum.

Therefore, as the Catholic Church has always maintained, we can say that relics are meaningful only to the extent that they help us to comprehend the mystery of Christ, as catechesis, or as a means to elevate the spirit to the reality of the Savior. By way of example, Antuñano Alea mentions that the Shroud of Turin, considered by many to be the most important relic of Christianity, is a detailed description of the tremendous passion and death of the crucified Jesus that leads to an understanding of the mystery of a God who not only surrenders himself, through love, to the most terrible of tortures, but who can also, through that love, conquer death itself and rise from the dead, leaving us evidence of the fact in the inexplicable three-dimensional impression of his body on the sacred linen. For Christians, relics, images, signs, and miracles do not form the foundation of our faith. They can help, but our faith never depends on them in such a way that if they didn't exist we could not believe. They are capable, however, of leading us to faith in Jesus, which has occurred in many cases with the Shroud of Turin, the Sudarium of Oviedo, and other relics. They can be a means of arriving at a personal encounter with the God who loves us, and are capable of awakening in us the same love felt by the saints for Jesus. The Holy Chalice of Valencia, for example, can be a powerful memory of the love of our Savior who consecrated his blood for our salvation, or of the intense love of Laurence for Jesus on behalf of that miracle, giving him the courage to suffer martyrdom for the Church, or that shown by the heroic actions of those who took extraordinary means to save the relic during the Spanish Civil War, simply because of what that cup represents for us as Christians.

This renowned relic, therefore, is much more than a simple agate cup. It is a symbol of Jesus' love for us, persecution and martyrdom during our life on earth, salvation, and our hope for eternal life. It still exists, safe in the bosom of the Church, because of what it represented for all those Christians – from St. Peter and St. Laurence, to the people of Valencia – who have done what was necessary to protect it from harm, so that all Christians might be inspired to a greater love for God and perhaps a better understanding of why the Eucharist must be defended from attack, especially in an age when the equality of religions is being widely proclaimed as the key to world peace. St. Laurence was not asked to renounce Catholicism, but to acknowledge the Roman gods by offering the required incense, and to pay tribute by surrendering Church property, an easy compromise for many today whose indifference prevents them from understanding that it is the Eucharist itself – the Body and Blood of the Lord – that makes it impossible to declare that all religions are equal. Jesus created the divisions, not man, when He instituted the sacrament of redemption: *"This is my blood of the covenant, which is poured out for many for the forgiveness of sins."* *(Mt 26:28); "Amen, amen, I say to you, unless you eat the flesh of the Son of Man and drink his blood, you do not have life within you. Whoever eats my flesh and drinks my blood has eternal life, and I will raise him on the last day." (John 6:53-54); "Do you think that I have come to establish peace on the earth? No, I tell you, but rather division." (Lk 12:51)*[7]

Relics, therefore, can help us to arrive at a greater love for Christ, enabling us to grow as Christians and become more focused on the things that are not of this world. Of course Christians know that neither relics nor images, nor even visions and miracles are the foundation of the faith. They cannot impart grace to the believer. Even if every single relic of the Catholic Church were false, it would not affect the certainty of faith, which has its origin and foundation in a personal encounter with the God who loves us. But, as Salvador Antuñano Alea has explained so well, it is precisely that encounter that gives meaning to relics, enabling us to better understand that mystery by means of the memory they arouse in us of the love that the saints have felt for the Lord, and because of their reminder of the person and life of Christ and the act of redemption. What is important is not the sign but the meaning. The Shroud of Turin is not important in itself, but because it reminds us of the Resurrection, and the Sudarium of Oviedo is meaningful, not as an ancient linen cloth, but because it is a very powerful reminder of the Crucifixion and its significance for humanity. A visit to the Holy Land only takes on meaning when the pilgrim meditates on the lives of Jesus, Mary and the Apostles, and one certainly does not need to leave home for that. Relics are treated as any holy image, such as a holy card or statue. They are venerated for what they represent, not for what they are. Non-Catholics often do not understand that we do not adore statues, wood, bones, and pieces of cloth, until someone explains to them that they serve the same function as a photograph

---

[7] See *The New Jerome Biblical Commentary*, which says: "Peace will not be obtained at any cost, esp. at the cost of compromising God's word. Yet even in nonpeaceful situations the Lucan Jesus calls for forgiveness and reconciliation and love of enemies." (Englewood Cliffs, NY: Prentice Hall, 1990), p.705.

of a loved one that is carried in the wallet or hung on the wall.

It is for this very reason that the Holy Grail has become such an important symbol for humanity, as the receptacle used by Christ to institute the Sacrament of the Eucharist. St. Peter employed this very same cup during the Consecration of the Mass for what it represented. It was a concrete link to Jesus, and the institution of his sacrament of salvation. This tradition continued in an unbroken chain for many years in Rome until the persecution of Valerian demanded that the relic be moved to safety in another country, Spain. When the Muslim invasion of 711 AD required that the Holy Cup be hidden in remote areas of the Pyrenees, rumors quickly spread, leading Christians of all nations to ask the question, "Where is the Holy Grail?" Popular imagination and the pious desire to preserve memories of the Lord gave rise to magical stories of adventure that continue today. Echoes of medieval tales about King Arthur and the Knights of the Round Table, beginning with Chrétien de Troyes in France, have arrived in modern times in the form of books and films such as *Excalibur*, *The Fisher King*, and *The Magic Sword*. Even the popular *The Lord of the Rings* involves the theme of the quest for an all-important object with supernatural powers. The Holy Grail, precisely because of its Christian religious significance, has acquired these powers of invincible force, curing properties, eternal sustenance, and the fountain of youth, all made concrete for the medieval readers of the Grail literature. It has become the relic of relics, the symbol of man's quest for the eternal.

Most people will ask, "But how do we know that the Holy Chalice of Valencia is that used by Christ?" The answer is that we can never know with absolute certainty, but the Church has always venerated it as such, and history, tradition, legend, and archaeology all point to its authenticity. Therefore, it is of little importance if science can never definitively prove its authenticity, because that is something that is simply not within its capabilities. The Holy Chalice of Valencia *is* the medieval Holy Grail, venerated in San Juan de la Peña, inspiration for the famous legends. Throughout its remarkable history, it has always been treated as the authentic Holy Cup of the Last Supper, used by Jesus for the consecration. Its history reflects a genuine conviction in its authenticity, firmly supported by tradition, and science can find nothing to indicate otherwise. We will examine all of these aspects: the extraordinary veneration of the Holy Chalice in Valencia, its early tradition in Rome, the St. Laurence tradition, the medieval presence of the Grail in the Pyrenees, the Arthurian legends, documented history of the relic in the Cathedral of Valencia, Beltrán's archaeological study, and the

ICON CALICIS PRETIOSISSIMI , IN QUO Dominus Noſter Jeſus Chriſtus Sacratiſsimam Euchariſtiam conſecravit ; qui Hicroſolymis Romam , Oſcam dein à S. Laurentio , Panon inde , & Cæſarauguſtam tranſvectus,Valentiam tandem Aragoniæ ab Alfonſo V. Rege tranſmiſſus, in ejuſdem Urbis Metropoli ſolemni cultu honoratur,

Que

18th-century xylograph of the Holy Chalice.

presence of the Holy Chalice in art and architecture. An extraordinary relic merits an equally outstanding past, and the Holy Chalice of Valencia is the only Grail of the world that meets that criteria. It has a story that demands to be told □

Chapter 2

THE HOLY GRAIL IN VALENCIA

I t is amazing how many people visit Valencia and its cathedral, and leave unaware that the Holy Grail is its greatest treasure. Although it is continually on display in the small chapel dedicated to it,[8] there is no publicity to speak of, other than a small sign at the entrance to the medieval passageway that leads to this impressive construction, which simply reads *Capilla del Santo Grial*. The agate cup, mounted on its golden, jewel-encrusted base, is preserved in a special tabernacle on the altar. Without prior knowledge of its history, which few have because it is not published in English, visitors tend to dismiss it as just another religious object, rather ironic considering the fervor that turned into "grail-mania" during the Middle Ages, and the profiles of courage of those who tried to save it throughout the centuries.

Before Antonio Beltrán's archaeological study of 1960, next to nothing was known about this precious relic, other than what has been contributed by tradition. At times it has been vaguely described through the epochs by various authors who often struggled with words, and at other times it was deliberately omitted from documents as the only defense against theft. Nevertheless, Beltrán affirms that the upper cup is indeed from the first century, and maintains that archaeology has found nothing that would be opposed to its authenticity.

Gaspar Escolano, in the seventeenth-century *Década primera de la Historia de la Insigne y coronada Ciudad y Reyno de Valencia*, describes it in the following manner: *"The entire cup of the Chalice is made of a single precious stone, similar to what they call chalcedony, according to what Pliney, in book thirty-seven, chapter seven, relates*

---

[8] The Chapel can be visited from Monday through Saturday from 10 a.m. to 1 p.m. and 4:30 to 6p.m. (7p.m. June to Sept.); 10 a.m. to 1 p.m. Dec. to March; public holidays all year 10 am to 1 pm; closed Sundays.

that the ancients prided themselves on making chalices of those stones. The color of ours is so strange and extraordinary that as it is turned, different lights and colors are formed that give off radiance when looking at it, so that the cup begins to lose its original color, although at first sight it is true that it appears to be like a dying ember." As will be explained, it was precisely the rare colors of the stone resembling fire that inspired the medieval writers of the Grail legends, which are deeply symbolic as well.

Escolano provides much interesting information about the Holy Grail. He talks later about a silver chalice, also supposedly from the Last Supper, cited by Baronio in the twelfth century and mentioned in the work of the Venerable Bede.[9] According to his description, the Cup of the Lord was placed in the hollow of a pillar in a plaza of Jerusalem, made of silver with a large cup that held the sponge that was offered to Jesus on the cross. The pilgrims would insert their fingers through the iron mesh that covered it. Escolano believed that the Lord used two cups on the night of the Last Supper, and that according to St. Jerome, one was used for the dinner of Passover lamb, and the other for the institution of the Most Holy Sacrament. He says that according to other authors, the cup that the Lord drank with at the meal of lamb was of silver, and that of the consecration, of stone. As will be seen, this second cup made of silver may be the only other serious contender to the title of Holy Grail, a claim that holds no weight because it was not used for the consecration.

Two other interesting pieces of information are provided in this account. Referring to a contemporary of his from another country, Escolano says that the man tried to make a drawing of the relic to take with him. He took the measurement of the cup with a cut piece of paper, and that having done this several times, God never permitted it to come out exact, but sometimes it was too large, and other times too small, so that he was forced to give up. The historian also refers to the death of Dr. Honorato Figuerola, Canon of the Church and inquisitor of Valencia and Murcia, who left in his last will and testament a generous sum of money to be used for an annual procession in which the Holy Chalice would be carried through the streets of the city.

The Holy Chalice is really composed of two distinct parts, an upper cup of oriental cornelian agate stone, semi-spherical in shape, often described in ancient

---

[9] César Baronio, *Annales Ecclesiastici a Christo nato ad ann. 1198*, Rome, 1588-1593, 12 vols.

manuscripts as the size of a half orange. This is the original cup that tradition maintains was sent to Huesca by St. Laurence during the Valerian persecution of 258 AD in Rome. The base, formed by an oval and inverted cup, is of the same color and similar material as the upper cup, although quite different and inferior in the quality of the workmanship and the stone itself. It is adorned with pure gold along the lower edge, with four golden bands that join the lower edging to the stem, on which are mounted 27 pearls, two rubies, and two emeralds of great value. The stem of the chalice, with a knot in the middle, serves to join the cup and its base, and it also has two handles, all finely engraved.

As will be discussed later in greater detail, Antonio Beltrán dates the upper cup to the period from the second century BC to the first century AD, made in a workshop of Egypt, Syria, or Palestine. He believes that the cup of the base is possibly from a workshop of Córdoba, made between the tenth and twelfth centuries, and added to the cup sometime between the tenth and fourteenth centuries. The handles, stem, and other gold work, just like the stones and pearls that adorn it, are later, from the twelfth to the fourteenth centuries, possibly the work of a Gothic goldsmith who was knowledgeable in Eastern, Mediterranean, and Mudejar techniques. He believes these were done when the Holy Cup was being venerated in San Juan de la Peña, since in 1399 it was exactly as it appears today, and was recorded that way in the inventory of 1410 done at the death of King Martín el Humano.

The Chapel of the Holy Grail

In the Cathedral of Valencia there is a beautiful Gothic Chapel to the right of the front entrance, called the Chapel of the Holy Grail. To enter, the visitor passes through a medieval passageway, with a precious vault of crossed diagonal arches and two side chapels constructed at the end of the fifteenth century by the Master stonemason Pere Compte.

This chapel dates back to the middle of the fourteenth century, ordered built by Vidal de Blanes, the Bishop of Valencia from 1356 to 1369. It still retains the characteristics of that epoch, constructed to serve as Chapter Room for the Faculty of Theology and as a burial place for many prelates and canons, among them St. Vincent Ferrer[10]. The Washing of the Feet on Holy Thursday was at one time celebrated in the Chapel, as well as other special ceremonies, among them a sermon preached in Latin on Christmas Eve and Easter. It was not until 1916, however, that veneration in the Chapel came to be centered on the Holy Grail.

It now consists of a square room, with four stone walls that are 24 meters wide and 16 meters high, that serve as support for a complicated vault of crossed diagonal arches with stars, formed by twelve oval arches that are joined together under a great central key that serves to sustain the vault on the roof that covers the chapel. The arches rest on many other small, decorated corbels.

On the wall facing the entrance wall, functioning as an altarpiece for the niched display case that holds the Holy Grail, there is an exquisite Gothic frontispiece of alabaster stone that consists of two parts with three arches superimposed in the center, with openwork, dossals, and pinnacles, and twelve compartments or vaulted niches with the Italian relieves of Guiliano Poggibonsi, all exquisitely crafted. The upper reliefs correspond to the lower ones, representing scenes from the New and Old Testaments, respectively.

Beginning on the left side, they are: "Crucifixion," along with the bronze serpent of the passage of Exodus; "The descent of Jesus Christ to Limbo," along with "Samson destroying the gates of Gaza"; The "Resurrection of the Lord," with the "Departure of Jonas from the belly of the whale"; the "Ascension," with "Elias pulled by the chariot of fire"; the "Coming of the Holy Spirit," with "Moses receiving the Law on Sinai," and, finally, the "Coronation of the Virgin," with "Solomon seating his mother Bethshebah on a throne to his right."

The reliefs are a collection of Biblical diptychs of opposites, or double panels, representing the concrete and the figurative, whose scenes are taken from the repertory of theological and artistic themes from the Middle Ages. The symbolism is remarkable, with esoteric significance such as the division of the day in twelve hours, that of the year in twelve months, the twelve signs of the zodiac, the sons of Jacob as heads of the twelve tribes of Israel, the twelve

---

[10] St. Vincent was born in Valencia, probably in the year 1350, and was ordained a priest during the great schism, acting as confessor and adviser to Pedro de Luna or Benedict XIII as he was called. The stress was so great that he became ill, and upon recovery he finally obtained permission to leave the court and become a missionary, quickly becoming famous for his eloquent preaching that produced innumerable conversions that included 8,000 Moors and many Jews. Although known to have exceptional good looks and a charismatic manner that attracted crowds, St. Vincent was remarkable for his humility, calling himself a "plague-spot in soul and body," as he wrote in his spiritual treatise.

Apostles, and many more. Numbers are not used merely as quantitative expressions, but as ideas, and in this case, the number twelve corresponds to the meaning of cosmic order and salvation, and has been a number of great significance from antiquity.

There are supports on the stone walls, two long benches of the same material, and in addition to the entrance, there are three other doors: one on the right side; another, with a pointed arch, located in the same wall to the right, that leads to the beautiful Gothic pulpit from which St. Vincent Ferrer would give his famous theology lessons, also done in stone; and a third door on the facing wall, decorated with a relief representing the Annunciation of the Virgin, that leads to the Museum of the Cathedral.

Throughout the course of time, historical remembrances were incorporated as ornamentation for the dark enclosure of the Chapel, such as the chain that closed the port of Marsella, broken in two unequal pieces of 50 and 70 links, as well as the instrument that broke this chain when King Alfonso el Magnánimo (the Magnanimous), with the Armada of Aragón, forced entry and took the city in 1423. The body of St. Louis, Bishop of Tolos, was taken along with the previous trophies. His remains are still preserved in the Cathedral of Valencia.

As one enters the Chapel, there is a cartoon of Vicente López on the wall to the left, depicting the allegory of "The Triumph of the Eucharist and the Expulsion of the Moors." To the right, next to the pulpit, there is a great fresco, an imitation tapestry that is now transferred to linen, called "The Adoration of the Magi" by Nicolás Florentino (1469). On the wall of the door, facing the frontispiece of Poggibonsi, is what appears to be the central part of a great altarpiece of the fifteenth century, dedicated to St. Christopher. In the central opening, under the three sculptured and staggered arches that have been mentioned, the tabernacle of the Holy Grail is in perfect harmony with the Gothic style of the altarpiece, formed by a very beautiful niche of alabaster, supported by a corbel and squared off by small columns that support a chest, all done in 1942 by Vicente Traver.

Vicente Traver and J. David designed the hexagonal glass case that covers the niche, made with protective glass on three of its sides. It is covered with bars of embossed bronze on those sides that have engraved allegories and Eucharistic symbols. In its interior, in an artistic reliquary of gold–plated silver with marble knots, the Holy Grail remains exposed for public veneration.

This reliquary, formed like a lantern and finished at the top with the sun of a small monstrance that can be detached for the benedictions with the Most Holy Sacrament, is also the work of Vicente Traver and J. David. It was donated by the mayor of the city of Alcoy, Enrique Oltra Moltó, on Sunday, May 5, 1959, as an offering made by the people of that city to the Holy Chalice of the Last Supper, in order to commemorate the 17th Centennial of its arrival in Spain.

The Chapel of the Holy Grail has recently undergone two important renovations. The first was solemnized on May 23, 1943, which included various restorations of the Cathedral to its original state, with a solemn Pontifical officiated by the then Archbishop of Valencia, Prudencio Melo y Alcalde, and in which the Administrative Apostolic Bishop of Vitoria, Dr. Javier Lauzurica, preached. After the chanting of the *Te Deum*, the procession with the Holy Grail took place, which was transferred to the Plaza of the Virgin where it was deposited on an altar of natural flowers. The Chapter Room was cleared of the tombs, funerary urns, and frescos that had obscured the original design, and these were transferred to other outbuildings. The reliefs were restored to their original positions, and a partition wall was removed, revealing the three staggered arches. Once the detachable items that had disfigured the chapel were gone and the original elements could be seen, the monstrance of the Sacred Relic was positioned, arranged in such a way that it would be part of the Gothic altarpiece, with the altar table placed in front of it, formed by a solid stone slab, thirty centimeters thick, that is supported on five pillars that were formerly on the main altar of the Cathedral.

The completion of the final restoration was solemnized on January 26, 1979, with a Eucharistic celebration in the same Chapel, presided over by the Archbishop, Dr. Miguel Roca, who was assisted by the most important authorities of Valencia. This restoration was carried out in order to remove the layers of filth that smoke and time had left accumulated on the vaults and walls, so that Valencia would once again see the splendor of its rich cultural tradition, in the words of Manuel Sánchez Navarrete. An exceptional team of artisans and artists set out to work wholeheartedly, under competent technical direction, seeking to restore to its original purity the beautiful vault of crossed arches that had been hidden under a thick layer of dirt. The beautiful central key, carved in stone, was revealed, now a wonderful polychrome relief that represents the "Coronation of the Virgin." The artisans uncovered the original richness of the pulpit, framed new artistic glass in the adorned windows, and restored the three images of the Virgin and Child, with St. Helen to one side, and St. Louis,

King of France, to the other, which crown the altarpiece and are also of polychrome stone.

On July 3, 1991, the Chapter enriched the appearance of the altarpiece by placing sixteen images in the pedestals that had been empty until then. Twelve of them represent the Apostles, and the others are of Pope Sixtus II and his deacon St. Laurence, and St. Valerius and his deacon St. Vincent, all of them created in the workshop of the renowned artist, José Esteve Edo. As will be seen, St. Laurence and St. Vincent were cousins martyred in a similar manner, but in different persecutions, the first in Rome in 258 AD, and the second in Spain, during the persecution of Dacian[11] in 303. They are always portrayed together in the churches of Spain, especially in Huesca.

The Chapel of the Holy Grail was highlighted during the Exposition of the year 2000, during which time there was a continual flow of visitors who came to venerate the relic and view a specially prepared video in Spanish that narrated the relic's illustrious past, including an explanation of how it would have appeared on the table of the Last Supper without its golden, jewel-encrusted base.

The Theological Vision of the Grail

From the theological point of view, the cup that Christ used at the Last Supper can be considered the relic par excellence because it is the symbol of redemption, having been the first receptacle for the consecration of wine into the blood of salvation, and perhaps, as the apocryphal Gospel according to Nicodemus relates, used later to collect the blood that flowed from the side of the crucified Lord. The iconography of the angels, or the Apostles, collecting the blood of Christ in the very same cup that he used during the first Consecration is a medieval tradition that is the origin of the idea of Christ as Source of Life, theologically based in the meaning of water as a symbol of Baptism, and blood as symbol of the Eucharist. In Christian imagery, therefore, wine mixed with water symbolizes the Church, eternally united with the water of the faithful, producing unity in Christ, whose members become imbued with the purifying and saving power of the blood of

---

[11] Dacian was the governor of Spain, acting under the orders of Diocletian and Maximian, who published their second and third edicts against the Christian clergy in the year 303, put in force the following year against the laity.

the Savior. It is associated with eternal life, from the words of the Savior, *"Whoever eats my flesh and drinks my blood has eternal life, and I will raise him on the last day. For my flesh is true food, and my blood is true drink. Whoever eats my flesh and drinks my blood remains in me and I in him"* (Jn 6:54-56). This springs from the Jewish sacrificial ritual in which blood represents the life and was symbolically offered to God, just as the blood of the Passover lamb smeared on the doorposts protected the Israelites from the angel of death in Egypt.

The blood of the Eucharistic drink departs from the Jewish prohibition of eating blood, but the sacramental significance retains the idea of blood as the life that is communicated from Jesus to his disciples through the Eucharist. This divine blood is that of the new covenant, and is also an atoning agent through which we are made righteous and become able to draw nearer to God, found represented in images of the mystical lamb, symbol of Jesus Christ, with blood flowing from a wound in the chest into a cup, such as that done by Jan van Eyck, painted in 1432. In John 1:29 John the Baptist refers to Jesus as "the Lamb of God (in Latin *Agnus Dei*) who takes away the sin of the world," chanted or sung in the Mass as the prayer that immediately precedes the reception of the Eucharist, and a symbol that already appeared in the Roman catacombs. The mystical lamb is always associated with St. John the Baptist, who is present throughout the entire history of the Monastery of San Juan de la Peña and is represented in the seventeenth century engraving in which he appears with the inscription *Ecce Agnus Dei*.

This symbolism is captured perfectly in the agate and precious stones of the Holy Chalice of Valencia. The agate stone of the upper cup, whose color has been described as blood and fire, has always been believed to possess magical powers. The early Christian text *Physiologus* reports that pearl-fishers tie a piece of agate to a string and drop it into the sea, because the agate is attracted to the pearl and "does not budge," allowing divers to follow the line and recover the pearl. The pearl is a symbol of Christ, and the agate refers to St. John, who announced to us the holy pearl when he said, "Behold, this is the Lamb of God, who takes away the sin of the world." *Physiologus* tells of a "purple oyster that comes up from the bottom of the sea, ...opens its mouth and drinks in the dew of heaven and the rays of the sun, moon, and stars, it thus produces the pearl from the lights above....The two halves of the shell are like the Old and New Testaments, and the pearl is like our Savior, Jesus Christ." According to the Book of Revelation, the gates of the "heavenly Jerusalem" are made of pearl, and a string of pearls is a frequent analogy for the multitude of God's powers.

The 28 pearls on the base are also a multiple of seven, a sacred and universal number, signifying the Cup of the New and Eternal Testament, the means of sanctification for all humanity. Seven appears frequently in the Church as a symbolic number: the seven gifts of the Holy Spirit, seven virtues, seven sacraments, seven deadly sins, and seven petitions in the Lord's Prayer, as well as in Revelation where it plays a major role as the seven churches, the seven horns and eyes of the Lamb (5:6), seven heads of the dragon (12:13), and the seven vials of the wrath of God (15:7) in the book "sealed with seven seals" (5:1). The sacred number also figures in Judaism and the Old Testament as the seven branches of the Menorah and in the Biblical scene where seven priests with seven rams' horns circled the walls of Jericho for seven days. On the seventh day they "compassed the city seven times," the Israelites gave a battle cry, and the walls of Jericho fell (Joshua 6:6-20).

Agate is the first stone of the breastplate of the high priest (Ex 28:17 and 39:10). In Revelation 4:3 John describes the Lord on a throne, whose "appearance sparkled like jasper and carnelian. Around the throne was a halo as brilliant as an emerald." Agate and emerald, two of the precious stones of the Holy Grail, also form the foundations of the heavenly Jerusalem: the fourth course of stones was emerald, and the sixth carnelian. As mentioned, the "twelve gates were twelve pearls, each of the gates made from a single pearl; and the street of the city was of pure gold..." (Rev 21:19-21). According to medieval legends, emeralds actually come from the depths of hell, and in some versions from Lucifer's crown, which makes them better suited to combat demonic forces. They symbolize faith and hope. Three of the four precious stones of the Holy Chalice – ruby, agate or carnelian, and beryl (emerald), adorned the breastplate of the Jewish high priest, as described in Exodus. The name of one of the twelve tribes of Israel was to be engraved in each of the stones.

The ruby is one of the most valued precious stones because of its red color, associated with fire and the planet Mars. The tradition of the ruby overlaps with that of the garnet or "carbuncle," which comes from the Latin diminutive of *carbo* or "coal": they were believed to glow in the dark like smouldering lumps of coal, reminiscent of the early descriptions of the upper cup. Albertus Magus (1193-1280) believed that it had the power of all the other stones, and Hildegard von Bingen wrote, "Wherever there is a carbuncle, the demons of the air cannot carry out their diabolical mission; ... so, too, this stone suppresses all human disease." It is a symbol of vitality, royalty, and passionate love, and in the Book of *Revelation*,

God's glory is compared to diamonds and rubies.

Oñate believes that the four precious stones of the Holy Cup – agate, emerald, ruby and pearl – could symbolize the four elements or the four points of the compass, a number also associated with the Cross in Christianity, as well as the four Evangelists, the four great prophets (Isaiah, Jeremiah, Ezekiel, and Daniel) and the four Doctors of the Church (Augustine, Ambrose, Jerome, and Gregory). There are also four letters in the name of God, written in Hebrew as YHWH or JHVH and often pronounced "Yahweh" or "Jehovah."

Hildegard von Bingen (1098-1179) describes Jesus speaking to God the Father at the Last Judgment as follows, "the world shall not pass away until you see my body and all its members... filled with precious gems, perfected in all those who... worship you, just as the gems glitter with the power of virtue." In her book *Liber Subtilitatum*, gems are described as having supernatural powers, originating in hell: "The devil draws back in fear before precious stones; he hates them and despises them, because they remind him that their brilliance was already manifest before he plunged from glory... and because some gems came to be, in that very fire in which he is punished... Thus gems originate from fire and water, and for this reason they also contain heat, moisture, and many powers and serve many good, decent, and useful ends..."

The symbolism of the Holy Chalice of Valencia is a perfect representation of Christian teaching concerning sanctification through the Eucharist, with the multicolored bands of the agate stone, reminiscent of the rays of blood that emanate from the side wound of Christ in iconography, symbolizing the purifying fire of the sacrificial lamb victim that symbolically cleanses the Christian from the blemish of sin. It is also the "fire from heaven," a sign of the presence of Yahweh in the Old Testament and a manifestation of the glory of Jesus Christ in the New Testament (Rev 1:14, 2:18), who has come "to set the earth on fire" (Luke 12:49). Partaking of the blood offering of the Eucharist becomes for the Christian a means of spiritual cleansing that is "poured out for many for the forgiveness of sins," renewed in the divine sacrifice that is celebrated in the Mass, united daily with the praise, sufferings, prayers, and good works of all the members of his Body, thus creating "gems" composed of water and fire that are capable of serving many good, decent, and useful ends as bearers of the saving and sanctifying action of Christ.

Wolfram von Eschenbach refers to the Holy Grail as *lapsit exillas*, often understood as "stone fallen from heaven." It is often read as *lapis exilis*, meaning "insignificant stone," scorned by the foolish, but sought by the wise, a description that explains to a great extent the relative oblivion the relic has experienced in Valencia, revered by some, but unknown to the vast majority of people. As Asunción Alejos Morán believes, the fact that Wolfram describes the Grail as a precious stone that fell to earth from the crown of Lucifer is thought provoking, because in the Christian sense the Grail represents Christ, who with the blood of redemption constructed a bridge between heaven and earth, or between God and man, as well as time and eternity. The contemplation of the Holy Grail, therefore, signifies the revelation of a God made man, whose blood is continuously present in the Eucharistic cup that makes it possible for a soul to ascend to a superior plane of existence, the aspiration of the mystics.

Melchizedek, the Old Testament king of Salem, or Jerusalem, whose name means "my king is righteousness," or "my king is Sedek" (Gn 14:18-20), met Abraham after his expedition against the four kings, gave him bread and wine, blessed him, and received a tenth of the booty of Abraham. In many ways, the cup of Melchizedek prefigures that used by Christ at the Last Supper, with Melchizedek presented in iconography as a High Priest carrying a cup, with such great Eucharistic significance that in the fourteenth century the support for the monstrance that encloses the Sacred Host for Exposition was called *melchizedek*. Although the priestly function performed by Melchizedek was not the offering of bread and wine but the blessing of Abraham, the connection between the bread and wine and the Eucharistic sacrifice was first made by Clement of Alexandria and Cyprian. From this interpretation Melchizedek entered the Canon of the Roman rite of the Mass.

The symbolism of the Holy Grail in general and the Holy Chalice of Valencia in particular is quite significant, therefore, and demonstrates well the theological vision of the relic par excellence and its importance within Christian eschatology. The cup represents both nourishment and the fire of purification. It is a spiritual drink that enables one to transcend the physical limitations of earthly existence in order to ascend to higher realms. It is a blessing and hope for salvation with great curative powers, scorned by many but sought by the wise for its powers of spiritual cleansing. Similar to the manner in which it is portrayed in the Grail legends, its importance cannot be perceived by the sinner, but only by the pure of heart, those who are able to leave the ways of evil in the quest for salvation that is a symbol of life on earth □

Part

2

EARLY TRADITION:
FROM THE CENACLE TO ROME

*The first generations of the Church were no
doubt accustomed to communicate their beliefs
by the means which were familiar to them from
the rabbinical schools: the oral transmission of
the material to disciples... It was of importance
that this tradition should be preserved without
deformation; and fidelity to the received
tradition was the ultimate assurance that
the doctrine proposed was genuine.*

John L. McKenzie, S.J.

Chapter 3

THE LAST SUPPER IN JERUSALEM

One of the most transcendent acts of the history of humanity, as Manuel Sánchez Navarrete so eloquently expresses it, was the extraordinary and emotional act of love of a God who made Himself flesh and blood in order to redeem the human race. This act of love, however, doesn't end with the birth of Jesus. The Son of God, in one of the most culminating moments of his life on earth, feeling nostalgia for his imminent separation and the desire of continuing to live among us, although hidden, instituted the Eucharist under two species, converting the bread into His Body and the wine into His Blood. And this precious Blood, the first time that the miracle of transubstantiation was performed, was contained in a Cup held by the hands of the Master.[1]

It is in this sublime mystery of the institution of the Eucharist that the Cup of Salvation came to be converted into one of the most precious relics of Christianity, described by tradition as embarking on a pilgrimage of love that begins with St. Peter, its first custodian; continues with the first Popes, who reverently maintain the original tradition begun by Christ by using the very same cup that was held by the hands of the Savior; departs for Huesca, Spain, after the Holy Cup is saved by Pope Sixtus II and St. Laurence at the cost of their lives; and stops for several centuries in San Juan de la Peña where, hidden and venerated, it becomes the fabulous and mysterious Grail, around which beautiful legends were invented, populated with heroes and leaders, who with their fantastic deeds, the grandeur of their virtues and the example of their chivalric courage, left a permanent impression on the Christian world. The Cup of Salvation has been

---

[1] *El Santo Cáliz de la Cena.* (Valencia: Cofradía del Santo Cáliz, 1994), p.15-16.

coveted by all, from kings to the godless, but protected by the Providence of God, it miraculously escaped all harm to be finally entrusted to the Cathedral of Valencia, where it is daily offered to the entire world as a witness of the most sacred mystery of all: that of the institution of the Eucharist on Holy Thursday.

On the first day of the preparation period for Passover, the day for sacrificing the Passover lamb, Jesus was in Bethany, a short distance from Jerusalem, in the house of Simon, whom he had cured from leprosy. According to the Gospel of Luke,

> ...he sent out Peter and John, instructing them, "Go and make preparations for us to eat the Passover." They asked him, "Where do you want us to make the preparations?" And he answered them, "When you go into the city, a man will meet you carrying a jar of water. Follow him into the house that he enters and say to the master of the house, 'The teacher says to you, "Where is the guest room where I may eat the Passover with my disciples?"' He will show you a large upper room that is furnished. Make the preparations there." Then they went off and found everything exactly as he had told them, and there they prepared the Passover (22:7-13).

The two disciples arrived and found everything to be as the Master had told them, and they prepared the meal. In the afternoon, Jesus took his place with the Apostles.

> He said to them, "I have eagerly desired to eat this Passover with you before I suffer, for, I tell you, I shall not eat it [again] until there is fulfillment in the kingdom of God." Then he took a cup, gave thanks, and said, "Take this and share it among yourselves; for I tell you [that] from this time on I shall not drink of the fruit of the vine until the kingdom of God comes." Then he took the bread, said the blessing, broke it, and gave it to them, saying, "This is my body, which will be given for you; do this in memory of me." And likewise the cup after they had eaten, saying, "This cup is the new covenant in my blood, which will be shed for you (22:14-20).

It is clear from the Gospels that Jesus used a *cup* to institute the Sacrament of the Eucharist, not the Christian chalice of later centuries. All of the Gospels agree, as well as St. Paul in verses 23-28 of Chapter 11 of his first letter to the Christian community of Corinth, that Jesus, after breaking and giving the bread, took a cup of wine and declared it to be the blood of the new covenant. The original word in Greek is *potérion*, which means *calix* in Latin, and *copa* in Spanish. The Spanish, however, prefer to use the word *cáliz* because it is used in the Liturgy to designate "the cup of the Eucharistic Supper of the Lord." Hence, the Holy Chalice of

41

Valencia is called in Spanish *"el Santo Cáliz"* rather than *copa*, a title that refers to the relic as it exists today, with its later additions of gold and jewels. As the word *cáliz* can be translated as either *chalice* or *cup*, the original agate cup will be called the Holy Cup of the Last Supper, but when referring to the relic as it now appears in the Cathedral of Valencia, *"Santo Cáliz"* will be translated as Holy Chalice.

In his book *El Santo Grial*, Juan Angel Oñate Ojeda explains the significance of the words of Jesus, "This cup is the new covenant in my blood." He says that in order to understand the meaning of these words of the Lord, it is necessary to keep in mind what is narrated in Exodus 24:1-8 concerning the ratification of the Old Alliance or Pact of God with the People of Israel in the Old Testament. According to this covenant, it was necessary to observe the commandments of God, and in exchange God would give them the Promised Land and protection (23:25-31). To ratify it, Moses sent young men of the Israelites to offer holocausts and sacrifice young bulls. Once they were offered in sacrifice to the Lord, part of the flesh was burned on the altar so that, converted into smoke, it would rise in a spiral toward heaven, known as the dwelling of the Lord; another part was eaten by the people. With this, an Alliance, or union between God and the people, was established. The blood could not be eaten (Lev. 17:10-14), because it was considered to contain the life, which is only from God. For that reason, Moses took half of the blood and put it in large bowls and sprinkled it, part on the altar, which symbolized God, and part on the people, saying, "This is the blood of the covenant which the Lord has made with you in accordance with all these words of his."

When Jesus took the Cup of the Last Supper in his holy and venerable hands, he consecrated the wine that it contained and gave it to his disciples, saying, *"Drink of it, all of you; for this is my blood of the covenant, which is poured out for many for the forgiveness of sins."* (Mk 26:27-28). It is clear, according to Oñate Ojeda, that what Jesus meant was that the Cup contained his own blood, which would ratify a New Alliance or Covenant between God and Man; it was being shed for that reason. *Drink of it, all of you,* because if life is in the blood, in this Cup is Divine Life, and this Alliance is precisely the union of God with man for the communication of his own Divine Life (Jn 6:40, 48-59). [2]

---

[2] *El Santo Grial*, p.28.

This cup that was used by Jesus to consecrate the wine is thought to have been a cup of common usage that belonged to the rich owner of the house or *Cenacle* where the Last Supper was celebrated. It was most likely expensive for that reason, because on such a special occasion, the wealthy proprietor would certainly have used the best drinking vessels and table service he possessed. Various details given by the evangelists indicate that the owner of that house was rich: 1) Jesus says to the disciples that upon arriving in Jerusalem they should follow a man with a jug, which implies that the owner of the Cenacle had servants, because normally the women went to the well for water, and 2) the Cenacle was on the upper floor, which implies that it was a large house with an upper level, not very common.

Several authors[3] believe that the owner of the Cenacle was Chuza, the steward of Herod (Lk 8:3), whose wife Joanna was one of the women who ministered to the needs of Jesus. Comenge Gabasa and Juan Maldonado maintain that it was Joseph of Arimathea, the disciple of Jesus who later brought the shroud he had purchased to his own garden tomb, in which no one had ever been buried, and who many believe later brought the cup to England, as legend relates. According to others[4], however, these opinions lack historical weight, because they are only founded on supposition, not on passages from the New Testament or testimonies from Christian tradition. These testimonies and passages favor those who maintain that the Cenacle was the property of the family of the Evangelist St. Mark, whose real name was John Mark. One testimony is that of Theodosius, who speaks of the Cenacle of Holy Sion when describing his visit to Jerusalem around 530 AD. He says: *Ipsa fuit domus Sancti Marci Evangelistae*, or "This was the house of the Evangelist St. Mark."[5] According to Oñate, Alexander, the monk of Chipre, writing in the sixth century, assures us that an ancient tradition affirms that the house of the Last Supper was that of Maria, mother of Mark, and that the man with the jug of water was St. Mark himself.[6] In addition to owning the house in Jerusalem, as Jorge Manuel Rodríguez writes, the father of John Mark was also

---

[3] Sanchis Sivera and Olmos Canalda, following the opinion of Agustín Sales.

[4] Oñate Ojeda and Jorge-Manuel Rodríguez. See also *The Navarre Bible: St. Mark* (Dublin: Four Courts Press, 2nd ed. 1992).

[5] *De situ Terrae Sanctae*, p.141.

[6] *Laud. St. Barnabae Apost.*, 1:13; *Act. Sanct.*, 2 (1867), 434.

the owner of an oil press on the Mount of Olives, where Jesus and his disciples gathered to pray because it was in front of the Temple mount and was the only place where they could pray looking at the Temple [7]. The writers of *The Navarre Bible* affirm this by saying that "it seems probable that the Garden of Olives belonged to this same Mary, which would explain Mark's presence there"[8]. They explain that most writers see in Mark 14:51-52, the episode of the young man who leaves his sheet behind him as he flees from the garden when Jesus is arrested, as "Mark's own veiled signature to his Gospel, since only he refers to this episode."

The Evangelist Luke also tells us that years later, Peter, after being freed by an angel from the prison in which he had been confined by Herod Agrippa, went to the house of Mary, mother of John who is called Mark, where there were many people gathered in prayer[9]. This John Mark, who later wrote his Gospel, accompanied Barnabas and Saul on their missions and served St. Peter in Rome as an interpreter. The passage makes it clear that the house of his mother served as a meeting place for the Christian community of Jerusalem, and it is the first place Peter goes after escaping the double chains with which he was bound, managing to escape the guards who kept watch. It seems likely that this house of Mary, mother of Mark, was the same house where Jesus celebrated the Last Supper and which later served as the meeting place for the Apostles awaiting the arrival of the Holy Spirit.

The Eucharist, as a new concept for the Apostles of the newly formed Christian Church, would have been indelibly engraved on them for its transcendental significance. Communion as a Eucharistic feast had been just established as a rite, and it is inconceivable that the receptacle that served to consecrate the wine into the blood of Christ would have been lost. Because the owner of the Cenacle was also a disciple of Jesus, he certainly would have valued the cup even more for having been the object of such an exceptional use, but even if that were not the case, the cup was an expensive piece of fine stone that was part of his property. And certainly, as a disciple of Jesus, it is logical to think that the owner of the Cenacle would have entrusted the relic to St. Peter as

---

[7] *LINTEUM* 17-18 (March-June 1996), p.24.

[8] p.56.

[9] Acts 12: 1-18.

José Estruch. Mystical Supper. 19th century, Valencia.

head of the Church. Peter even calls Mark his son (1 Pet 5:13), which implies a long-standing and deep relationship, and supports the hypothesis that Mark gave the precious cup of salvation to the first Pope. Although it is not possible to find documentary proof of something so remote in time, most would agree that the sacred vessel had to have been preserved. That such a significant relic would have been buried or lost is impossible according to most Christian writers, simply because it was so important for the early Christians to use their relics in the liturgy, and certainly, if the cup was in the possession of St. Peter, it would have gone to Rome, just as tradition maintains ☐

Chapter 4

EVIDENCE OF THE HOLY GRAIL IN ROME

Most historians agree that St. Peter was executed in the reign of Nero in 64 to 67 AD on the Vatican hill, described as being crucified head downward in the apocryphal Acts of Peter as he himself insisted, because he believed himself unworthy of imitating Our Lord's Passion too closely. Excavations in the 1940s confirm that there was a shrine to St. Peter from the middle of the second century immediately under the great high altar of the present-day St. Peter's. If Mark turned the agate cup over to Peter, and Peter used it in his Eucharistic celebrations until his martyrdom in Rome, what would have happened to the cup after his death? It wasn't an easy time for the Church, because Nero had ordered a great part of the city to be burned, Christians were fed to lions in terrible spectaculars for the entertainment of the Romans, and the Christian community met secretly to celebrate the Mass. After Peter's martyrdom, the Christians buried his body in the cemetery on Vatican Hill, along with a recently discovered sign that reads *Petrus est hic,* or "Peter is here." Pope Paul VI announced in 1968 that the skeletal remains of St. Peter had at last been found and identified, a statement that he explained rested on long and intensive study by experts. The bones were found under the Basilica, exactly where the ancient tradition of the Church had located the original grave of the apostle. It is believed that during the Christian persecutions of 250-260 AD, under Decius and Valerian, the bones were transferred from the grave to a concealed repository in a third century graffiti wall and were later returned to the grave when the danger was past. The fact that the church was built directly over the grave demonstrates in a rather dramatic manner the importance of relics for the early Church as a testimony of faith.

Linus, the second Pope, guided the Church for about ten years through the tribulation and during the brief moment of peace after the death of Nero. We know little about him, but by the end of the second century he was recognized as the first Bishop of Rome, appointed by Saints Peter and Paul. He was followed by Cletus, who some believe was a slave originally called Anencletus, converted and baptized by Peter. After his death in 88 AD, Clement became Pontiff, whose name is mentioned by St. Paul in the letter to the Philippians, ordained by Peter and who collaborated with him in the pastoral care of the Church of Rome. The Roman prophet Hermas refers to him as the official who wrote letters on behalf of the Roman Church to other Churches. One of these still survives, the first *Letter of Clement to the Corinthians*, which was given an authority in the early Church second only to Sacred Scripture, a masterpiece that shows us how the Roman Church exercised pastoral responsibility over other churches.

Almost nothing is known of many of those who followed: Evaristus, possibly of Greek origin, Alexander I, credited with the inclusion of the reference to the Passion in the Canon of the Mass, Sixtus I, attributed with the insertion of the Sanctus, and Telesphorus, who added the Gloria and began the tradition of Christmas midnight Mass. Hyginus was a philosopher from Athens, the writings of Pius provide evidence of the status of the Roman Church as the center of Christian intellectual life, and Anicletus resolved a difficulty over the celebration of Easter, although the nature of the dispute is not certain. At the start of the persecution of Decius in the year 250 there had been 20 Popes in all, including Fabian who was one of the first to be arrested and martyred. All are canonized saints of the Roman Catholic Church, and their importance for the history of the Church is that each one of them safeguarded the depository of faith, transmitting it to the following generation and fulfilling a role that was not merely a primacy of honor, as many non-Catholics might believe, but an effective ministry that confirmed the churches in their faith and gave unity and truth to the entire Mystical Body of Christ. Tradition strongly maintains that these first popes safeguarded the Holy Grail, as well as many other relics, using it to say the Mass in imitation of Christ.

This transmission of faith, headed by the first pontiffs, finds its expression in the formulation of the Eucharistic rite: the "Roman Canon." It is here that many find evidence of the traditional belief that the relic was in Rome. As Antuñano Alea explains, the Roman liturgy is quite different from the liturgies of Eastern origin, with its original elements dating to the first Christian times, especially in the essential parts, like the formulation of the transubstantiation. In fact, there is a common origin to the two basic liturgies – Latin and Eastern – that seems to be the primitive liturgy of the community of Antioch, whose formula is recorded by Luke and Paul. But beyond that, the two have evolved differently, with the western communities creating a dynamic liturgy rich in formulas for every occasion, while the eastern communities focus more on the contemplation of the mystery, with a liturgy that is more fixed or static, but quite beautiful and mystic. Nevertheless, the western liturgy very early on also established a series of invariable parts, in addition to the words of the Eucharistic consecration and built around them. That invariable part is called the Canon or the rule of the Mass.

The nucleus of both liturgies, of course, consists of the words of the consecration of the bread and wine. In essence, with respect to these words, the two liturgical sources coincide, showing the unity of the faith and of the Church. But there are also notable differences in the ordering of the sentences and rites that precede and follow these words, a variety that enriches the Church with the plurality of the rites. There is one that is particularly relevant: the Divine Liturgy of St. John Chrysostom, the Greek rite of the Eucharist, ordained by that Bishop of Constantinople in the sixth century. Based on the Eastern tradition, at the moment of the consecration of the wine it says simply: "In like manner he took *the Cup* with the wine, saying…." On the other hand, the Roman Canon of the Mass, at that moment, says: "In like manner, after He had supped, taking also *this excellent cup* into His holy and venerable hands, and giving Thee thanks, He blessed, and gave to His disciples, saying…" The difference may be small, and certainly doesn't affect the validity of the consecration, but scholars believe that it is important for the question of the Grail. As Antuñano Alea asks, "Why does the Roman tradition specify *this* Cup – *"hunc praeclarum calicem"* – while the Greek does not – *"tò potérion"*?

Although this could never be considered as conclusive proof, the Spanish authors agree that this demonstrative adjective seems to point to a very special Cup, as if to insist that the *very same Cup that is here now* was the one that the Lord took in his holy and venerable hands. The Greek tradition would not use that adjective because it did not have the Holy Cup of the Last Supper in its possession. The Roman Canon, on the other hand, originated in the celebrations presided over by Peter and his successors. It is quite likely, as we have seen, that Mark turned over the Cup to Peter, who would have used the words *"this Cup"* when saying Mass. The Popes who followed received the Cup from Peter, and continued the very same formula that was consolidated in the second century and continued intact into the third, until it was finally recorded in the fourth century as a stable part of the formula of the Roman Canon.

Antonio Beltrán offers the following quote from Agustín Sales as an example of an explanation for how the Cup was taken to Rome by St. Peter, showing the author's desire not to leave a single space of time unaccounted for:

> I hold as very probable the belief of our venerable bishop of Córdoba, don Marcelino Siuri, and this is that St. Peter, visible head of the church, brought from Jerusalem to Rome this sacred object and that, until his death, he used it to celebrate, as did his successors up to Sixtus II. And it is more likely that he brought it after the assumption of the Virgin Mary and long after establishing his pontificate in Rome, because as the sovereign Lady kept the Passion of her Son so present and lived until her death in the house of the Father of Families, she would have had it in her oratory, in sight, along with other Relics, renewing with them the dolorous Passion of her Son. Nor is it unlikely that as St. John said Mass every day, he consecrated in this Cup, giving Communion to the Virgin with it, in the species of wine. After the death of Our Lady, as the Holy Apostles and disciples were present at her passing, it is very natural that they would have divided among themselves her Relics and those that she possessed from her holy Son, and then St. Peter, as head of the church, would have brought the Cup to Rome.

Further evidence for the hypothesis that the Cup was in Rome is the tradition of St. Laurence, which asserts that the agate cup of the Cathedral of Valencia was the Papal Eucharistic Cup of the first two centuries. The tradition of Aragón has always maintained that at the moment when Pope Sixtus II surrendered the treasures of the Church to his deacon Laurence, with instructions to give the money to the poor, he asked him to save the relics, among them the very same Cup that Jesus had used to institute the Eucharist at the Last Supper. St. Sixtus knew that the Papal Cup was in fact the original cup used by Jesus, and Laurence had assisted him often at Mass, listening to the words of the Roman Canon, "He took in his holy and venerable hands *this excellent cup.*" Until now, however, there has not been much historical support, with the exception of two pieces of evidence, both lost today. The first is parchment 136 from the collection of King Martín el Humano in the Archives of the Crown of Aragón, in which, when referring to the Cup that the king demanded from the prior of San Juan de la Peña, it says that St. Laurence had sent the Cup to Spain "*cum eius littera* – with a letter he wrote." The letter no longer exists, but the reference remains. The second is the ancient mosaic in the central nave of the Basilica of St. Laurence Outside the Walls in Rome that was destroyed by a bomb during World War II. There one could contemplate St. Laurence entrusting the Holy Cup to a soldier of the Roman army who received it on his knees. The Basilica was built over Laurence's original tomb in the Campo Verano.

The life of St. Laurence according to St. Donato is very possibly the earliest surviving written reference to St. Sixtus II surrendering the precious Cup to Laurence, translated in 1636 from a Latin manuscript believed to have been written by St. Donato in the second half of the sixth century. Because it contains so many unknown details about his life, and clarifies many of the contradictions that are found in his biographies, concerning such things as his birthplace, when he left Spain and whether or not he ever returned, his relationship with St. Vincent, how he met Sixtus II, and the events that took place before his martyrdom, it is translated in its entirety. It not only provides historical support that has been lacking until now, but is also a moving story of Christian life in the third century, written with a love for accuracy that is not often seen in early historical records. The surrender of the Grail to Laurence by Pope Sixtus II is also mentioned by Francisco Diago in his seventeenth-century *Anales del Reyno de Valencia*, which further confirms the tradition.

It should also be noted that after peace had been restored after the Edict of Milan in 313 AD, there are no references to the Holy Cup of the Last Supper, which would certainly have been the case if it had been in Rome or Jerusalem. The travels of Etheria, the Spanish pilgrim to the Holy Land, mention many relics, but not the Holy Cup.

The Bollandists are a group of Belgian Jesuits who edit and publish the *Acta Sanctorum*, a great collection of biographies and legends of the saints. They took this name in Amberes, Belgium, in the middle of the seventeenth century, when they began the enormous task, still unfinished, of examining the abundance of history, traditions, and legends having to do with the lives of the saints and Christianity in general, using the most rigorous scientific methods of investigation and critical research, for the purpose of revising and purging all existing texts, separating from them all that popular legend could have invented. As a consequence, they intended to proceed with the suppression of liturgical celebrations, as well as references found in the readings and hymns, that lacked a solid historical foundation.

This colossal work was conceived and initiated by the Jesuit priest Heribert Rosweyde, who gathered together a large amount of documentation, but never lived to see the first two volumes of the *Acta Sanctorum* published. His death in 1629 paralyzed the project for a time, but it was reinitiated with another group of Jesuits, presided over by Jean Bolland. The first stage of publication – fifty monumental volumes of *Acta Sanctorum* – began in 1643 and ended in 1773 when the Society of Jesus was suppressed. The work was reborn in 1837 with renewed activity and growing scientific prestige that can be attributed to the progress made in historical methodology. There are now 67 published volumes, as well as a quarterly review, *Analecta Bollandiana*, a bulletin of recent hagiographical publications, and inventories of texts previously published.

This formidable work, which involved an incalculable number of trips, studies, verification, and examination of archives, has left very few traditions out of its reach. Concerning the study of everything related to St. Laurence, the Bollandists confronted the problem of the tradition of the Holy Grail, which has always presented difficulties because of lack of documentation. In light of that, the Bollandists issued a prudent dictate, which stated that "in spite of the difficulties mentioned, it is possible that St. Laurence really sent the Holy Cup to Spain, from where he seems to have originated, and as there are no concrete documents that might convince us of the falsity of the event, we therefore leave tradition in the state in which it is found."

Christian belief, especially when referring to the institution of the Eucharist, is the object of tradition, important in the teaching of the primitive Church. Tradition is not legend, but rather a common body of information that is meant to be preserved without deformation, and was always considered more trustworthy than written records, at least until most recently. In the case of St. Laurence, tradition insists that Pope Sixtus II entrusted the Holy Cup of the Last Supper to his deacon and treasurer, Laurence, and that he, in turn, gave it to a Spaniard for safe-keeping. Modern scholars tend to cast doubt on the tradition due to the style of literary accounts that manifests the intentions of individual authors, but the tradition nevertheless remains on firm ground. Many of these will be examined in order to understand the difference between literary technique, tradition, historic truth, and legends[10], which often only serves to underscore the tremendous similarity between the various versions, in spite of variances in language, greater emphasis on certain events rather than others, omission of scenes, and amplification of conversations. Artistic technique can perhaps be understood better in terms of modern historical films and novels, which while they can hardly be considered as accurate as a video, they are solidly based on what we know about real people and events from written records. Although the style may change – illustrated in the differences between two films about Joan of Arc, for example – the veracity can still be trusted. So, while the stories of Laurence are all unique in a certain way, it is still possible to have confidence that this momentous act, the surrender of the Holy Grail to a Spaniard, really took place, because it is far more than conjecture, legend, or medieval fiction, having its roots deep within the Church that has always been the guardian of the truth □

---

[10] Unlike tradition, legends resemble folktales, and may include supernatural beings, elements from mythologies, or explanations of natural phenomena. They are generally considered as purely fictional, but the line varies, and even in the most sophisticated societies many strange legends are believed by the populous, one notable example being that of St. George and the dragon. Legend and tradition are often confused, but they are really worlds apart. The Laurentine tradition is supported by historical and physical evidence, but legends have woven implausible tales regarding his life, such as that in which Pope Sixtus II wanders through a forest in Spain, discovers the baby Laurence under a laurel, and raises the child. Although the Arthurian legends are clearly medieval fiction, a recent documentary on the Holy Grail actually questioned why Sir Galahad and the other Knights of the Round Table would have set out in search of the famous relic, as if they were historic personages rather than literary creations. It is perhaps for this very reason that the Spanish writer Cervantes set out to destroy the genre by inventing the ridiculous knight, Don Quixote, who read so many of these romances that he could not distinguish between reality and the human imagination.

Chapter 5

THE VALERIAN PERSECUTION

As mentioned, tradition maintains that the Holy Grail was used by the first Popes until Pope Sixtus II, who when forced to relinquish the property of the Catholic Church, including its most precious relics, chose martyrdom. Before his death, however, he entrusted the treasures to his deacon, St. Laurence, predicting that he would soon suffer the same fate as the Pontiff. Laurence, although certain that he would suffer greatly at the hands of the Romans, entrusted the Grail to a Spaniard, and gave the money to the poor, thus openly defying the established authority who responded with a dreadful punishment at that time fairly unknown: Laurence was cruelly tortured, and then roasted on a gridiron. Anyone who has seen the film *Gladiator* can understand that in spite of the magnificent successes of Rome in terms of roads, architecture, and political dominion over many nations, they were barbarians at heart with little regard for human suffering and death. Life was an expendable commodity, and torture and martyrdom were means to achieve control.

Those scholars who insist that Laurence was probably beheaded like Pope Sixtus II do not comprehend the series of events that took place. The Pope, as the highest authority of the Church, refused to surrender Church property and was beheaded. Laurence, the only surviving deacon, young and with far less authority, knowing that he would also be killed, not only refused to surrender the goods, but also publicly appeared to be mocking Roman authority by declaring in front of the crowds that the poor were the treasures of the Church. The authorities simply could not respond with the same punishment without losing face and seriously damaging the power they wielded over the population through fear tactics. It became absolutely imperative for them to make an example of Laurence that would not be soon forgotten.

The Valerian persecution of the third century in Rome, often difficult to understand so many centuries after it took place, was grounded in the fact that it was impossible that any system of morality such as that of the Christians could coexist with the Roman Empire, since Christianity was opposed to the very existence of the pagan creeds and cults and threatened the foundations of political and social life. Toleration was impossible, because Christianity and Heathenism were too different to allow for compromise, as Rev. Patrick J. Healy explains. He comments, "On the one side was all the strength and power of a magnificent empire, identified with a system of religion dear to the hearts of its patriotic citizens and closely interwoven with their history and traditions; on the other was this new creed, destitute of earthly grandeur and possessing neither temples nor history." The two parties could not be more unequally equipped, and the struggle ensued with great bitterness, with all the resources at the command of a vast empire directed against people whose only weapons were their doctrines, and whose only strength were the virtues they practiced. Christians faced scorn, contempt and social ostracism, but even worse was the enactment of laws that made Christianity a felony punishable by death.

Healy's perceptive analysis of the situation sheds much light on the historical backdrop for the surrender of the Holy Grail to Laurence, and its subsequent flight to Spain. The persecutions that took place during the reigns of Decius and Valerian marked the peak of the antagonism between Christianity and pagan Rome. Peace could not be achieved until one side or the other was completely eradicated, because the Roman Empire was not merely a physical union of different nations and peoples living under one centralized government. It was a union based on universal goals, the same beliefs and a common culture. The greatest possible liberty was permitted in the worship of new deities, but Christianity was opposed to this tolerance and syncretism, having firm beliefs that these practices were mere superstitions. Because it denied all existing forms of worship in the Empire, the new religion became a problem that had to be resolved. Its declaration that there was no difference between Jew and Greek, or between slave and freeman, cut at the root of society and threatened political stability. Christianity denied the authority of the state to regulate marriage, education, and religion itself, and was considered to be anarchistic and a serious threat to the future of the Empire.

Before the reign of Decius, Christian persecution was sporadic, but in January of 250 AD the new emperor issued an edict ordering all citizens to perform a religious sacrifice in the presence of commissioners. It was the worst trial that the Church had yet suffered. Many Christians resisted, and the government responded by arresting and killing many of their leaders, including the bishops of Rome, Jerusalem, and Antioch. Besides the large numbers of Christians who were put to death, many apostatized, and the Church was faced with the problem of deciding how they should be readmitted, which resulted in two schisms that left the entire Christian organization in disarray. In the final analysis, however, Christianity was strengthened rather than weakened, perhaps because public opinion favored the passive resistance of the martyrs. The persecutions ceased just a few months before Decius' death in 251.

Under Gallus, emperor from 251-253, Valerian held a command on the upper Rhine and was summoned to bring his armies from the north to aid in the struggle against the rival emperor Aemilian, who stood out in contrast to the cowardly and irresolute Gallus. Valerian did not arrive in time to save Gallus, but did manage to succeed him in power. During his short reign, Gallus had renewed the persecution of Christians when they refused to take part in the sacrifices that were offered to appease the gods because of the famine and plague that were devastating the Empire, which for a time claimed a total of five thousand victims a day. Seasons of drought were followed by terrible hailstorms and tornadoes, which ruined the crops, causing famine that killed thousands more; earthquakes, floods, and tidal waves followed. Never was the conflict between Christianity and the paganism of the Romans more intense. Christians were seen as the cause of the disasters and loss of life, simply because they refused to worship the Roman deities.

Valerian initiated his reign along with his son Gallienus, who was made co-regent, and continued the persecution of Christians with even greater vigor, determined to complete the unfinished work of Decius by uprooting Christianity from the Empire. This did not take place immediately, however. During the first years of his reign the Church was not molested due to the schisms that had occurred during the time of Decius, which weakened its power in the eyes of the emperor. Besides, Valerian was a man of high moral standards who was at first attracted by the virtues manifested by the Christians. His household was composed of many Christians, and his daughter-in-law was also Christian. When Valerian suddenly reversed his policy, however, the internal strife within the Church was quickly forgotten, and it became clear that something had induced the emperor to change his attitude. According to Healy and other scholars, Denis of Alexandria provides the answer, writing that Macrianus, the master of the Egyptian Magi, persuaded him to abandon this course, exhorting him to persecute the Christians as enemies and obstacles to their incantations. Valerian was advised to study rites of initiation and acts of sorcery, to perform sacrifices, to kill infants, to sacrifice children, and to mutilate and dismember newborns. Although some historians disagree, this information also appears in the manuscript of Donato, and certainly makes sense, given Valerian's abrupt reversal of policy.

The Empire had been daily sinking into a deeper state of ruin and disorder, which made Valerian more susceptible to Macrianus' influence. Every calamity was seen as a sign of the anger of the deities of Rome, who seemed to be punishing the entire Empire for the dereliction of Christians, considered to be outlaws as long as they refused homage to the gods of Rome. Persecution of the Church also seemed to promise relief from the financial burden that was threatening political stability. The government was bankrupt because sources of revenue had been cut off by the ruined commerce and agriculture. Reserve funds had been exhausted by the luxury of the court, the people were completely impoverished, and there were no resources to fight the many wars that had ensued.

In striking contrast to this deplorable state of the Empire was the apparent prosperity of the Church, which always possessed sufficient means to support the clergy, provide for services in the churches, maintain the cemeteries, and support the poor, the widows, and the orphans. Large sums of money were obtained through voluntary contributions made by members who were eager to renounce their worldly possessions, donations of wealthy converts, weekly collections, and a monthly tax. The Romans suspected that there was some immense fund available that was being used to seduce the people.

A decree was issued in the middle of the year 257, which clearly shows that Valerian's earlier benevolent attitude toward Christians had changed radically. According to the instructions given with the decree, the leaders of the Christian communities, the bishops and priests, were to be seized immediately. The members of the Christian hierarchy were to be compelled to render homage to the gods of Rome, but without requiring them to renounce their faith. In the case of refusal to perform acts of worship to pagan deities, the Church leaders were to be sent into exile. Finally, the Christians were to be warned that holding any assemblies or even entering their cemeteries would be punished with death. For the Christians, the cemeteries were not merely places for burial, but meeting places for the living, devoted to prayer and sacrifice. The edict was aimed principally at the clergy. Although the measures seemed milder than those of Decius, they were far more effective in depriving Christianity of its vitality, Healy explains.

Pope St. Stephen died on August 2, 257, and was succeeded by Pope Sixtus II on the thirtieth day of the same month. St. Stephen was slain at the altar and buried in the cemetery of St. Callixtus on the Appian Way, where the Christians continued to meet in spite of the prohibitions of the edict. A young acolyte named Tarcisium was killed when he refused to surrender the Blessed Sacrament that he was carrying to some of the confessors. A large number of the faithful who had assembled in a crypt to celebrate the first anniversary of the death of the martyrs Chrysanthus and Daria were also martyred. As they offered the Holy Sacrifice of the Mass, the soldiers stationed themselves at all of the exits so that no one could escape. Thus trapped, the Christians were put to death by being buried alive under a mass of stones and sand. Years later Pope Damasus discovered their skeletons, along with the sacred vessels used in the Mass, which were still clasped in the hands of the priests and deacons.

The clause of the edict that prohibited the use of the cemeteries and the holding of assemblies was the only one under which the laity could be convicted, and its punishment was usually death, although some were condemned to the mines. These Christians were first beaten with whips and rods, and then branded on their foreheads. Their heads were shaven on one side so that if they managed to escape they would be easily recognized as criminals. The prisoners included nine bishops who had sat in the Council at Carthage, as well as many other Christians of all ages.

When the first edict of Valerian was issued, Rome was at peace, having won back the territory that barbarian invaders had attempted to take. During the summer of 258, the emperor assembled all his great commanders near Byzantium, an occasion that was marked with great pageantry. Valerian conferred Aurelian, the future emperor and his favorite general, with the highest honors, extravagantly praising him in the presence of officers from all parts of the Empire in an attempt to restore order and public confidence. With the restoration of Roman power in the provinces, Valerian took advantage of the moment to issue his second edict of persecution against the Christians. Promulgated very shortly after the assembly, the rescript of 258 seemed to acknowledge that the law of the preceding year had failed in its goal of destroying the Church, although it certainly had caused the Christians some suffering and inconvenience. The exiled bishops had continued their supervision over the Christians, and the priests, although in hiding, had been able to continue their ministries. The removal of the bodies of St. Peter and St. Paul to temporary hiding places seemed to reinforce Valerian's belief that the decree was not strong enough.

The rescript commanded that bishops, priests, and deacons be immediately put to death. Senators, men of high rank, and knights of Rome were to be degraded and deprived of their possessions, and if they continued to be Christians, they were also to be punished with death. Matrons were to be deprived of their property and banished. The intent was to wound Christianity by eliminating its leaders, and to cut off its source of income by taking away its means of support. Its aim was the destruction of Christianity without trying to exterminate all those who professed faith in Christ, which would only depopulate the towns, fill the prisons, and tax the resources of the Empire. By cutting off all sources of power, influence and resources, the Church would be left impoverished and fatally weakened.

As soon as the edict was issued, Pope St. Sixtus II was seized and martyred on August 6 in the cemetery of Praetextatus, opposite that of Callixtus on the Via Appia, along with four deacons. Many have believed that the martyrdom took place immediately after his arrest, but the *Liber Pontificalis* relates that the pontiff was first led away to offer sacrifice, indicating that he was then brought before a tribunal to be sentenced according to the legalities of the time. After being condemned to death, he was sent back to the same place where he had been seized, in order to be executed in the place where he had broken the law. He was beheaded along with the deacons Januarius, Vincentius, Magnus and Stephanus. Two other deacons, Felicissimus and Agapitus, were martyred on the same day but in a different place. This event left the Church with only one surviving deacon, Laurence.

Recent criticism has stripped the martyrdom of St. Laurence of its most dramatic features, admitting only that he was martyred on August 10, 258, probably beheaded as were Sixtus II and his deacons. The story, however, that has been preserved by tradition is one that immediately captured the attention of the faithful. It was preserved in poetry, celebrated in medieval literature, and remembered in art and architecture as perhaps the most singular martyrdom of history: the story of the deacon St. Laurence who defied the Roman authorities' demand for the treasures of the Church, mocked them by gathering together the poor and lame, presenting them at the praetorium as the real treasures of the Church, and courageously suffered a cruel and painful death on a gridiron, after having endured every torture known to the Romans. It is not only the memory of his remarkable martyrdom that has endured to the present day, however, but also what might be considered to be one of the most transcendent acts of history: how St. Laurence saved the Holy Grail from destruction, at the cost of his life. In spite of the lack of written documentation, this heroic act is still immortalized in tradition and art, and cannot be eradicated even after nearly two thousand years.

It is at this point that Patrick Healy's arguments fail. Like other modern scholars, he objects that both Decius and Valerian are represented as taking part in the trial and condemnation of the martyr, whereas Decius was dead and Valerian in the Far East at the time. He writes that the quality of the dialogue between St. Laurence and his bishop "throw the gravest doubt on its authenticity," and "it can scarcely be believed" that Laurence would expose beggars and cripples to the fury and cruelty of a prefect of Imperial Rome. Doubt is also cast on the martyrdoms of Hippolytus, Romanus and Crescencius, canonized saints of the Church, and therefore, the conclusion by Healy and other modern scholars has been that the story of St. Laurence is nothing more than a legend, "pure and simple." The force of tradition, however, is not a simple matter that can be dismissed with the stroke of a pen.

It is true that both Decius and Valerian are represented in nearly every account of the passion of St. Laurence, but this is not surprising for the period of time in question, which lacked our modern means of communication, absolute accuracy in recording historical events, and electronic methods of publishing and disseminating material. What was most important for Christians was the fact that Decius had begun the persecution, which was intensified under Valerian. This made such a strong impression in the early Church that both were represented in later literary interpretations, as an article in the *New Catholic Encyclopedia* states[11]. Although written accounts may have amplified events to some extent, they did not invent things out of thin air. The undeniable fact of the terrible third-century persecutions under Decius and Valerian was important to those who endeavored to preserve the story for their readers, and if neither emperor was physically

---

[11] *New Catholic Encyclopedia* (New York, 1967), vol. 4, p.701.

present in the Roman praetorium when Laurence was arrested, that detail does not affect the authenticity of the tradition. Furthermore, St. Donato indicates in his biography of Laurence that the Decius mentioned in the tradition was not the Emperor Decius who initiated the persecution in 250 AD but a prefect who happened to have the same name.

Certainly, if Pope Sixtus II entrusted Laurence with the treasures of the Church, including the Holy Grail and other relics, there would have been a dialogue between them containing the essence of the tradition: that the Pontiff knew he was about to die, that he wanted to entrust Laurence with the responsibility, as treasurer of the Church, of distributing the money and saving the relics, including the Grail, that Laurence also desired martyrdom as the highest crown possible for a Christian, and that Sixtus predicted that Laurence would be martyred only a few days later, in a much crueler fashion. If some of the accounts embellish this conversation, it is not proof that it never took place.

It is evident that Laurence believed that he would soon be martyred, because he immediately carried out the last wishes of the Pontiff, and his actions demonstrate that he did not fear death. Tape recorders didn't exist in the third century, but events, including the essence of the words that were spoken, traveled quickly and were preserved orally, which was the only means possible at the time. To conclude that the tradition is false, or invented, nearly two thousand years later, in a different epoch with a totally distinct culture and way of life, is a form of modern arrogance that changes the past to fit the mindset and technology of the present. The words that were exchanged between Pope Sixtus II and Laurence were undoubtedly amplified, but that does not throw the "gravest doubt" on the essence of the tradition.

It is certainly without doubt that Laurence would have been given the responsibility for the treasures of the Church, including the Holy Grail and other relics. He was the treasurer of the Church and the only deacon who was not killed along with the Pope. It is also certain that the Roman authorities would have arrested him in order to obtain the wealth. The story of how he presented the poor and lame to the authorities is very consistent with what we know about Laurence, especially his love for the poor and his strong desire to suffer for Christ, as well as his love for evangelization. St. Donato indicates that he loved to teach the doctrines of Christianity, converting many in the process. Although martyrdom on a gridiron was fairly unknown at the time, it shortly thereafter became the norm. It is therefore quite likely that Laurence was one of the first, which would have inspired Christians everywhere, leading to the multitude of hymns, poems, and narrative accounts that were later recorded. Furthermore, without the scene at the praetorium, in which the young and fervent Laurence appears to be mocking the governmental authority, "asking for it" in the eyes of the Romans, his exceptionally cruel death makes no sense whatsoever. Laurence distinguished himself as unusual, someone who would proclaim his faith and defy Rome, in spite of whatever dangers were involved in doing so. The authorities responded with an equally unusual punishment.

The life of St. Laurence according to St. Donato is the most detailed account in existence about his childhood and youth: his birth in Valencia, the shipwreck in Italy as a small child on a pilgrimage to the Holy Land with his parents, his involvement and move to Rome as a disciple of Sixtus II, his love for the poor, and possibly the most complete and moving account of his martyrdom, which although it closely follows the major events of the fifth-century Latin *Passio Polychronii*, includes mention of the surrender of the Holy Grail. The story preserves the ancient names of towns, reflects the mindset and values of the third century, is written in accordance with early documents that begin their narration with the story of the flood, and shows a remarkable love for accuracy and detail. It is an exceptional document that explains how many of the errors about Laurence have occurred, including the reason why so many have mistakenly believed that he was born in Huesca, rather than Valencia. The details about his early life, the shipwreck, the crucifixion of his parents in Rome, and so many other details do not appear in any other existing account.

St. Donato was an abbot who came to Valencia from Africa, along with many companions from the Augustinian order of monks. According to this document, because of the generosity of the matron Minicea he founded the Servitano Monastery, dedicated to St. Martin, on the side of the promontory of Ferratia, between Setabicula and Dianio, instituting for the first time the monastic discipline in that area. According to this document, his duties as an abbot required him to go down to Valencia quite often, where he was informed about the details of the life of St. Laurence by the older presbyters of the Church. At that time there were still monuments in honor of Laurence and his family: the place where his parents, Orencio and Paciencia, had their hut, the house and bedroom where Laurence was born, and the jail cells where Bishop Valerius and his deacon Vincent were held with chains. St. Donato confirms that Vincent was the son of Paciencia's younger sister Enola, that Laurence was born on December 26, 225, and that the account of his martyrdom is based on books and other information that he considers trustworthy, a certain indication that many more sources were in existence in the sixth century than now.

This information can be confirmed from *Libro V* of the seventeenth-century *Anales del Reyno de Valencia*, which states that although some modern writers believed that the Monasteries of the Servitano and San Martín were different, as did Ambrosio de Morales and Esteban de Garibay, they were indeed one and the same, located on the promontory of Ferratia. Fray Francisco Diago writes in the Anales that Donato was a saint who came from Africa with seventy monks and many manuscripts, and that in the time of King Leovigild he had already been in Spain about seventeen years. Minicea Elfa helped Donato found the Monastery, being a descendent of those of her family who came to Spain in the time of the Romans.

Diago also confirms that Laurence was born in Valencia, not Huesca, a belief shared by every ancient writer. He write that Orencio and Paciencia were originally from Huesca, where they had a house that is now a church, but due to the Roman persecutions of the time, they came to Valencia where Laurence was born. *The Anales* mention the surrender of the Holy Grail as well, saying that Laurence was entrusted with saving the important relics by sending them to other parts, *"among them the Cup of the Lord, a piece of great worth for being made of a precious stone, similar to chalcedony and incomparable for being that in which on the night of the Last Supper the wine was consecrated by Christ into his own blood when he instituted the Most Holy Sacrament of the Altar."*

Given the fact that there is nothing in existence that could contest the accuracy of Donato's account, it is translated in the following chapter as the most complete biography of St. Laurence, shedding great light on the details surrounding the flight of the family to Italy, Laurence's upbringing and education under Pope Sixtus II, and his eventual martyrdom for the faith. It also provides substance for the tradition that Laurence entrusted the precious relic to a Spaniard, mentioning even his name □

Part 3

ST. LAURENCE AND
THE HOLY GRAIL

*Among those who had taken refuge there
he found Precelius, his co-disciple and fellow
countryman, because he was a Spaniard from the
city of Hippo in Carpentanea. To him he entrusted
some memorable relics so that he could send them
to Spain, and among them was the most renowned
Cup in which Christ our Good, and Master,
consecrated his precious blood on the
night of the Last Supper.*

Life and Martyrdom of the Glorious Spaniard
St.Laurence,taken from some ancient writings
of the celebrated Abbot Donato

Chapter 6

ST. LAURENCE'S LIFE
ACCORDING TO DONATO

The account that follows is a translation of the manuscript in the Biblioteca Nacional of Madrid, entitled *Life and Martyrdom of the Glorious Spaniard St. Laurence, Taken from some ancient writings of the celebrated Abbot Donato, Founder of the Servitano Monastery of the Order of St. Augustine*, published in Salamanca in the year 1636 by Father Buenaventura Ausina, Doctor of Theology, Professor of Huesca and current rector of the Augustinian College in the city of Salamanca. Although the original is not extant, it is reputed to be a seventeenth-century translation of the only known early manuscript (sixth century) mentioning the surrender of the Holy Grail to St. Laurence, entrusted by Pope Sixtus II to his treasurer and deacon only days before his martyrdom. It is translated into English with an attempt to preserve the language and tone of the original.

CHAPTER 1: *Condition of Spain when the glorious Martyr St. Laurence was born.*

The valiant and noble Spain was for much time the unfortunate scene of cruelty and tyranny. Tubal, son of Japheth and grandson of the holy patriarch Noah, populated it in the year 142 after the flood, according to the most accepted calculations. Hercules of Egypt tyrannized Spain. The Greeks devastated it, coming from Zacinto, and together they decorated it with sumptuous temples, sowing idolatry that remained for many centuries. The Argonauts arrived on its beaches, and the Rutulos of Aldea invaded it, dominating the country for many years, until the calamity of drought left it almost unpopulated. It was restored from this lamentable destruction; and envious of

Spain's treasures, many Jews lived there from whom Adoniram, minister of King Solomon, demanded tribute; when taken by death his greed was buried in Sagunto. The Phoenicians from Tyre also inhabited it; afterward the Phocaeans from Ionia, and consecutively those of Carthage, whose tyrannical ardor was reason for those of Sagunto to resist, forming a confederation with the Romans whom they emulated. The Romans, under the pretext of favoring them, conquered them, which in the beginning was no more than amicable protection.

In this state the universal Redemption took hold of Spain, which was dominated by Romans who changed it into the battleground of their civil wars, and with the yoke of slavery, established their rites and rituals, founding different colonies in order to make itself secure from the warlike nations. The Alans, Vandals, and Goths withdrew when the faith of Jesus Christ had become deeply enrooted, having been spread by the Apostle James, son of Zebedee, favored by the Princes of the Apostles St. Peter and St. Paul, and watered with the blood of innumerable martyrs. And thus, although the northern nations arrived infected with the epidemic of Arian, the ancient Spaniards practiced the Catholic religion with burning devotion; especially the people of Carpentania (La Mancha), Illergetes (the region of Lérida including Huesca), Celtiberia (Valencia, from Segorbe toward Aragón), Edetania (from Almacora to beyond the Albufera), and many others.

CHAPTER 2: *Origin of the parents of the Martyr St. Laurence.*

Before the arrival of the calamities that the nations of the south brought to Spain with Arianism, there was in the towns of Illergetes (whose borders extended to the edge of the Pyrenees), a famous city called Osca (today Huesca), valiant in arms, celebrated in letters, renowned in nobility, and abundant with all the good things that Heaven, with a liberal hand, generally endows. It was known throughout the world, because in this region *bigatos* and *quadrigatos* were made, silver coins envied by all, which they commonly called *argentum osense*, or silver of Huesca[1]. Almost all of its inhabitants were Christians, who with reverent devotion and pure faith, observed the doctrines taught by the holy Apostles of Jesus Christ, and remained free from error for a long time.

Among all of them, a patrician named Orencio was noted as much for his virtue as his nobility, from the most ancient lineage of the city, awarded with military trophies by his elders and peers for having been a captain in the Spanish army, but much more for those people he brought to the service of the Most High. He was married to a noblewoman, a matron called Paciencia, Orencio's equal because of her generosity and the virtuous habits of her blood. They were the most frequent visitors of the old Church of St. Peter[2], which is understood to be the first in Huesca dedicated by its inhabitants. They were conscientious in all acts of devotion, those who most uplifted the people with their example, and those who most generously helped the poor, as much with money as with everything else needed by the afflicted. Although Orencio was of noble blood, his ordinary occupation was farming, because in the pure simplicity of those times, the first-rank nobility did not in lazy idleness feed themselves with vanity. In times gone by they occupied their time employed in honest endeavors, dignifying themselves when they supported themselves by their own work. *Labores manum tuarum quia manducabis: beatus es, et bene tibi erit*[3]. Once in Israel the prophet Elias had been seen farming, and those who had been chosen for the Kingdom were selected from the fields, those of the staff for the power. And later in Rome, the most famous heroes were taken from the fields. And even more recently in Spain almost the same thing has been seen: that this virtue no longer involves the nobility, but was formerly the polish that ennobled Spain the most.

Orencio owned a hacienda in the country, (opulent for that time), about a half league from Huesca. And although it had an overseer, and lads who took care of it, when other work didn't prevent him he enjoyed putting his hand to the plough, or taking the hoe or the pruning knife to the ploughed field,

---

[1] A large number of ancient coins of Huesca have been found in many archaeological excavations throughout all of Spain. Coins of silver were in circulation 2,000 years ago, and in the time of the first Roman emperors, they were made with the Latin name *OSCA* on one side, with the faces of Augustus, Tiberius and Caligula on the reverse.

[2] San Pedro el Viejo, where according to tradition St. Vincent was baptized. As will be seen, Donato believes that Vincent was the son of Enola, Paciencia's younger sister.

[3] Work with your own hands so that you may eat: you will be blessed and things will go well for you. Translated by Mark Guscin, historian of the Spanish Center for Sindonology, responsible for the historical investigations on the Sudarium of Oviedo.

humble but decent work that gave him the utmost consolation because he was imitating so many patriarchs, monarchs, potentates, and princes. O fortunate times, in which vanity (if the nobles were familiar with it) consisted of meeting one's obligations more fully, not in boasting of having been born a noble, in order to apply oneself more immoderately to the vices! O happy time in which it was only considered indecent to be lazy, because when the clamor of arms was sleeping, the most famous captain and the most valiant knight who didn't work, didn't eat, and was not considered to be a reputable person!

CHAPTER 3: *A cruel persecution comes upon Orencio and he tries to leave his home.*

According to what has been said, ambitious Rome dominated all of Spain, and as the Caesars and Magistrates vilely followed paganism and idolatry, in order to foster that fabulous superstition, they procured, by means of its presidents and ministers, that Christianity would not be permitted in any province of the Empire. The Roman Laurel had tightened around the temples of Severus Pertinaz, when the Most Holy Prelate of León, Irenco, communicated to the world the light of his doctrine. And the bloody Emperor, in order to exterminate the faith in one blow, ordered that all of the Christians who lived in that city be put to death with a knife, and with such a leader as Irenco, they happily suffered martyrdom, and flew to the celestial city. The Pastor was happy a thousand times over, who knew how to bring into his fold those whose upbringing had been entrusted to him.

Severus immediately sent Cornelius to Spain to govern as president. He landed in Tarragona, and left for Valencia (maritime city in Editania) as soon as he entered the city, having been informed that there were many Christians there, issuing the cruel message: *Non quid post Severi Principis, Severam, laudabilenque Lagdunensium trucidationem, in his locis Christianitatis inditia remanserunt?* Which says in Romance: *How is it that, after the laudable and severe rigor of Prince Severus toward those who were cut to pieces in León, there remain in these towns indications of Christendom?* Thus it is that Severus ruled (not Valerian or Diocletian, as some have said without basis) when Cornelius came to Spain. Nor could he terrorize with the fact that there were fifty or one hundred years that passed.

He found out that the presbyter Feliz, along with his deacons Fortunatus and Archileus, was preaching the Gospel there. He ordered them to appear, and as they remained constant in the Faith, with exquisite torments he crowned their perseverance, and they, victorious, flew to Heaven, martyred in the same place where they had their humble shelter [4], on the 23rd of April, in the year 243, which corresponds to the year of Christ 205 in Valencia, which was in Editania and not in the region of the Delfinado, because there Cornelius did not rule; nor in Alcántara because at that time it didn't have such a name, but rather that of Mendicalea, and the *Acts* clearly state that they suffered in Valencia.

Cornelius was president the entire time that Severus ruled, as well as his son Antoninus Caracala, who ruled until the year 217, continuing his cruelties with the Christians with more or less activity, as the events of that time permitted. He resided in Valencia most of the time he governed, where he left witnesses in the form of many relatives of both sexes. Macrinus and Diadymedus had hardly warmed the Imperial seat when the soldiers killed them. Heliogabalus, the successor, didn't have dealings other than vileness, and Alexander, acclaimed by the legions of the Alps, although he didn't hate the Christians as son of Mamea, who esteemed them, because he was occupied totally with arms, he entrusted everything political to Domicius Ulpianus, celebrated jurisconsult and prefect of the praetorium, cruel persecutor of the name of Christ. He began to bloody Rome, and so that the Church didn't rest in Spain, he sent as president a friend of the same inclination, named Alexander. The blood shedding began later, and as the beginning of a government usually gives signs of its intentions, when he was going to Toledo he martyred the Holy Matron Julita in the nearby town of Yepes, who, fleeing the persecution, had come there from Seleucia with her son Quirico, not much more than three years previously. The cruel tyrant threw the child against the stones because he understood him to be a Christian, resisting the pleas of the mother who had him in her arms. After giving the mother an extremely cruel lashing, he ordered that she be cut to pieces. Those who say that this martyrdom took place in Tarsis of Cilicia are mistaken, because, as Yepes is called Hyppo, the matter is easily resolved. This truth is proved after having

---

[4] As Donato explains later, this abandoned hut in Valencia was later found by Orencio and Paciencia, Laurence's parents, and it is where Paciencia gave birth to her son Laurence.

discovered her holy relics a few years later in Carpentania in a place called Histonium, today Hyto, located between Saelices and Villaeseusa, not far from the old Valeria. They remain in Burgos in a special church consecrated to St. Quirico,[5] whose Abbey dignifies that church and is commonly called St. Quirce. The finding of her remains occurred in the year 300, during the rule of Diocletian and Maximilian. The result of this is that if, in Cilicia, others suffered who had the same name, it was not these people because they were martyred in the first year of Alexander Mamea. Some say that it was 222, but I believe it was 224, which corresponds to the time of 262.

CHAPTER 4: *The parents of St. Laurence try to leave, and they go to Valencia.*

Such a horrendous evil as it was to kill by your hand an innocent of three years of age flew through all of Spain, making the hearts of all the faithful who lived there tremble. Those most constant in the Faith conceived such horror that even though they had their necks put to the knife or the rope, their bodies put to the knife or to other torments, they wisely preceded the great blood shedding that threatened this early stage: the storm of evils that was about to be unleashed upon Christ's flock and the detriment foreseen for the Catholic religion, because among such a multitude they feared there would be some whose weakness would be a scandal to the others. St. Orencio grieved more for his dear wife than for himself because it seemed to him, rightly, that that sex ran a greater risk, because of its natural weakness and the dangers of modesty that come before life in women with obligations like his wife. He wanted to encourage her and couldn't find the way. He wanted to dry her tears, so much more obvious to him because they were repressed, and the way did not occur to him. Because the solid virtue that she possessed sealed her lips, he didn't want to offend her with mistrust. He was perhaps going to propose it, and couldn't manage to get it out. In the middle of this confusion, St. Paciencia guessed the battle that as going on in his chest and said to him with sobs and tears:

---

[5] The hermitage dedicated to Sts. Julita and Quirico still exists in Burgos.

Sweetest husband and my lord, it is not time to cover up your feelings. It is no longer possible to hide the pain that afflicts us. The blow that threatens us is no longer just a threat, but evident. The cruelty of the tyrants that rule us already brandishes the whip and the fire in the persecution; there is no longer any sex or age that is safe from danger: Julita, irreprehensible matron, and Quirico, innocent child. She had hardly arrived to these western regions when, enclosed by tyranny, she saw the lamb torn apart, and its neck cut with barbarous rigor. He, in the orient of his tender age, experienced the infernal fury of Alexander, even before having the sagacity to offend anyone. Happy were they who so quickly died to the danger, and were reborn in eternal rest, crowned with martyrdom. Happy are we who see ourselves exposed to the risk of hesitating because of our weakness, or through our own fault. They already say that the President rules Carpentania, and is approaching Celtiberia, for in Salduba the Christians are experiencing his cruelties. Who doubts that from there he would come to this city, which he has so close by, although he wouldn't have any motive other than that of visiting the coin factory, that those of our nation esteem so much? And who doubts that the same Magistrates, who are idolaters, must accuse us because of how many of us march under the standard of the Cross, either to please themselves, or to destroy us? We must rightly wait for divine clemency, so that when placed in the midst of the danger it will assist us with the necessary constancy; but we don't have to search for it, because he who seeks, perishes. We must thus fear that as miserable people the Divine Justice can find itself irritated against us, and if it were thus, what refuge would there be for us? The essential truth of the Gospel advises the body to flee the persecution. Let us flee, my Lord, to regions where they won't know us. Let us abandon the conveniences of our house and hacienda. Let us follow the example of so many illustrious men in sanctity who have done the same. Let us put everything in the hands of God, who is a good father, and if it is necessary to his holy service, he will favor us in the pilgrimage. And if it were ordained that we die in martyrdom, it would come through his Divine Plan, with which it will be certain that He must contribute with the gift of strength, and on our part we will have to add the pain of this voluntary exile, on behalf of his love.

St. Orencio was amazed by the prudence of his wife in considering the same things that he had been thinking. And lovingly giving her many thanks for the warning, he spoke to her in this way:

Who will be able, dear wife, to explain the esteem with which I hear such beneficial advice: is it only that fulfilling what you are proposing to me would declare the pleasure with which I have listened to it? These tears, as much as I want to drink them, take from my eyes the tenderness with which I hold you in esteem, they confirm the love with which I accept your pleas. I recognize the evidence of the danger, the certainty of the harm, the little reason there is to trust in human frailty, but in the middle of all of this, I know that the prudence of men is very limited, and the more they presume to be secure, the more they are lost. We will place our doubts with God, who cannot err, nor is He accustomed to permit that those who take refuge in his holy will, with all their hearts, will err. Let us take advantage of the intercession of his Most Pure Mother Mary. Let us compel them with a three-day fast and incessant prayer during all of this time, so that with this we will be able to hope for their mercy, that it enlighten us in so much confusion.

Paciencia was very consoled seeing her husband so attentive in using the means necessary to choose what was best, so that the fire not soften the iron that is far-off, nor the water fertilize the earth from the cloud, fountain or brook. Implementation is what makes activity have an effect on suffering, and without it nothing can be done. The devout ones fasted religiously in those days, without ceasing from praying, in which with tears and sighs they asked the Divine Majesty to inspire them as to what would be his greatest desire. God is very faithful with his servants, and when the petitions are for his greater glory, He is very honest in showing them what is necessary by different means; He does not always have to send an Angel to reveal it, or work a miracle to point it out. He knows how to speak to the depths of hearts, and by subtle means governs the souls that serve Him. They both knew clearly that God wanted them to leave their homeland, and thus they resolved to obey, without paying attention to the difficulties or the inconveniences, because his Divine Majesty subdues everyone when he wants it to be. And when he doesn't, what seems easiest cannot be done, nor does one know how to obtain it. As they feared being discovered, they prepared for the day, without any of the family knowing it[6]. Which could be facilitated, having that hacienda in the country that they frequented during many seasons of the year, because their friends in the town

---

[6] This corroborates the tradition that the family of Laurence's parents remained in Huesca where his cousin Vincent was later born of Paciencia's sister Enola, and baptized in the church of San Pedro el Viejo. Hence, the reason why the Grail would have been sent to Huesca is clear: there were no family members living in Valencia.

[7] According to tradition, Orencio and Paciencia had two residences: one in the town of Huesca, and another on their farm just outside the city.

believed that they were there, as at other times, and the servants of the village wouldn't miss them, even knowing that they had left their house, and were not coming to the country estate or farm.[7] The most precious of their belongings they had sold covertly, whose price they distributed almost entirely among the poor, reserving a minimal part for the expenses of the trip. It was their intention to embark and go to regions where they wouldn't be known. And as the closest beach was that of Valencia, they directed their steps there, always going by paths apart from the actual road. The solitude of those lands gave them reason to raise their thoughts to the Creator, and praising the works of his omnipotence, displayed by the beauty of the Heavens, the light of the Stars, the making of the world, the amenity of the fields, the coolness of the forests, the highness of the mountains, the fecund humility of the valleys, the leafiness of the trees, the fragrance of the flowers, the flavor of fruits, the eternity of the fountains, the lightness of the birds, and the variety of animals. From this they speculated on the infinity of his wisdom, because everything was ordained so perfectly, that lack or excess cannot be noted. They came to meditate on his tender love, because He did everything for the service of men. And when mankind had most ungratefully and perfidiously irritated his goodness, He sent his eternal Son, so that with his own blood He would redeem them. And confessing to owe Him all of this goodness, they gave Him humble thanks, and reverently praised his glorious name. Once more they meditated on the journey that Most Holy Mary, Joseph, and the Child Jesus made to Egypt, fleeing the tyranny of Herod. They reminded the Queen of the Angels of the cares, pains and trials that she suffered, so that she would be their refuge, northern star, and guide on that journey that they had undertaken to flee from another tyrant. With these thoughts the discomforts of the pilgrimage were made easier for Paciencia, who felt frail, seeing herself exiled from the gift of her house, the company of her relatives, the assistance of her servants, on foot, through mountains, and forests, exposed to the inclemency of the weather, to the dangers of solitude, and to the insults that she rightly feared, at the time that Spain was agitated by the cruelties of the President. Orencio consoled her with gentle and prudent reasons, and gave her whatever his scant wealth permitted, in the barrenness of the places through which they were passing. They didn't even go into the small towns, where one rarely finds what is sought. Divine Providence guided them, so that they arrived healthy and happy in the city of Valencia.

CHAPTER 5: *The way of life that they adopted in Valencia.*

Valencia has always been amenable, because favored by Heaven with a very mild climate, it is hardly familiar with frost and ice. The entire year it enjoys the mildness of springtime, that not even winter disturbs with excessive rigor in that plain that the city dominates; nor does the heat of summer inflame it much, which would be intolerable; the light sea breezes refresh it, which the Mediterranean sends in gentle waves, that fall very close by, at a distance of two miles. Turia inundates its fields with beauty, always crowned with roses and orange blossoms, that neither the flowers of the Hibleos envy, nor the fruits of the orchards of Pomona. For that reason it is rare that the foreigner, having enjoyed its delights, knows how to leave it, without feeling sorry that he is leaving it. The natives, being warlike people, take care to give a royal welcome to strangers; and shelter them in their necessities with generous politeness.

It was necessary for them to stop, as much to recover from the fatigue of the trip, as because Orencio lacked the means to continue, because the modest savings that he had taken from his house had been consumed during the pilgrimage. Those who put all of their hope in earthly things, think that prudence, when they have to walk, consists in having enough money so that they lack nothing, and often this fails either because they are robbed, or because they consume it all so quickly that they suddenly realize that nothing is enough. On the contrary, the Saints place all of their hope in God, without paying attention to human means, and thus find themselves taken care of in their necessities by such a powerful hand. It would have been easy for Orencio to walk with more conveniences, and to have provided himself with enough money so that he would lack for nothing for many years, but as a lover of poverty, he chose to give it to the poor, and to leave everything for Jesus Christ, with which he was assured of the greatest achievement, and more and more he found himself accompanied by such a precious virtue.

He determined to acquire the means to support himself and his wife by the sweat of his brow, and happily undertook this endeavor, taking refuge in a humble hut (half burned and almost destroyed) that he found without an owner in the eastern part of the city, between the border of Turia and the wall. He fixed it as best he could with branches. And it was, without doubt, Divine Providence, because it was the same house that twenty years previously had given refuge to the Holy Martyrs Felix, Fortunatus, and Arquileus[8], and they left it enriched with their blood, because it was in that same place where they were beheaded for the Faith. In this hut, happier than the monarchs in their rich and magnificent *alcázars*[9], they lived as poor people, but happy, exiled on behalf of Christ, but more consoled than in their homeland. They lived more like angels than men, because given with fervor for every kind of virtue, they only breathed to bless the Lord, and they didn't take a step that wasn't directed to serve Him.

In Valencia there was a great Sanctuary, consecrated by the Apostle Santiago (James)[10] to the Holy Sepulcher of our Redeemer that remains even today, and the Cathedral Church of the Invocation of San Salvador, that at the time was governed by the Holy Bishop Felicianus. Orencio and Paciencia came to one of these Churches every morning to commend themselves to God, to hear the Holy Sacrifice of the Mass, when it was celebrated, (which was not every day in those troubled times, nor was it without danger that they came to the House of God) and to pray as much as they were able, in which they would ask his Divine Majesty to grant peace to his Church, consolation to the Faithful, and help in all of their necessities. For themselves, that He take them in his hands, and that He illuminate them with how they could serve Him.

Paciencia was able to pray more than Orencio, because for her it wasn't necessary to go out to earn a living by manual labor. Thus, one day, when she was very devoutly asking all this of His Majesty through the intercession of his Mother, Felicianus noticed the appearance of that woman: Her honesty and composure, the modesty of her beautiful appearance, the humble and clean clothing, and the devotion with which she prayed. He called to her and asked her who she was, and from where she had come, inspiring her humility with pious exhortations. Prostrate, Paciencia asked for his blessing, and answered his question by relating the entire story, and concluded by saying that her petitions were being directed toward being able to know the holy will of God, in order to fulfill it with complete submission. The Bishop was completely attentive listening to the discretion and great modesty with which the Saint spoke to him of their work. And penetrating the depth of that virtuous simplicity, he consoled her with his doctrine, and encouraged her with spiritual consolation. He promised to

---

[8] In Chapter III, Donato mentions that they were martyred in Valencia on April 23, 205, during the reign of Severus.

[9] Royal palaces.

[10] The tradition that James the Apostle went to Spain finds support in many ancient documents.

help her and her husband (although in that time the Prelates were richer from tribulation than from income) and to ask the Divine Majesty in his sacrifices to inspire them with what they need most.

Paciencia, consoled by his words, informed Orencio that night of what had happened with Bishop Felicianus, and encouraged by the persuasion of his wife, he looked for him on the first feast day, and prostrate at his feet, told him who he was, and asked him affectionately if he, as Pastor, would take them as his sheep, so that they not err in their voluntary exile. The Holy Prelate comforted him, so that he would continue on that road, adding that according to his understanding, God was arranging something pointed to his service; he thought that at that time it was necessary to persevere in that state. The interior consolation that Orencio received from this advice manifested to him that the Holy Spirit was speaking to him through the mouth of Felicianus. The spiritual fathers tend to be the voice of the Most High, whom he uses to speak with his creatures, when they humbly consult the doubts of their consciences.

CHAPTER 6: *Paciencia discovers she is pregnant, and how God helps her in the delivery.*

Orencio returned happily to his hut, and told Paciencia what had happened, and both, with complete resignation, accepted as compulsory the advice that the Pastor had given them. They continued that way of life, and within a few days the Saint realized that she was pregnant, which was the cause of great joy for both of them. Orencio quickly began to realize how much in need the pregnancy had caught them, and how much harm it could give his wife, which would wrap the newborn in a helplessness such as what he was suffering. He placed his confidence in the mercy of God, and put this worry at the feet of the Most Holy Mary, begging her to obtain the help of her pious Son. His pain was not so secret that it was hidden from Paciencia, and without neglecting to ask the supreme Goodness, he tried to find the means possible. And the pious Lord, who gently grants what he wants, used this instrument in order to console them. Paciencia was skillful in making linen. She had looked for someone who could give it to her, and found no one; because as no one knew her they feared losing it. Because of those who pretend to be poor, discrediting the virtue, those who are really poor are placed in greater distress.

She had suffered some rejection, but exercising the virtue of her name, persevered in being diligent. One day, when she was praying in front of the Holy Sepulcher with her customary devotion, a woman who was a widow, rich, and a good Christian, noticed the honest goodness of the foreigner, and her reverent attendance at the Sanctuary that she also frequented. She sat down at her side, and asked her where she was from. Paciencia satisfied her question with such gentleness of reasons, (pointing out the helplessness in which she found herself), that the women, moved to pity, begged her to say how she could help her. Then Paciencia said:

My greatest affliction consists of not being able to help myself by means of my work. I do it reasonably, but as a foreigner, no one trusts me. And as the necessity of the pregnancy is pressing on me (because my poor husband must earn a living for both of us), it is necessary to beg you to take pity on me, and find me linen to make for the price to which you are accustomed; my punctuality would not present you with any risk. I ask you this for love of God, and I beg it of you on behalf of his most holy Mother.

The affliction could not stop the tears that with copious abundance wet her cheeks. It is a great sorrow, when one has nothing, to have once had money, and even more if necessity is pressing. The integrity of the Saint gave signs of what she was feeling with her tears. Columba was taking a liking to her (this was the name of the matron) and from the fondness was born compassion; and taking her to her house, after having welcomed her to the use of the land, she gave her linen to make.

The cloth was for blouses for her single daughter, who was tormented by the devil, although she never declared it. She gave it to her, and sent her off happy. Paciencia, with much skill and promptness, finished the work. And taking it to her much sooner than expected, she found that the woman was very generous in paying her for her promptness and for the quality of the workmanship. And she offered to tell her friends, so that she would have as much work as she was able to complete. God willed that when the miserable daughter was dressed in the first of those blouses, the foul spirit, by virtue of such hands, left that body screaming, saying: *That the foreigner was expelling him from his dwelling.* Sanity returned to her, and Columba, understanding, because of the effect that the unexpected declaration had on her, went out in search of her, in order to thank her for such a great favor. Although she had given signs of her whereabouts, she only managed to find her with difficulty, because she hadn't been convinced that the foreigner would have lived in such humble dwellings. She was amazed seeing the extreme poverty of the hut, whose bed was nothing more than some straw where they reclined, and the few pieces of furniture necessary to put together a tenuous meal. After having given her infinite thanks for the health of her daughter (which left Paciencia confused, because she was ignorant of what had happened), seeing her pregnant, and in such an inadequate dwelling, offered her a room in her own house with compassion, along with everything that would be necessary for the birth. She made her understand how much risk she would suffer by giving birth in a poorly constructed hut of hay with weak branches, easily penetrated by the harsh winds of the winter that was expected.

Paciencia thanked her for the offering (knowing that the hand of God was behind it), but added that without the permission of her husband she could not allow it, no matter how much she wanted to. Columba could not resist such diligence based on reason, and agreeing with what she was doing, returned to her home, admiring such rare virtue, with the joy that comes from expecting to have such holy guests in it. Paciencia was much happier, and did not cease praising God, because in such an unexpected way He was consoling her in her greatest affliction. When Orencio returned from the field he realized what was happening, and the holy Farmer agreed to allow this act of charity, thanking the Lord for such a great favor.

Columba had a very large house in the heart of the city, close to the meat shops, and not far from the port of Sucronense. In one of the family bedrooms, separated from the others, she ordered a bed to be placed from those that served the women servants, with other furnishings that the farmers might need, because at that time she did not understand that they were more than that. And although, without doing without, she could have given them a larger room, adorned with better furnishings, she didn't dare, realizing that such virtuous people would reject anything that wasn't necessary. Orencio, a lover of true poverty, on the one hand hated to leave the hut that he so loved, but on the other hand, recognizing that his wife was close to childbirth, desired her comfort and safety. But seeing that the preparation of the lodging contained nothing superfluous, he happily moved into the new dwelling, offering himself at the service of Columba and her daughter Eleuteria. And she, noticing Orencio's politeness, realized that his way of speaking, and such sensible and justified attention were not from a rustic farmer, but from someone with much greater bearing, and with time came to know that she was not mistaken.

CHAPTER 7: *Happy birth of Laurence, and the signs that began to let it be known what he was to become.*

Paciencia, the more the pregnancy advanced, the more she enjoyed spiritual delights in her soul, from which she prudently deduced that the Fruit of her womb would be such that the name of the Most High would be praised through it. And she was not mistaken, because with suffering being the lot of Saints, that tender plant, even before being born, was beginning to possess her. With continuous prayer she begged the Omnipotent One to free her from the dangers of childbirth, so that what she was carrying in her womb would be born with the happy event of receiving the most holy Baptism, and that if it were desirable he would grow up in the exaltation of the Faith. She felt within herself a gentle zeal, but passionate; sweet, but active; tender, but strong; that made her desire Martyrdom, inflaming her completely, as if her chest were burning with a flame of Divine love. The inspirations enlightened her, understanding that that Child very soon would be great in the eyes of God. On the other hand, although she was paying the debt contracted by the first mother, in the exertions brought by pregnancy, either the love in which she was burning smoothed them, or the blessed offspring tempered them, who had been conceived in the midst of tribulation and groans, in the middle of exile, work and fears. Because she was not experiencing the distress, fainting, and other mishaps that normally accompany pregnancy, nor was she feeling that weight or impediment that in similar cases normally accompany it, she deduced that it all was a gift from the Most High, because his powerful right hand was comforting her.

The day of the birth of our Savior arrived, and both celebrated it, with religious ceremonies and profound devotion. On the feast day of the martyr St. Stephen, before daybreak, Paciencia began to feel the pains of childbirth. She tried to hide them, but in vain, because later Orencio would see them. Foreseeing what would be necessary, according to what was possible, Orencio tried to call someone to assist her, as is customary. But Columba hardly managed to come down with one of her maids, when a beautiful Infant was born, whose robustness and beauty was the admiration of all who saw him. The tradition is that Felicianus saw a globe of light come down and settle on that happy dwelling. And wanting to find out the cause, he found that Paciencia had just given birth. And guessing the presence of the grace that that sign demonstrated, he gave him the sacrament of Holy Baptism by his own hand, on the day of the Adoration of the Kings, in the year 226, or 262 of Caesar. The Holy Prelate thought that the tender Infant was conceived with pain and exile in a hut, the receptacle of Martyrs, born on the day of the martyr Stephen and baptized on the Feast of the Epiphany. And from all of these signs he gathered that he was to have been born an illustrious hero in the Holy Church; that he offered to God in grateful thanks (as another Stephen) his blood in the sight of the entire world, so that the blind, most Gentle Child would know and adore him. He gave him the name of Laurence. No special reason is known besides understanding the common belief of having been Divine ordination, so that it be known that a *Laurel* was born that would crown the triumphs of the Faith. He put the parents in charge of the care of that Infant, and giving them his blessing, left them very much consoled. Paciencia nursed him at her breasts with the love that she let herself understand, and more, noting that the more the Child grew, the more she discovered a modest beauty, a reverent grace, a composed joy, and an exquisite constancy, because he neither cried as other children are accustomed to, nor demonstrated feeling the miseries of nature. Because being the coldest season of the year, and his poor parents having so little protection to free him from the cold when they wrapped him, he neither complained, nor gave any indication of feeling. He was always smiling like the dawn, and charming his mother with his gurgling and the movements typical of his tender age.

The president, Alexander, was wandering at that time through Spain, bloodying his cruel hands on the Christians that he found, without reservations for sex or age. It was necessary for him to stop in Baetica before going on to Celtiberia, and when he was approaching Valencia through the Contestanos, he heard the news of the miserable death of Ulpianus su Mecenas, whom the soldiers had stoned for his cruelties, and whom God refused to free from the evils of the punishment that he deserved, even in this life. Alexander had to relax his rigor, because he wasn't ignorant of the fact that Caesar liked very few of these ravages, and that if they had continued, Orencio and Paciencia would have been the first to suffer. Because as the light cannot hide itself so much that its very rays are unable to reveal themselves, likewise the two spouses managed in little time to disseminate the Faith and their virtues; especially since they were living within the city, because Columba spread the news among her friends about how her daughter had regained her health, and because of this, other sickly people sought them out in order to obtain their help. And consequently, by the chance that this made them venerated among the Christians, they came to be hated by the

Gentiles. Alexander embarked briefly in Dianius, and Laurence had time to grow up without danger, drinking the Faith of Jesus Christ with the milk, and stealing the hearts of whoever knew him, because the modest beauty of the Child, the courtly brightness, the innate modesty, and the childish discretion that he was discovering were an attractive magnet of the will.

When he began to be in charge of his actions, his entire entertainment was to adore a Crucifix that was in the bedroom of his parents. He gave it the veneration dictated by such a tender age with particular inclination. All of his works led to virtue, and his motivation to suffer for Jesus Christ. The young plant was generous, and was watered with the holy upbringing of his parents, naturally producing flowers of sanctity, assuring that when he arrived at the years of discretion, he would be overflowing with abundant fruit, for the gift and glory of the Church. He would be little more than five years old when God began to inspire Orencio to make a pilgrimage. He gave him the reason for it by disturbing the peace of the faithful in Spain with the news that was coming from Rome concerning the cruelties that the Prefect Almachius was employing with the Christians. These echoes resounded in Spain, where at that time they martyred the Presbyter Graciliano and the Virgin Felicissima after he had cured her of the blindness of her soul and body. Resolved to make the journey, they said goodbye to Columba and their other friends, who felt their absence very much, and generously helped them with what was necessary for the road. They embarked on a ship that was going to the East, desiring to visit the Holy Places where Christ lived and died, if His Majesty would allow them to arrive in Jaffa, Palestine, where the ship was headed.

CHAPTER 8: *A storm hurls them to Italy; they take shelter in a village of Capua in Campania, where Orencio devotes himself to agriculture.*

Until now (says Donato) I am able to have written with exactness what I discovered, because although I am African, I have lived for many years around Valencia, having gone to Spain with many companions from my order. And because of the generosity of the renowned Matron Minicea, adorned with Christian virtue, I settled on the side of the promontory of Ferratia, between Setabicula and Dianio, and founded the Monastery Servitano, dedicated to

St. Martin, an Augustinian Hermitage, instituting in these parts the monastic discipline, which had been lacking in Spain until now. My duties as Abbot made it necessary for me to go down to Valencia many times, where I have visited the Sanctuary of the Sepulcher of my Redeemer, and next to it the place where Saints Orencio and Paciencia had their hut, made holy before with the blood of three Martyrs. The house and bedroom where the glorious Laurence was born, the jail cells where Bishop Valerius Caesaraugustanus and his Deacon Vincent were held with chains[11], the arena of the Martyrdom of Saint Levita, the lavatory where she died on a soft bed that the tyrant made for her, full of flowers, in order to deny the glories of her triumphs, the dung heap where they threw her blessed body, so that the beasts would devour it, and finally the sepulcher where her Holy Relics are kept. The Clergy of that city showed me these indubitable monuments, venerated by all of the Faithful with great devotion.

The oldest Presbyters told me what I have written, adding that the relationship of St. Laurence with St. Vincent was because St. Paciencia had a younger sister, called Enola, who was the mother of St. Vincent. They also affirmed that St. Orencio, the Archbishop of Aix in France, was not the son of Orencio and Patiencia[12], but rather the grandson of one of Orencio's brothers, named Facundo. They indicated that the birth of Laurence was on December 26 of the year 263, or year of Christ 225. The martyrdom of St. Vincent was on January 22, in the year 341 or year of Christ 303, under the rule of Diocletian and Maximian. What follows I have not been able to verify except through books and information that I hold to be trustworthy.[13]

---

[11] This site is now called the St. Vincent Archaeological Crypt, a small Visigoth chapel with a sepulcher surrounded by four finely decorated screens and two Visigoth stone sarcophagi.

[12] The Huesca tradition maintains that St. Orencio, who later became the Archbishop of Aix, was Laurence's brother, and that they both spent their childhood on the family farm outside of the town; in fact, a sign close to the Hermitage of Loreto proclaims that Paciencia would meet them at that spot as they came home from school. Ambrosio de Morales strongly disagrees with this assertion, giving reasons why the people of Huesca erroneously came to the conclusion that Laurence was born in their town, which will be discussed in another chapter.

[13] I am not aware of any other source that provides information about St. Laurence's early life in Capua, Italy, an indication that there were other early books that are now lost. Donato affirms that he is certain of the early life of the family in Spain because the information had been passed down orally through the clergy of Valencia, and the sanctuaries still existed in the sixth century, but now he says he is relying on written sources.

Orencio and Paciencia sailed happily with the sweet treasure that God had given them, desiring to leave Italy behind, because they thought that in this lie their safety. But God wanted something else; with his providence that is incapable of error, He led them to this country, as a demonstration of his judgment. On the sixth day of sailing, when they were passing the gulf that is between Melita and Sinacuya, a seasonal downpour battered them, that disturbed likewise the sailors and captains, with the navigator being unable to steer the vessel. The rudder, rebellious to his command, obeyed the storm; rigging and sails, oppressed by the hurricane, had to give way, serving danger more than the safety of the route. The mast and poles could no longer resist the battering of the waves and winds. With it reduced to disorder, fears and crying, that small republic had to follow the whim of the storm, having no other remedy than the divine. After three days of shipwreck, they discovered land, and although they didn't succeed in finding a place, they tried to take the closest port, hoping to repair the battered vessel. Arriving then in the inlet of Puteolanus, the holy Pilgrims landed. Orencio, understanding that it was no mystery that he survived that accident, determined to remain in that land. He discussed it with Paciencia, and as she had such a gentle disposition, with no other will than that of her husband, they easily agreed, hoping that God would open the road to their peace and safety.

Because that place didn't seem suitable for their purposes, they went to the interior of ancient Lazio, in fertile Campania, and chose to reside in a hamlet of the town of Capua, with pleasant and fertile fields, so that Orencio could take advantage of the very opportune cultivation. As the wealth that he still had was very little, it wasn't enough to buy a pair of domestic oxen. He bought them unbroken, but the merciful Father, who helps with the greatest necessities, allowed them to submit to the tether as if they were gentle lambs. A wolf ate up one of these broken oxen, and the Saint, capturing it, assigned it to the plough, and along with the one that remained it supplied his needs, with the admiration of whoever saw it. Because with its natural ferocity and voraciousness laid aside, it neither envied the life of its companion, nor resisted the precepts of the goading. Here he was educating Laurence in the exercise of every virtue, imprinting on that invincible spirit (of wax in everything related to Religion) the dogmas of the Faith and the precepts of the Gospel so perfectly, that neither hail nor fire could tear them from his heart.

Laurence was discovering a subtle ingenuity, deep capability, and great inclination to study. His father did not want to violate his natural talent, because many do not thrive when they are separated from it, and allowed him to go where his capabilities led him. Orencio himself taught him to read and write, and when he was old enough to learn the sciences, he sent him in the mornings to the neighboring city, where there were teachers of the first literatures, Latin and Greek. Laurence's inclination was great, and thus he prospered in knowledge, among all of those who attended similar schools. And although in the beginning he was shocked by the mixture of fables and lies that he heard from the teachers (in which the Gentiles had based almost all of their learning), his father warned him that he had to hear all of that without believing it, only as knowledge to be refuted later. With that the holy student, with great caution, avoided all that seemed superstitious and profane. He desired that God would give him a Christian teacher and begged him incessantly for it; because he had already begun to enjoy the sweet nectar of prayer, which, hardly an adult, he could read as an expert among many older individuals. He loved his teachers dearly, many of whom had a close relationship with him, because besides his kind presence, modest appearance, and pleasant conversation, he had a polite attractiveness that obligated everyone to like and respect him. No one ever heard from him a brazen or crude word. Profane actions or harmful pranks he never committed, because of which the parents of the other students tried to have their children accompany him, so that by his example they might learn composure and modesty, and for this they lavished attention on him, endeavoring to go to his house at noon, where they would give him whatever he needed. And thus, although in the beginning Paciencia provided food for him, later he told her that it was no longer necessary, because God was providing it through other means. And he even perhaps gave his mother what seemed best to him, without reservations.

God was already beginning to awaken in Laurence a passionate desire to teach the Faith to his fellow disciples. But as his father had warned him of the great danger of showing himself to be a Christian, without necessity, he would proceed with much caution, trying to discover the intentions of those young men by beating around the bush. And some who were inclined toward our Religion drank the first light from Laurence, and others who were sons of Christians, easily understood that he was too, and from this knowledge, many were highly consoled. And being able to speak plainly with them, he always discovered if among those who were teaching there was one who was Christian, and it bothered him very much when the answer did not agree with his desire.

CHAPTER 9: *Laurence meets St. Sixtus in Capua. He follows him. He wants St. Sixtus to take him with him, and obtains permission from his parents.*

St. Sixtus was going through those towns at that time, preaching the word of God, by orders of the Holy Pontiff Fabian, and comforting them because of the persecution that Maximinus had started. After arriving in Capua, it so happened that he was in the house of a Christian with Laurence, who was eating there that day with a son of the owner, a great friend of his. Laurence heard a remark that Sixtus made to those present, while explaining some mysteries of the Faith. Because it seemed to him that he had found the Teacher that he desired, he knelt down at his feet, asking him with tears that he teach him that doctrine, and to allow him to be a Disciple. His look and appearance, and even more his fervent petition, pleased Sixtus very much. He asked him some questions, and discovering in his answers a great depth of talent and virtue, he replied that he was not able to stay there for very long, but that if he wanted to follow him to Rome, he would take him as his companion from then on. Laurence thanked him very much for such a great favor, adding that he was indeed ready to accompany him to the most remote climate, but because his parents were living it wasn't right to leave them, but to obtain their permission and blessing. It also seemed so to the Saint (Presbyter at that time, although High Pontiff later), so he promised to go to visit his parents and intercede so that they would concede the permission that he desired. This happened shortly, and Sts. Orencio and Paciencia, although modestly, put him up in their home. And having heard his celestial doctrine, and knowing what he was trying to achieve, believing that with such a Teacher their son would have to make progress in the service of God and his Church, they agreed to his pleas, giving their consent for him to take him to Rome.

This is the reason for the mistake that some have made by saying that he was taken from a neighboring hamlet of Osca. I am not absolutely certain, but I don't believe that Sixtus came to Spain, nor that Orencio and Paciencia ever returned, but that those towns of Campania were formerly called Bolscos, and Capua Osca; those who heard that he was taken by Sixtus from a hamlet of Osca (not realizing that there was another, other than that of Spain) were convinced that he took him from there, so that it was necessary to conclude that Sixtus came to these Provinces. But I understand this, and believe that it is the truth.[14]

The Holy Spouses were very lonely without Laurence, the only son that the Most High had given them for their consolation. But in accordance with his holy will, they overcame their love and desire so that their son could have such trustworthy teaching, because good parents must not pay attention to what their love dictates, but to what is most necessary for their children. They followed that humble and virtuous life, until the Divine Majesty rewarded their virtues, as I will say, compensating the difficulties of his absence with the joy of knowing that their son was making much progress in sanctity and letters, dedicating everything to the service of the Church.

Laurence, (who was fourteen years old)[15], thus came to Rome, with Sixtus as his godfather, with the caution that the turbulence of that time demanded, devoutly visiting the tombs of the glorious Apostles Sts. Peter and Paul, the place of their passion, and of the other Martyrs, who with their blood consecrated that Holy City, already rich with such treasures, although still filled with idolatry, evils, and abominations. He implored the support of such Saints, by means of which, along with the doctrine of such a great Teacher, he hoped to obtain the mercy of God. He applied himself completely to the study of the sacred letters, and with his great talent he surpassed all of the Disciples of Sixtus. He served him in every ministry possible for his vocation and age, which were those that did not require Sacred Orders, but so attentively, punctually and devoutly in whatever was related to the Divine Devotion, that he was an example for his contemporaries, and the admiration of his Superiors.

He was, since he reached the age of reason, so inclined to help the poor, that he was the first to visit the hospitals, console the afflicted, and help the needy. So much so, that if Sixtus did not temper that fervent charity with prudent admonitions, Laurence would have often been without clothing, and hungry, for having helped the necessities of those around him. The Catechumens, who were many at that time, he served with charity, and assisted them with love and

---

[14] This is very important, because it explains the reasons for many of the errors in the Huesca tradition, which maintains that Sixtus came to Spain and brought Laurence back to Rome with him, not at all likely given the difficulties of travel in the third century.

[15] If Laurence was born in 225, the year is now 240, twenty-one years before his martyrdom according to Donato, which he believed to have occurred in the year 261. Although the year 258 is believed to be correct, many ancient writers recorded 261. The mistake was common.

complete punctuality. He encouraged them with fervor, explaining to them the doubts they were experiencing, looking on them as tender plants that with time would adorn the Garden of the Church. The most pre-eminent priests of Rome recognized him as an individual of the greatest hopes, and already the Pontiffs since Fabian (upon whose head the innocent dove came down suddenly at the time of his election) saw him as one of the most useful ministers of the Holy Apostolic See, and began to see him as a vessel of election. I have found records that the first ecclesiastical office held by Laurence was that of Archdeacon of Zaragoza, or Salduba,[16] but I have not been able to verify who gave it to him, nor be certain if he returned to Spain to exercise it. It is certain that he left Rome many times, accompanying Sixtus, who would go to different jobs in which the High Pontiffs had employed him, throughout different provinces of Italy, but it is not certain that he came to these parts.

CHAPTER 10: *While Laurence was absent, they martyred his Holy Parents in Rome.*

During one of these absences, occasioned by the cruel persecution that had been started by Gordianus, that lasted until the first year of the Emperor Philip[17] (who was still a Gentile when he took the Laurel), with Laurence having gone away with Sixtus to confirm in the Faith the Christians, his elderly parents were arrested, known by those faithful to Jesus Christ in all of the area surrounding Capua. Taken to Rome with the extortions that the cruel ministers were accustomed to, with no respect for the venerable age of Orencio, nor for the modest humility of Paciencia, they presented them to the Prefect. And as they remained constant in the Faith, without pleas, promises or threats separating them from the true Religion (after being imprisoned with cruel rigor) they were condemned to death on the Cross, and victorious, they were crowned on the first day of May, 284.[18]

---

[16] This possibly is the basis of the tradition that Laurence and Vincent were deacons in Zaragoza, but there appears to be little substance to this belief.

[17] Marcus Antonius Gordianus, Gordian III (255-244), was succeeded by Philip the Arabian after he was murdered by the troops on a campaign against the Persians.

When Laurence heard such happy news, he was greatly afflicted, not because he was sorry for the death of his Holy Parents, who being so glorious, had already filled him with incredible joy, but because it pained him not to have accompanied them in their moment of peril, because he already desired to suffer for Christ, and his heart was burning, as well as his entire being. He held himself to be unworthy, because God was delaying the triumph to which he aspired. He moaned his misfortune, offering his life over and over again to the Lord Most High, pleading with ardent zeal that He allow him to imitate his parents in their constancy, and come to suffer for his Holy Name. Sixtus comforted him, with whom he didn't agree at that time, because Laurence was useful to the Church in the matters that he was in charge of, and Laurence, resigning himself humbly, hoped that the eternal Goodness would reward his desire.

Once again in Rome, he proceeded with his duties, and when Decius[19] incited the terrible persecution, he did marvellous deeds, comforting the Martyrs in their passion. He would visit them in the jails during the afflictions, encourage them in their anguish, accompany them to their torture, and help to bury the blessed bodies, without sparing work, or rejecting danger. He was already sub-deacon of the Roman Church, whose job it was (besides the attendance and ministry of the Altar) to take care of the hospitals, and attend to the help of the poor, by the express obligation of his institution[20]. Pontiff Cornelius, knowing the promptness that Laurence demonstrated in this exercise, ordained him Deacon, and the Saint fulfilled this ministry superabundantly. It was Divine Providence that the Ministers of Decius (who precisely saw him fulfill such duties with the Martyrs) didn't arrest him. It was perhaps because the Majesty of God wanted to raise him to a greater degree, so that this bright Torch would shine from the highest mountain,

[18] 246 AD. Laurence is now twenty years old. The early Roman Martyrologies considered Laurence's parents to be martyrs, a classification that was later changed to that of confessors to agree with Huesca's tradition that they had remained in Spain.

[19] In January 250 Decius issued an edict ordering all citizens to perform a religious sacrifice in the presence of commissioners. A large number of Christians defied the government, and many bishops and Church leaders were arrested and martyred. Pope Fabian was one of the first, martyred on January 20 and buried in the Catacombs of St. Callixtus.

illuminating the entire earth.

He hardly had a job of importance in the Roman Church that he didn't have the disposition for or the ability to fulfill. Because the High Pontiffs were very aware of how prudent, wise and virtuous Laurence was, they consulted him in everything, and many times followed his example. And as ordinarily the fulfillment of a duty is entrusted to the person who originated the idea, and his activity was so considerable, later on he was entrusted to carry out whatever he conceived. And Laurence gave such a good account of everything that he was then entrusted with other duties, being certain that the stairway up is composed of skill in everything related to the first job. Because on the contrary, the guile of the lazy one, who after obtaining the office wants to enjoy it without work, is to err in the first commission so that he is not given another.

Lucius[21] died in Holy Office, crowned with martyrdom before completing the year of his election. Stephen[22] succeeded him, who although he enjoyed the seat longer, ultimately shed his blood for the Faith, and the fortunate Sixtus II[23] was elected in his place. And as he had full knowledge of the profound capacity, eminent letters, solid virtue, and deep charity of his disciple, finding him already

---

[20] According to Michael J. Walsh, "a surviving fragment of a letter of Cornelius (Pope from March 251 until June 253) boasts of the presence in the Roman Church of '46 presbyters, 7 deacons, 7 sub-deacons, 42 acolytes, 52 exorcists, readers and door-keepers, and more than 1,500 widows and persons in distress, all of whom are supported by the grace and loving-kindness of the Lord' (i.e. the Roman Church). These statistics, unique for the third century, are particularly interesting for the stress laid on widows and the destitute, who were to be described in the legend of St. Lawrence as the true wealth of the Church." *Lives of the Popes* (New York: Barnes & Noble Books, 1998).

[21] Lucius I followed Cornelius, who was banished by the Emperor Callus to Civitavecchia near Rome, where he died a year later. Lucius was also exiled by the same Emperor, but returned to Rome after the death of Cornelius. He died after a pontificate of only nine months, on March 5, 254. According to Bishop St. Cyprian of Carthage, Lucius continued the liberal policy of Cornelius toward apostates who renounced Christianity because of the persecution of Decius.

[22] Stephen I was Pope for little more than three years. He was beheaded during a religious function on his pontifical chair in the Catacombs of St. Callixtus, on August 2, 257.

[23] Sixtus II was elected on August 30, 257, whose pontificate was remembered for the renewed persecution of Christians initiated by Valerian.

prepared for the highest offices, he made him cardinal, archdeacon, treasurer, and chancellor of the Roman Church, whose duties, for the short time that he had them, he administrated with holiness. Such offices were at that time all work, care and toil, because as income and glory were lacking, the entire weight fell on the shoulders of the person who held them. He had to attend to so many jobs by himself. There were no servants to help him, nor many officials to relieve him. And as he was in his prime, and was a Spaniard with spirit and untiring energy, the illustrious Levite [24] fulfilled completely so many obligations. And God, who saw that the fruit was ripe in the garden of the Church, wanted to pick it at the precise moment, so that it would enlighten the universe with wonderment, which still celebrates his triumph.

CHAPTER 11: *The glorious martyrdom of the Holy Pontiff Sixtus, and the imprisonment of St. Laurence.*

As Valerian had treated the Christians kindly at the beginning of his reign [25], he admitted them into his palace, and to his conversation. He knew St. Sixtus very well, and his archdeacon Laurence, whose doctrine and pleasant talk he had enjoyed, showing more than a slight inclination to follow it. An Egyptian magician perverted him [26], teaching him those detestable arts to the point of offering human victims, exploring the coming events in the entrails of the miserable innocents with barbarous cruelty. This convinced him to persecute the Church, and taken from his advisors, he came to be so violent that the faithful began to think that he was the Antichrist, of whom such atrocities were prophecied. He slowly introduced it in Rome, without publishing new edicts, but giving orders to all the ministers of the Empire to execute those of his predecessors, conceding a good part of his haciendas to those who would discover the Christians, and for this reason the aroused rancor of greed produced

---

[24] In the Bible, a Levite is any member of the tribe of Levi, chosen to assist the priests in the Temple, used here because of Laurence's job as one of the deacons who assisted the Pope.

[25] Donato has been historically accurate in naming the Roman Emperors responsible for the persecutions. Valerian became Emperor in 253.

[26] This is in agreement with what Patrick J. Healy has written about the Valerian persecution.

lamentable havoc. He became furious. It was 297. More and more, until in 299 [27] Sixtus was accused, without his venerable age, his applauded doctrine, or his delicate condition being able to preserve him from the danger. With Valerian having forgotten the old friendship and benevolence, he ordered him arrested, and after having tried to persuade him to offer to the idols, with smooth talk, endearments and promises, and seeing that nothing was sufficient to erode his firmness in the Faith, he ordered that he be taken to the temple of Mars, and that if he didn't offer incense, they cut off his head.

In order to execute this sacrilegious decree, they returned Sixtus to the Mamertine jail. Laurence looked for him there, already thirsty for martyrdom, and having found him (preparing himself for the combat) he threw himself at his feet, and with tears said to him:

Where are you going, Most Holy Father, without your son? Where, High Priest, without your minister? Where, beloved teacher, without your disciple? Since when do you come to celebrate without your deacon to assist you? How have I displeased you that you so disdain me? How have I failed that you thus leave me? By chance you saw something that departs from your teaching? Is there something unworthy of the office in which you placed me? Try to see if you knew how to elect a good minister. Examine the constancy of that minister, to whom you entrusted the distribution of the body and blood of our Redeemer, and to whom you entrusted the celebration of the other Sacraments in your consortium. As you deny me to mix my blood with yours, when will you allow me to assist you in all of the sacred ministries? See that the reputation of your office is not damaged while you are proving your strength. The dishonor of the disciple always implicates the teacher. How many illustrious men praise the victories of their soldiers more than their own? How many famous heroes are more ashamed of the cowardice of those whom they instructed, than of their own defeat? Consider that Abraham was about to sacrifice, with the victim being his son, and not himself. St. Peter sent his deacon to Stephen so that he would suffer. And thus most loving Father, show clearly in me, your son, your virtues. Offer to God in the sacrifice that you are going to celebrate the disciple that you taught, so that your judgment be distinguished by such

---

[27] Although Donato's dates are from the old calendar, the year now is 259, or two years before the deaths of Sixtus and Laurence, according to Donato's belief that they were martyred in 261. This is a mistake that is common in ancient manuscripts. We now know that Sixtus II was elected on August 30, 257, and died on August 6, 258.

illustrious company, you are receiving the victorious crown, or send me first, so that I prepare the mansion.

This said, the fervent Laurence, bathed with copious tears, desired death, pain and martyrdom more than others desire consolation, gifts and life. The Holy Pontiff answered him tenderly:

Don't despair, beloved son, before I announce to you that your battle will be crueler. God is saving you for a more illustrious triumph. A greater struggle is awaiting you on behalf of the love of Christ our Good. I, laden down with years, can resist less; already tired, I will surrender my life with a lighter blow; but I will quickly reach the end. A tougher battle awaits you, an invigorated combatant with robust youth. But you must win a glorious victory from the tyrant. Understand that your torments must be much greater. Don't be distressed thinking that this will be delayed much longer. In three days time you will follow the old Priest as a valiant Levite. It wasn't necessary for you to suffer with me, because they could severely reprimand you as weak, appearing that you needed the teacher in order to die for the Faith, and you would not obtain all the honor that you would get by dying alone. Dry your tears. Elias left Elijah, and he had the virtue and courage to work greater wonders. Thus, without me, you will have the strength to suffer a glorious death, and obtain a greater trophy than the one that I will obtain, with such widespread fame that it would give honor to the Church. If you suffered in the shade and umbrella of your teacher, all of the triumph would be attributed to him. You do not need, beloved son, this help. So that you would yearn for my company in your passion? The weak (although teachers) precede their brave disciples in martyrdom. The strongest follow them so that they triumph by themselves, when they do not need their help, or their example. One thing alone I entrust to your care, and it is that you put out of harm's way the treasures of the Church. Later see to distribute them among the poor, because it is dangerous to delay. It cannot happen that they fall into the power of the tyrant.

Laurence, happy with the certain hope that his teacher gave him that he would achieve his desire for martyrdom, accepted the commission of distributing among the poor the treasures of the Church, of which he was the trustee, and which consisted of things of value that some people had given for the Divine worship: the ornaments to celebrate, some money to help the needy, and what was most valuable, some memorable relics that had been taken from Jerusalem. Getting everything together, he left to comply with his legacy, happily and obediently.

CHAPTER 12: *Laurence distributes the treasures of the Church. He is present at the martyrdom of St. Sixtus, and they arrest him by order of the Emperor.*

With what he had collected Laurence went up to Mt. Caelsus, and went to the house of Cyriaca, a Christian widow, where he knew that many of the faithful were accustomed to hide in similar tribulations. He gave them an admirable sermon, encouraging them to suffer for Christ, and persevere in his holy law. He began to distribute to them what he had brought, and to wash the feet of the men, with great humility and devotion. And God wanted it understood that the works of his Levite pleased him, with the wonders of his power. Cyriaca was about thirty years old, but suffered from great maladies. She threw herself at the feet of Laurence, and said: *I beg you, on behalf of Jesus Christ our Good, and Lord, that you put your hands on my head, so that with your virtue you heal me, because there I suffer many infirmities.* The Saint made the sign of the Cross; he laid his hands on her head, as well as the towel he had used to dry the feet that he had washed, and left it healed of the pains that she was suffering, with the admiration of those present, who praised the Lord, marvellous in his servants.

He went from there to Canaria Street to the house of Narsus or Narsisus. He found there many Christians; he washed their feet, took care of their necessities, and admonished them to persevere in the Faith and prayer. Crescencius the blind was among them, who begged him to take pity on his misery, and touch his eyes. Laurence, crying with tenderness, said to him: *Our Lord Jesus Christ, who opened the eyes of the one who was born without sight, will restore your sight.* And after he made the sign of the Cross, Crescencius recovered his sight. He went from there to the Patrician neighborhood; and between the two hills, Esquiline and Viminal, he went into the Hepociana cave, where there were many Christians, with the Presbyter Justin. They were having among themselves a holy contest, in which they had to kiss each other's feet. Laurence prevailed, and placed on him all the sacred vestments. He washed the feet of all the men, to whom he gave copious alms, and to the women also, confirming them with his doctrine and example. Among those that had taken refuge there he found Precelius, his co-disciple and fellow countryman, because he was a Spaniard from the city of Hippo, in Carpentanea. To him he entrusted some memorable relics so that he could send them to

150

los quales, y à las mugeres tambien diò copiofas limofnas : confirmandoles con fu dotrina, y exemplo. Entre los que alli fe alvergavan encentrò à Precelio fu condicipulo y paìfano , porque era Efpañòl natural de la ciudad de Hippo, en la carpentìnea. A efie le entregò algunas memorables reliquias para que las remitieffe à Efpaña ; y entre ellas la mas feñalada *el Caliz en que Chrifto nuestro Bien, y Maeftro confagro fu preciofa fangre*

151

*gre la noche de la Cena.*Defta fuerte fue diltribuyendo aquellas alajas , y dinero: dexando confolados à los Chriftianos,con fus obras, y fus palabras.

Hecho efto,bolviò en bufca de S. Sixto , à tiēpo , que yà le avian facado de la carcel. Alcançòle en el vmbral del templo de Marte, donde le llevavan, à que ofrecieffe incienfo.Pero el fanto Pontifice no quifo; antes esforçando la voz, dixo al idolo: *Deftruyate el bijo de Dios vi*
K 4 *vo.*

Copy of the page from the seventeenth-century translation of Donato's Latin manuscript by Mateu y Sanz that specifically mentions the surrender of the Holy Grail to St. Laurence.

Spain, and among them the most distinguished *Cup in which Christ our Good, and Master, consecrated his precious blood on the night of the Last Supper.* [28]

He distributed those relics and money, leaving the Christians consoled with his works and his words.

This done, he went again in search of St. Sixtus, in time, who had already been taken from the jail. He found him at the threshold of the temple of Mars, where they took him to offer incense. But the holy Pontiff refused; before, raising his voice, he said to the idol: *The son of the living God will destroy you.* Laurence

---

[28] This reference is unique to the manuscript of Donato, as is the mention of the name of the Spaniard to whom Laurence entrusted the relics, Precelius.

responded, along with the other Christians, Amen, and immediately the image of that false god fell from the altar, along with the greater part of the temple. The Gentiles were terrorized, and the happy Christians praised the name of Christ, who had such power. But the soldiers of Valerian, irritated much more with the miracle, took St. Sixtus from the City, in order to execute him. Laurence, distressed, followed him, and when they came to the place of the torture said to him: *You do not want, beloved father, to abandon me in this moment of peril. I already distributed the treasures that you entrusted to me, according to your command.* They did not give the Holy Pontiff the chance to answer him, because arriving at the designated spot, they executed their cruelty, cutting off his head, as well as those of six companions, Felicissimus and Agapitus, deacons; and Januarius, Magnus, Innocence,[29] and Stephen, sub-deacons, so that the sacrifice be complete, with the Priest dying along with his Ministers, whose souls flew to celestial glory on August 6, 299, which corresponds to the year 261.

There wasn't lacking the person who made objection to the words referring to the treasures, of which the Emperor was informed, who greedily ordered the Holy Levite to be arrested. The soldiers later executed his command, and turning him over to the Tribunal, called Paternus, they advised Caesar, who very happily ordered it told to the Prefect Decius,[30] who entrusted his custody to a Roman soldier who was called Hippolytus. He took him to the jail that he cared for, and locked him in a strong cell, where there were many others, Christians as well as Gentiles. One of them, whose name was Lucillus, was blind from crying over his misfortune, because he had been a prisoner for many years; hearing that Laurence was there, he told him of his work. The Saint said to him: *Son, believe in our Lord Jesus Christ, who is the true son of God, who will give you life if you are baptized.* Lucillus answered, *I have always wanted to be baptized in the name of Jesus Christ.* Laurence taught him, baptized him, and he was instantly healed, with perfect vision in his eyes.

This miracle spread throughout the city, and with the desire of being cured, many blind people came to the jail, whose vision was restored by the Saint when he made the sign of the Cross with his venerable hands. Hippolytus couldn't help

---

[29] Vincent is listed by Butler as the fourth deacon martyred, not Innocence.

[30] The Prefect Decius is very possibly a coincidence of name, as it was the Emperor Decius who began the first persecution in 250.

knowing (from the marvellous tales), the supreme power of the one through whose power he worked these miracles. And fond of the modesty and virtue of Laurence, he gave him these reasons:

I beg you on behalf of who you are, O brave Spaniard, tell me where you have hidden the treasures that Caesar demands from you: it is a shame that you suffer your youth in this way. It would be better to turn them over than to risk your life. Healthier to find them, than to suffer the dire torments that await you, because it is certain that you will die otherwise. And because your courtly appearance pleases me, I will be sorry that you die before your time.

St. Laurence, understanding the intention behind the words, and full of fervent desire for his health, answered: Hippolytus, friend, if you want to acquire treasures with which you can become rich forever, I will find them for you. The Saint, with Christian elegance, preached to him the incomprehensible treasures that God has waiting in Heaven for his own. He explained to him the mysteries of the Faith, declared the lie of the idols and the abomination of idolatry, and finally he said so much to him that Hippolytus converted and was made a Christian with his entire family, and there were nineteen people who were baptized by St. Laurence. God, to confirm the faith of Hippolytus, allowed him to see the souls of those baptized, beautiful, radiant and happy.

CHAPTER 13: *Martyrdom of St. Laurence.*

With this heroic action completed, Laurence was called by the Prefect. And when the Prefect had him in his presence, he said to him: *Leave your obstinate rebellion, forget the obstinacy. Tell me where you have the treasures that I have found out are in your possession. Turn them over, before you come to experience my severity.* The valiant Spaniard answered: *Give me a time period to collect them. Give me two or three days delay to turn them over.* Decius [31] intervened in this matter, conceding him that

---

[31] Again, Donato mentions the Prefect Decius, not the Emperor or Caesar, which was Valerian at the time. This may also explain why both Decius and Valerian appear in most accounts of Laurence's martyrdom. In ancient Rome, a prefect was any one of various high-ranking officials or chief magistrates in charge of governmental or military departments, and it is logical to think that the prefect in charge could have had the name Decius, which was common. Donato explicitly states that Valerian was in power.

limit, ordering Hippolytus not to lose sight of him, with all three being happy: the Prefect, believing he already had the treasures that he coveted; Hippolytus, seeing that all that time he would enjoy Laurence's doctrine; and Laurence, because he would have time to distribute what he still had, and finalize certain matters related to the duties that were in his care. For everything the company of Hippolytus was very suitable, because as a Christian, before he began to help him he had prevented such safekeeping. In this way God confuses the advice of men, when they intend to oppose his holy will, because the instruments that they apply to a contrary end serve so that it is executed with greater speed. The holy Deacon went about exercising that will in works of charity, distributing among the poor the goods of the Church, which he couldn't do before; comforting the weak, and encouraging the strong. And when the time limit was already over, he brought together the blind, lame, disabled, and paralytic, and leaving them hidden in the house of Hippolytus, he presented himself very consoled before the Tyrant, who at that time was in the palace of Salustius.

He, seeing St. Laurence, said to him: *You were punctual in returning to my presence, but I don't see that you have the treasures in your possession, which you have promised me. Where, then, are they?* The glorious Levite went for the poor that he had ready, and showing them to the Prefect, in a loud voice (so that the crowd gathered there could hear him) answered: *Here are the eternal treasures of the Church, which are never lessened or diminished. They are distributed in each one of them, and are found in all, when they are searched. These cannot perish, nor are they subject to those who steal.* Decius replied, furious at seeing that he was being made fun of: *Why do you switch to such diverse things? Sacrifice to the gods, and forget the magic arts in which you trust.* And the Saint with the greatest courage said: *Do the demons have all of you so subject to their slavery, making you send for the Christians so that they can sacrifice to the infernal spirits? Those you call gods are statues without feeling, and he who answers through them is the Prince of Darkness.*

That tyrant could not withhold his rage, and ordering that his clothes be taken, he had him scourged cruelly, with extremely hard scorpions, which were really steel claws, made similar to the tongue of that venomous animal. The Saint, joyful in that terrible battle, said: *I give infinite thanks to my God and Lord, because He made me worthy of being counted among his servants. But you, wretch, will have to pay by seeing yourself tormented with your own rage and fury, without an end to your misery.* Then Decius, blind with rage, said: *Stop this torture already, and put in his presence all of the instruments of torture, so that he can see what awaits him.* They later executed the lashes, and press, sheets of steel, pincers, claws, and combs, lead beds, racks, thin ropes, and clubs. But seeing that nothing frightened him, nor made him lose his constant courage, he was fastened with heavy chains and ordered taken to the palace of Tiberius, in order to solemnly find out the reason.

Tiberius sat down in the tribunal that he had close by in the temple of Jupiter; they presented Laurence as the accused, laden down with chains, to whom he said: *Sacrifice to the immortal gods, and do not have faith in the treasures that you have hidden.* The Holy Martyr, with true Spanish spirit, responded: *It is true that I have faith, and with such treasures I am certain of your severity.* They ordered him to take off his clothing, and beat him with sticks or poles, a very atrocious torment, because besides being very painful, it bruised the flesh, and broke the bones. Laurence said to him, when this was being carried out: *See, wretched one, that you are lost, and that you must know, although it weighs on you, how I triumph from your cruelty, by means of the treasures of Jesus Christ, because I do not feel your torments at all.*

Decius ordered the poles to be repeated with more violence. And when he recognized that they (smoother than his chest) were breaking apart in splinters, and the executioners were fainting from fatigue, he had a bonfire lit, and the steel sheets heated. And when they were glowing with heat, he ordered that they be applied to the sides of the invincible soldier of Christ. And he, in the middle of such horrible torment, raised his eyes to Heaven, and said: *My Lord, Jesus Christ, son of God, have mercy on me, your servant, because accused I did not deny your Holy Name, and when asked I acknowledged my Lord, Jesus Christ.*

The rage of the tyrant did not stop with this; driven by two such violent emotions as hate and greed, and seeing that nothing was making Laurence waver in the Faith, he ordered that he be beaten once more with the *plumbatas.* They were straps with small metal plates and lead balls. Filled with rage, the executioners worked without pity. And having done it for a long time, the invincible combatant exclaimed: *My Lord Jesus Christ, who for love of us deigned to take the form of a slave, in order to free us from the snares of the devil, receive my spirit.* With this prayer hardly finished, a voice resounded in the Heavens, heard by all of those present, even the tyrant himself, that answered: *You must still overcome many combats.*

That heartless one did not relent with such a rare sign; even more furious, he ordered that he be placed in the *catasta.* It was a rack, like a trap, in which all of the limbs of the subject were extended, dislocating bones and nerves. There he ordered that the lashes be repeated with scorpions. St. Laurence suffered all of these pains smiling, and gave thanks to the supreme Lord, saying: *May you be blessed and praised Lord God, all powerful Father of my most beloved Lord Jesus Christ, who grants us because of your infinite goodness and mercy, what we do not deserve. And for me in particular, because you ease the pains for me, so that all of those present will recognize them as gifts and consolations for your servants.*

Among the soldiers present at the martyrdom was one whose name was Romanus. He attentively heard the prayer of the Saint, and contemplating his wounded body, his unbeaten spirit, and his happy appearance, recognized that it did not come from human virtue, but divine. Because of this he believed that Jesus Christ was the true God, and approaching St. Laurence, said: *Brave Spaniard, who with invincible spirit resists so much violence, I recognize that the Deity that you invoke is helping you. I see close to you an extremely handsome young man, who is wiping your wounds with a delicate towel. I beg of you on behalf of Christ, who has sent his Angel to ease your pain, that you not abandon me.*

Laurence could not answer, but with his face let him know that he would not be without his help. The Prefect, seeing such unbeaten constancy, ordered him to be taken from the rack. He turned him over to Hippolytus without shackles, so that they would keep him in that same palace, and went to inform Valerian of what was happening. While all of this was going on, Romanus, anxious for the remedy, took a jar of water, and prostrate at the feet of the Holy Levite, begged him with great fervor to baptize him. Decius found out, and ordered him summoned. Romanus, before they could ask him anything, said dauntless, *I am a Christian*, and they ordered him to be beheaded. They took him through the Salarian gate, and executed the sentence there. Blessed soldier, who so quickly triumphed gloriously. Romanus, a thousand times happy, in a few short hours was fixed on Heaven, that already began to enjoy the fruit produced by the formidable martyrdom of Laurence.

They consulted the Caesar and his Prefect about what ought to be done, and agreed that the torture of Laurence would be finished completely the following night, so that the horror of the darkness would reduce that constant spirit to what they hoped for, or so that in its silence he would lack the exhortation of friends and the applause of victory, if he achieved it. In order to execute this agreement, Decius arranged that in the baths or thermals of Olympia, on Mount Viminal, next to the palace of Alustius (that the Emperor Decius[32] had enlarged and lived in) what might be necessary would be prepared, in order to execute his wicked intent. In the short time granted to the glorious Spaniard for rest, Hippolytus, with many tears, asked for permission to show himself as a Christian, so that he could suffer martyrdom in the company of Laurence, which he already desired. But they denied him permission, persuading him to hide Jesus Christ in his chest for a short time, so that the Faith could strengthen in his heart, assuring him that his desire would not diminish, because very quickly (by confessing himself for Jesus Christ) he would give his life for his love. Hippolytus, consoled, dried the tears, hoping to attain martyrdom, and a short time later they called Laurence by order of the Emperor.

CHAPTER 14: *Glorious death of the Holy Levite.*

Night had already fallen when the Emperor and Prefect [33] met in the thermals of Olympia, finding ready the instruments of the most methods of torture that until that time had been invented by evil, or the tyrannical despotism of the Gentiles. The Caesar ordered (unworthy action of the Majesty) that Hippolytus arrange that Laurence be presented before him. And having obeyed, he showed him infinite instruments, and said: *Forget already the treachery of the magic arts that you use: obey our precepts, and declare to us who you are, and from where?* The illustrious archdeacon responded: *As for the homeland, I am Spanish, born in Valencia, Maritime city, close to Sagunto, of noble parents from Huesca, raised in Rome, where I learned the sacred letters. I am Christian from birth, and my parents were also, and they taught me how much is contained in the Holy Law that I profess. Then it is necessary for you to abandon it (added Valerian) by sacrificing to the gods, because if not, we must spend the entire night torturing you, with the most painful means ever seen.* And St. Laurence: *If you execute this, my night will not be at all dark, everything will be radiant and clear; the darkness will be converted to light, and the horrors to consolations.*

It seemed to the tyrant that that answer was contemptuous, and ordered the soldiers to batter his mouth with stones. How quickly was evil carried out! How quickly is obeyed that which yields to the harm of the fallen! The heartless

---

[32] It is clear here that Donato is distinguishing between the Emperor Decius, who had lived in the Palace of Alustius, and the Prefect Decius in charge of the execution.

[33] According to Donato, the Emperor Valerian gave the order for the execution and appeared along with his Prefect Decius to execute it in the thermals of Olympia.

executioners hastily wounded the most resonant clarion of the Gospel. But he was comforted with the wounds themselves, saying: *I give you thanks, Lord, for your supreme power that you use in Heaven as on earth, and because you bestow on this worm gifts that he doesn't deserve.*

Filled with fury, Valerian and his minister,[34] ordered an iron bed to be brought, formed with feet and bars crossed in the form of grating, capable of sustaining the weight of a human body. They stripped Laurence of his clothing, stretching him out on that bed, and extended him with some forks so that he couldn't move. He then said, looking at Heaven: *God, and my Lord, you have offered me for days to your Supreme Majesty. Lord, let my body serve as material for the fire that they have prepared for me, and my spirit as sweet perfume in your Divine Presence, because I know that the sweetest thing for you is a surrendered heart and a suffering spirit. Lord, give me your grace and let come what may.* He had hardly finished this prayer when the diligent executioners, in sight of the Caesar, began to put lit coals below the grating, so that with a slow fire his flesh would be roasted little by little, and the pain would last a long time. It was a spectacle never before seen until then, seeing a young man of noble appearance, extremely polite, modest and well-liked; a youth with a handsome face, known by everyone as the universal benefactor of the poor, for whom no one had ever had a bad word; who would soon help the many who were imploring his aid; who was uplifting everyone with his example as he was being roasted alive with a slow fire, done so that the many things that could aggravate the pain would not be absent, because even the season of the year seems to have been chosen for pain, in the middle of the burning midsummer heat, and in Rome the alleviation of breathing fresh air was not allowed, which would have at least diverted his burning insides, his fiery heart. With his limbs already altered from the heat, so many mouths complained as the penetrating voracity of the fire raised blisters. Already the blood, and the fluid that exuded from as many wounds as the live coals had opened, were putting them out, as though complaining of how inhumanely they were treating him. The odor of the roasted flesh was already demonstrating the effectiveness of the torment, but none of this was enough to temper the cruelty of the tyrant.

And Laurence, considering all of this, said: *Be advised, wretched one, how great is the virtue and power of my God, because these live coals serve me as relief, but for you they*

---

[34] It is clear that Valerian and his minister, the Prefect Decius, are present for the martyrdom.

must be eternal punishment. See how this sovereign Lord knows that, although accused, I do not deny him; when questioned, I confessed to serve him; and roasted alive, I am thanking him, because he grants me the privilege of suffering for his love. The fire from the coals that were toasting his members was not as active as the burning volcano of the love that was burning in his heart, and thus, insensitive to the one, and inflamed from the other, he was refreshed with the pains, and desired to have even more lives to offer to his Creator. The abominable torment went on without wearing away his constancy. And giving thanks once again to God, as he continued with an extremely beautiful appearance, he raised his eyes, and said to Valerian: *This half of my body is already roasted. Order them to turn me over, and you will be able to eat.* It wasn't Spanish boastfulness, but a burning desire to suffer more for Christ, because there is no doubt that he could no longer feel the burned side. And fearing that he would lose his life before the rest would suffer the same pain, he wanted them to turn him, so that nothing of his body would remain without having suffered. How is it that the feelings of that beast did not soften? How is it that a human heart resists compassion in the presence of such a pitiful spectacle? All of hell must have been in possession of Valerian's spirit, because such courteous reasoning did not soften him, nor such extraordinary constancy and patience that had never before been seen. The invincible Martyr, exclaiming once again, said: *I give you thanks my God, and my Lord Jesus Christ, because through your mercy I deserve to enter into the gates of your Kingdom.*

When he said this, already the smoke that was moving the spilled blood (because veins and arteries were bursting from the heat, and dripping on the coals) served as sweet perfume to the Divine Majesty, because penetrating Heaven it came to his throne in sacrifice more pleasing than incense. The unofficial executioners surrounded the gridiron, and tying his hands (not completely burnt)[35], they turned his saintly body so that there would not remain one part undamaged by the tyranny. And Laurence, as if he were on a bed of roses and jasmines, did not cease praising his Redeemer, repeating his thanks for having chosen him to suffer. The executioners tired of tormenting him long before the Saint tired of suffering, and lying on the ground, full of confusion, they neither

---

[35] On August 10, 1307, King Jaime II, who had great devotion for St. Laurence because he had been born on his feast day, gave the Basilica of St. Laurence in Huesca a relic of one of his fingers, obtained from Pope Boniface VII in 1297. Another is in the Escorial.

had the strength to persevere, nor dared to approach the gridiron, because the fire was already tormenting them much more than Laurence. Neither Decius nor Valerian gave the order, but they gave up, recognizing Laurence's courage as unconquerable.

With the happy Spaniard raising his eyes to Heaven, he saw the eternal dwelling open up, and a large troop of radiant angels come down, who with sweet hymns celebrated his victories. They received that invincible spirit, and presented him at the throne of the Most Holy Trinity, where he will enjoy glorious laurels for all eternity. The body remained the rest of the night on the grating, until in the early morning, Hippolytus and Justin took possession of it, giving it burial in the Campo Verano of the Via Tiburtina, where God, through his intercession, worked infinite miracles. His passion was on August 10, 261, under the reign of Valerian and Gallienus, and with the Seat of St. Peter vacant because of the death of Sixtus II.[36]

This is the essence of what I have been able to extract from the ancient writing that I found in the College of St. Fulgentius[37] of our order, being Lector there, whose title is said to be of Donato, Abbot of the Servitano Monastery, dedicated to St. Martin, which was founded in the time of King Leovigild. Donato flourished in doctrine, holiness and miracles. And that this writing is his can be determined only from the title, and from what is read in Chapter 8, because of the Servitano Monastery, destroyed in the loss of Spain, there are only the remains of its ruin. Among them it is tradition that said writing was found by those of our Order, who after the Kingdom of Valencia was restored, went to that place to inquire if there remained some trace of the antiquities of the Sanctuary. From this ancient writing I faithfully wrote this treatise, adjusted, according to my limited understanding, to what it contained in vulgar Latin, without having added anything of substance except this or that word to give better cadence or clarity to the sentence, without changing its meaning. May it be for the greater glory of

---

[36] At this point Donato's narration ends, followed by the commentary of the translator.

[37] St. Fulgentius was an Augustinian monk, born in Carthage in 468, who became Bishop of Ruspe in Tunisia in 508, but never wore the orarium, the stole then used by bishops, and often went barefoot. He converted a house at Cagliari into a monastery, worked miracles, and refuted Arianism. The translator is reputedly an Augustinian priest, and it is logical that his order would have Donato's Latin manuscript of the life of St. Laurence in its possession, as Donato was also a canonized Augustinian who embraced the monastic life and founded the Servitano Monastery.

God, subjecting what I say to the correction of the Holy Mother the Church, and the censure of its scholars. Amen.

The original for this new printing is kept in the Library of the Monastery of Preachers in Valencia.

DECLARATION *of some ancient names of this history, taken from P.M. Diago, in the Anales del Reyno de Valencia, and from Antonio Braudant in his Lexicon Geográfico.*

Baetica. Region that includes Upper and Lower Andalucia. *Campania.* The land of labour, whose capital is Naples. Capua and Puzzol belong to this region. *Carpentania.* Its capital is Toledo. Its kingdom is extensive, and includes La Mancha. *Celtiberia.* Its capital, Segorbe. This region comprises the parts of Valencia from Segorbe to Aragon (where it extends to Tarazona) and to Castile, up to Toledo. *Contestanea.* Its capital, Cocentayna. It extends up to the sea by Orihuela (although this city was of Bastitonia) and to the west just past Xucar. *Dianio.* Is Denia. *Edetania.* Its capital, Liria, it extends from Almazora, to beyond the Albufera, including the land within, from the boundary of Castile, and thus consists of Sagunto and Valencia. *Ilice* is Elche. *Illergetes.* Town of the Region of Lerida that consists of Huesca and other cities. *Insubres* is the Milanez. *Idubeda.* Part of Espadan, up to the River Mijares. *Lacio antiguo* is the countryside of Rome. *Melita* is Malta. *Osca,* Huesca. *Phocences* de Phosea, in the Region of Ionia, in Asia Minor. *Promontory of Ferraria* is next to Xabea, and divides the *Sucronense* bay, of Cullera, from the bay of the sea *Illicitano,* or of Elche. *Sagunto* is Murviedro. *Salduba* is Zaragoza. *Seleucia* is next to the Tigris, a day's journey from the ancient Babylon. *Seno Puteolano,* or from Puzzol in Campania, next to Naples. *Setabicula* is Xabea. *Sinacuya* would be Syracuse of Sicily or of some Island of the Archipielago. *Sedantia,* the Region of Xativa, and its area up to Xocar. *Sucro* is Cullera. *Valesia* is Cuenca. *Volcos,* towns of the countryside of Rome. *Yppo* is Yepez. *Zazintho* is Zante, island in the sea of Lepanto □

Chapter 7

ST. LAURENCE FROM PRUDENTIUS TO GONZALO DE BERCEO

"There are few martyrs in the Church whose names are so famous as that of St. Laurence, in whose praises the most illustrious among the Latin fathers have written, and whose triumph, to use the words of St. Maximus, the whole Church joins in a body to honor with universal joy and devotion," as expressed in *Butler's Lives of the Saints.* He has been one of the most venerated martyrs of the Roman church since the fourth century, and he is named in the Canon of the Mass. It is paradoxical, therefore, that all that is really known for certain of his life and death is that on the fourth day after Pope St. Sixtus II was put to death by the Romans under Valerian, Laurence followed him to martyrdom. Many scholars insist that good reasons have been given for doubting the historical reliability of various details traditionally provided concerning his life, such as his presentation of the goods of the Church, and even the manner of his death, and assert that "Christian piety has adopted and consecrated as its own the details supplied by St. Ambrose, the poet Prudentius, and others."[38]

This argument, however, does not explain the tremendous popularity of St. Laurence, especially in fifth-century Spain when Prudentius composed his verses and the *Passio Polychronii* was written, and during the Middle Ages at the time when rumors of the whereabouts of the Holy Grail were spreading like wildfire among the pilgrims on the Road to Santiago, igniting intense interest not only in the Holy Relic, but also in the saint said to have saved it from destruction at the hands of the Roman persecutors. The reality of the historical events

---

[38] Herbert J. Thurston, S.J. and Donald Attwater. *Butler's Lives of the Saints*, Complete Edition. Volume III. Allen, Texas: Christian Classics, 1996.

surrounding the Holy Grail in Spain indicate that Laurence's popularity for medieval pilgrims was based on more than mere Christian piety. It will be important to examine briefly these accounts, and then compare them with that of the Abbot St. Donato, because the latter differs considerably from the others, pointing to other sources of information that may be lost today, and as many of the details he provides are not mentioned in any other biographies of the saint it seems likely that this manuscript has never been considered by hagiographers. As Thurston notes, "Much confusion and inconsistency prevail in what purport to be the 'acts' of St. Laurence...Is (the poem of Prudentius) merely a poetical fiction, or does it represent some genuine tradition handed down either orally or in documents which have perished? St. Ambrose undoubtedly shared the belief that the martyr was roasted to death, and so did other early fathers."[39] An examination of these accounts against the information provided by St. Donato will help clarify the confusion.

Before entering into that discussion, it is necessary to explain the existing sources, especially those from Spain. Prudentius was the greatest Christian poet of the Late Antique period, writing Latin verses during the transition from the world of classical, pagan Rome to the New Christian Roman Empire, and it has been said that "his poetry gives expression to the new confidence felt by contemporary Christians."[40] He was born in Caesaraugusta, modern–day Zaragoza in 348 AD, a city close to Huesca where the Holy Grail was reputedly sent by St. Laurence, less than 100 years after its arrival in Spain. One of his major works is known as the *Peristephanon* ("Crowns of Martyrdom"), which contains 14 lyric poems on Spanish and Roman martyrs including the eighteen holy martyrs of Caesaraugusta, among whom was Vincent, Laurence's cousin of Zaragoza, who died in Valencia. The passion of St. Vincent is sung in Book V, and he and St. Laurence are the most well known of the martyred saints in this work.

Early *Acta* of St. Laurence have not survived, and most scholars believe that if they ever existed, they perished early, since fourth-century writers such as Augustine seem to base their knowledge of Laurence only on oral tradition. Whether through oral tradition or through lost written records, as Jan

---

[39] *Butler's Lives of the Saints*, Volume III, p.298.

[40] Anne-Marie Palmer, *Prudentius on the Martyrs*. (Oxford: Clarendon Press, 1989), p.1.

M. Ziolkowski points out, the main events of the life and martyrdom of St. Laurence are also recorded in works by Pseudo-Peter Chrysologus and Leo the Great, which include the traditions about the treasures of the Church and death on the gridiron.

The oldest surviving *Acta* of St. Laurence is the *Passio Polychronii*, a reasonably detailed record of both the words and the actions of all the main people important to the tradition. The passion of Laurence is only one in a series of narratives about the deaths of Roman martyrs, including Polychronius, Abdon, Sennen, Olympias, Maximus, Sixtus, Romanus, Laurence, Hippolytus, Irene, Abundius, Cyrilla, and Triphonia. Although the dating is uncertain, it is believed that it was composed at the end of the fifth and the beginning of the sixth century, which would place it somewhat earlier than St. Donato's manuscript that was written during the time of King Leovigild (d. 586); therefore, the *Passio* was most likely known by Donato. During the Middle Ages this account was quite popular and was copied frequently both in full and in abridgments, providing information for the accounts of the last days of Laurence's life in martyrologies, particularly that done by Ado of Vienne in the ninth century.

It is certain, however, that the existing accounts of the early life of Laurence are scarce, and all differ considerably from that of St. Donato, in the sense that they are not nearly as complete or accurate. In the martyrologies, Laurence would have been born in Osca in Spain (Huesca), and was sent to Zaragoza[41] to complete his humanistic and theological studies, where he met the future Pope Sixtus II who was teaching in what at that time was one of the most famous centers for learning. Laurence, who excelled in virtue and intelligence, became close to the future pontiff, and both grew in love for Rome as the center of Christianity. For that reason they left Spain together where they could realize their ideal of evangelization. This hypothesis appears to be quite unlikely and was rejected by Ambrosio de Morales; in fact, some versions even speak of the Pope coming to Spain and taking both Laurence and Vincent to Rome, historically impossible as Vincent was martyred nearly fifty years later than Laurence. The alleged manuscript of Donato, however, explains the reason for the mistake, which occurred because the town in Italy where Laurence was raised had the same name in Latin as Huesca: *Osca*.

---

[41] This belief appears to be based on a document mentioned by Donato, which he does not believe to be accurate.

The *Passio Polychronii*, which Brian Dutton believes forms the basis for Donato's account of the passion, nevertheless differs considerably. Donato's attention to detail and concern for accuracy are not so apparent in the *Passio*, which at the very beginning proclaims that Decius was the Caesar, or Emperor, and Valerian, the prefect, impossible historically as the martyrdom took place during the Valerian persecution. Donato, however, explains the reason for the widespread error that has led modern scholars to reject the tradition entirely: the Prefect Decius was the high-ranking Roman official in charge of the execution, coincidentally sharing the name of the Emperor Decius who began the Christian persecution in 250, while the Emperor Valerian gave the order for Laurence's death on the gridiron on August 10, 258, but was not physically present during his tortures until the very end. The differences between these two documents will be examined more closely in the discussion to follow.

The next biography is the *Passio* of Nigel of Canterbury, a poet of unknown birthplace, born around 1130 or 1140. He is now known by that name because Canterbury is where he was a monk and where he spent most of his life. It is not known whether or not he was schooled in that town, but it does appear that he was raised in a culture in which many people were bilingual either in French and English or French and Latin, or even trilingual in French, English, and Latin. Although raised in a home where all three languages were spoken, he uses very little French and English in his writings. Once again, modern scholars insist that the "colorful legend" of Laurence that is related by Nigel "bears little relation to the events that must have led to the martyrdom of the historical figure." Using the same arguments given by Patrick J. Healy, other scholars also point to the mistake made by hagiographers charging Decius with the crime, when it was Valerian who ordered in August of 258 that all bishops, deacons, and priests be executed immediately upon identification, insisting that this proves the inauthenticity of all existing sources. They also argue that the report that Laurence distributed the treasure of the Church "appears to be false," and state that Laurence's martyrdom was "probably achieved through the sword, rather than through torture on a grill." As previously mentioned, these arguments are based on little more than mere conjecture, because whether or not early *Acta* have been lost, the events are based on oral tradition, which in the first centuries after Christ was considered to be a more reliable source than the written word that was subject to the objectives and manipulation of an individual. It is clear, however, that Nigel embellishes the essential truths considerably with pious additions, which might lead one to doubt his credibility, although it must be remembered that this is a work of literature, not a historical document.

Several scholars believe that Nigel's *Passio* is based both on the brief account in Ado's martyrology, as well as the long prose version of the account in the *Passio Polychronii*, which was known in Anglo-Norman circles. Another Anglo-Norman poet, who composed the rhymed *Vie de St. Laurent*, most likely in the period from 1140-70, also followed the *Passio Polychronii* rather closely. In fact, there are striking similarities between Nigel's account and the *Passio*: Nigel not only incorporates many words and phrases from the *Passio Polychronii*, but some of the events described in his work are only found in this longer version of the St. Laurence tradition, and do not appear in Ado's martyrology. In some cases, he appears to have consulted other accounts of Laurence's passion, such as the etymologizing of Laurence from the word "laurel," a detail that does appear in St. Donato's account, but not in *Passio Polychronii*. Nigel's account of the passion and martyrdom of Laurence also follows Donato's account quite closely, which would lead one to conclude that both are based on the same source, the *Passio Polychronii*, although there are still considerable differences.

The final account that will be discussed is that of Gonzalo de Berceo, a poet of thirteenth-century Spain educated at Santo Domingo de Silos and San Millán de la Cogolla, who wrote in the then popular *mester de clerecía*, best known from the twelfth-century epic poem *Cantar de Mio Cid*. His surname comes from the village of Berceo where he was born and where the Monastery of San Millán is located. Very few vital statistics are known about this famous medieval writer and deacon of La Rioja, apart from his undeniable talent that produced the well-known *Milagros de Nuestra Señora (Miracles of Our Lady)*, a work taught in undergraduate-level courses of Spanish literature as composed by the first known Spanish poet to write verses in Castilian, with the intent of gaining rapport with his rustic, uneducated audiences by using the first person, a technique that had strong appeal when poets recited before groups of listeners. Gonzalo's *Vida de Sant Laurençio* is a blend of two varieties of religious literature: *passio* (Jesus's passion on the Cross), and *vita sancti* (saint's life), that is believed to follow most closely the account of St. Ambrose.

Prudentius' Peristephanon

The Hispano-Roman poet Prudentius wrote the *Peristephanon* in fourth-century Spain, not long after the Holy Grail was in Huesca, and in a culture in which both oral and written forms of discourse were cultivated. It must be emphasized that in Roman Spain there were several important Latin writers, such as Séneca, Quintiliano, and Marcial, but the language spoken by the people was very different from that used by writers. The popular Latin that prevailed in Spain was that spoken by the Roman legionaries who came from every part of the Empire, with infinite varieties of pronunciation, syntax, and structure, quite different from the literary Latin that was far more stable. Within Spain each region had its own peculiar phonetic characteristics, differences that became more pronounced after political ties were broken with Rome. Prudentius wrote in a very formal form of literary Latin that contrasts sharply with the tosco Latin used by Donato.

After the persecution of Diocletian in the very early fourth century, the culture was very Christian and highly literate, but attitudes toward writing were nevertheless complex and contradictory. As Françoise Desbordes has recently asserted, writing was considered to be both an arbitrary, external, and imperfect representation of speech and a powerful tool of logic that enables the human mind to master the world,[42] an attitude of ambivalence shared by St. Ambrose. Prudentius, however, adopted the second posture, departing from the popular prejudice toward the written word with sophisticated wordplays and anagrams that invite the reader to engender meaning in a literary discourse that is seen as a force capable of achieving redemption for Christians. Far from bearing any relation to the popular, communicative style of Gonzalo de Berceo, Prudentius "hopes that his poetic text will enable him to communicate with the martyrs, who will then themselves assume a textual role in that they will instantaneously relay his words to God: 'audiunt statimque ad aurem Regis aeterni ferunt' ('they listen to our prayer and straightway carry it to the ear of the eternal King,' (Pe 1.18)."[43] The role of the martyrs as intercessors between human beings and

---

[42] Françoise Desbordes, Idées romaines sur l'écriture (Lille: Presses Universitaires de Lille, 1990), p.99.

[43] Jill Ross, "Dynamic Writing and Martyrs' Bodies in *Prudentius'* Peristephanon," *Journal of Early Christian Studies* 3:3 (The Johns Hopkins University Press, 1995), p.325-355.

God is made concrete by the literary text whose function is not that of providing a historic record, but is rather a kind of indirect speech that will acquire a redemptive power.

It is important to clarify this point, because although the *Peristephanon* certainly represents genuine oral tradition, it was neither intended to be a complete historical record nor a didactic oral poem. In that respect, it can be considered to be a rather arbitrary and imperfect representation of the oral tradition to which the first generations of the Church were accustomed to communicate their beliefs. As John L. McKenzie explains, tradition was an integral part of the primitive Christian community. It was of great importance that the common body of material, summed up as gospel and teaching and which was traced to the apostles and witnesses of the life of Jesus Himself, should be preserved without deformation, and fidelity to the received tradition was the ultimate assurance that the doctrine proposed was genuine. Revelation was the *word* of Jesus: the word incarnate, his life and person, and his sayings. This revelation was the object of tradition, the oral transmission of the material to disciples, following the means of the Jewish rabbinical schools, and forms the basis of Christian belief.

This concept has changed dramatically throughout the centuries, being replaced by reliance on the written word rather than speech; in fact, recent centuries have witnessed such a complete reversal of this idea that many mistakenly believe that tradition is nothing but legend and folklore, rather than the aggregate of customs, beliefs, and practices that give continuity to a culture, including its laws and institutions. In many religions, among them Catholicism, tradition signifies essential doctrines or tenets that are not necessarily set down in sacred scriptures, but are accepted as equally authoritative, and are sometimes used to interpret them. The modern tendency, therefore, is to dismiss traditions lacking written documentation as inauthentic or at the very least untrustworthy, but it should be remembered that they are the foundation of societal beliefs and practices, and have been considered more reliable than documents written by individuals.

This explains many of the problems and contradictions found in so many of these sources of the life and martyrdom of St. Laurence, which are in reality works of literature, not historical documents, that manipulate oral tradition to suit their purposes. In the case of Prudentius, the intent is to formulate the restructuring of Rome's mission in the world and to establish

Laurence as the new Augustus who will be the leader of the spiritualized Rome, *Rome caelestis*. The encounter between Laurence and the prefect is therefore portrayed as a kind of battle in which victory is achieved by the martyr's death.

Prudentius expresses his Christian vocation in the *Praefacio*, in which he speaks of each stage in his career, overwhelmed by the realization that all his achievements are nothing in the face of death. For the poet it is now time to reject the world in order to celebrate God with his verses, represented as the result of a spiritual conversion that leads him to review his past life in a negative way, make a last confession, and resolve to repent by composing verses dedicated to the glorification of God. He does not speak of conversion to Christianity from paganism, but rather of a withdrawal from the world resulting from a decision to live out a fuller commitment to Christ. The theme of *ubi sunt*,[44] prevalent in Spanish literature throughout the Middle Ages and epitomized in the fifteenth-century "Coplas of Jorge Manrique for the death of his father," finds its source for Prudentius in the *Confessions* of St. Augustine and is repeated here: life flies rapidly past and old age creeps up suddenly. The poet, in fact, speaks of himself as already dead, reminiscent of the Epistles of St. Paul that exhort Christians to die to the world by living in Christ.

The poet writes for an audience that is familiar with the classical models that he evokes, "like-minded *literati*" with the background of the same form of secular education. In this epoch there was a renewed interest in the authors of late Latin poetry, among them Virgil, Livy and Juvenal, who are seen in the *Peristephanon* as "Christians without Christ," inhabitants of an Empire that was founded providentially by Christ for the promotion of universal conversion. Rome's traditional greatness is reestablished in the remains of its new heroes, the martyrs, and the new monuments in their memory that now decorate Christian Rome, as Anne-Marie Palmer explains.[45] This new patriotism of the Empire could be somewhat countered by the local pride of Spanish towns over their martyrs, which might explain the intense desire of Zaragoza to claim St. Vincent, although

---

[44] *Ubi sunt* is an ancient Latin theme meaning "where are they...", which questions what has become of the great people and civilizations of the past. Fame, prosperity and greatness all come to an end with death and are eventually forgotten.

[45] Anne-Marie Palmer, *Prudentius on the Martyrs* (Oxford: Clarendon Press, 1989).

he suffered martyrdom elsewhere, in Valencia, and the long-standing dispute between Huesca and Valencia over the birthplace of St. Laurence.

The oldest written sources of information about Laurence are the inscriptions composed by Pope Damasus, and the writings of Bishop Ambrose. The first speaks of the many tortures suffered by the martyr, but gives few other details. Ambrose's account, however, follows that of Prudentius quite closely. In the form of a hymn, he relates how Laurence met with Pope Sixtus II before his martyrdom, and tells of the order of Valerian's prefect Cornelius to hand over the treasures of the church, and of Laurence's presentation of the poor as the true riches of the Church. The account includes the saint's condemnation to the grill and the martyr's ironic reply to the judge: *Assum est, uersa et manduca.*[46]

Prudentius' account is essentially the same, but he differs on the form of Sixtus's execution, which he believes to have been crucifixion, even though Cyprian of Carthage affirms in his correspondence that the Pope was beheaded. Anne-Marie Palmer attributes this to a misinterpretation of a Damascene inscription which refers metaphorically to Sixtus's deacons as *crucis inuictae comites.*[47] He also adds the anti-Christian speech of the persecutor, and Laurence's prayer for Rome, which are most likely the result of poetic imagination rather than information from another source, and includes the death of Laurence on the gridiron.

It is clear that Prudentius was not the source for St. Donato, despite being of the same country. In the poem of Prudentius, there is no information on the early life of the saint, nor material concerning any aspect of his life other than his passion and martyrdom. The language is poetic, with abundant classical references and a syntax and structure clearly intended for a sophisticated, highly educated audience. Unlikely additions are made to the story, such as Laurence's prayer for Rome that does not appear at all in the longer account of Donato.

St. Donato presents Laurence's famous words on the gridiron in a spiritual manner, "And giving thanks once again to God...he raised his eyes, and said to Valerian: *This half of my body is already roasted. Order them to turn me over, and you will be able to eat.* It wasn't Spanish boastfulness, but a burning desire to suffer more for Christ, because there is no doubt that he could no longer feel

---

[46] *It is cooked, turn it over and eat.* Translation by Mark Guscin.

[47] Ibid. p.245. This is a Latin phrase meaning "companions of the unconquered cross."

the burned side," a passage reminiscent of Christ consecrating the Eucharist. This same detail from tradition is quite different in Prudentius: "Laurence on his own part hails the judge and addresses him briefly from the gridiron: *This part of my body has been burned long enough; turn it round and try what your hot god of fire has done.* So the prefect orders him to be turned about, and then *It is done,* says Laurence; *eat it up, try whether it is nicer raw or roasted.* These words spoken in jest, he then looks up to heaven, and sighing deeply prays in pity for the city of Romulus." The prayer that follows is a discourse so academic that it is completely implausible that it could have been delivered during such a moment of agony; the words, rather than prayerful, are rather insulting and grotesque, and the prayer is a perfect reflection of the author's intent to reestablish the greatness of Rome.

Although Prudentius used prose accounts of martyrdom as the basis for his poems, these were composed for a different purpose, as readings of the accepted martyrdom account in the Mass alongside, or in place of, the usual Scriptural readings from the Old and New Testaments. The solemn reading of the *Passio* held an important place in the Mass of the *catechumens* between readings from the Scriptures and the sermon, and readings from the *Acta* were allowed in Spain as early as the end of the fourth century and the beginning of the fifth. These earliest forms of martyr-literature fulfilled an important didactic function and were popular as devotional reading among educated Christians. They were not, however, written records of the Laurence tradition, but rather pious manipulations of the major events.

The Passio Polychronii

The *Passio Polychronii* is a document of special importance because it is the first written account of the entire story of Laurence's martyrdom, or at least the only one that has survived. Dated around the year 500 AD, the work revolves around the passion of Sts. Sixtus and Laurence, and it is believed that it was gathered together by St. Damasus, a Spaniard who became Pope at the age of sixty, after the death of Pope Liberius in 366. He is especially remembered for his concern for relics and sepulchers of the martyrs, as well as for his work in draining, opening out, and adorning the sacred catacombs, in which he set up inscriptions and epigrams in verse.

The author of the *Passio* is unknown, but it is believed that he worked from the popular and historical traditions that were prevalent at the beginning of the sixth century. This Latin document is the source for all later histories of Laurence's passion, and is reflected in art and literature. Its complete title is *The Passion of Polychronius and his Companions*, and narrates the story of this Christian bishop who was martyred with his clergy in Babylon during an expedition that the Roman emperor made there, instigating a persecution. His companions included Irenaeus, Sixtus II, Laurence, Hippolytus, Romanus, the deacons of Sixtus II, Felicissimus and Agapitus, and the presbyter Justin, among others, called companions not because of friendship or acquaintance, but for the proximity of their Christian martyrdoms that all took place during the Valerian persecution in the year 258. The author follows a chronological order, beginning with the persecutions that were initiated in Persia during the emperor's campaign in that part of the Roman Empire, and ending with the persecutions in Rome.

The *Passio Polychronii* is silent on Laurence's life before the Valerian persecution, beginning with the account of Pope Sixtus II being ordered to appear before the Emperor Decius[48] and the prefect Valerian, along with his deacons Felicissimus and Agapitus, who after refusing to sacrifice to the gods, are led to the temple of Mars to offer incense to that god. They refuse, and are incarcerated in the Mamertine jail. Laurence visits him there where the famous conversation takes place, in this account fairly succinct, and limited to Laurence's repeated questions along the lines of "Where are you going, father, without your son?" and Sixtus' reply that greater torments await his disciple in only three days' time, that will lead to a far greater triumph over the tyrant. He entrusts to Laurence all the belongings of the Church with orders to distribute them among the poor, without specifying what they are. Laurence complies with his wishes, and then goes to the house of Cyriaca, the Christian widow, on Mt. Caelius, and washes the feet of the Christians who had taken refuge there, giving them part of the treasures and healing Cyriaca of the maladies from which she was suffering. From there he goes to the house of Narsisus where he distributes more of the treasures to the Christians and washes their feet, healing also Crescencius the blind man, whose vision is restored when Laurence makes the sign of the cross on his eyes.

---

[48] A mistake historically speaking, as the Emperor Decius was already dead.

In the part of the story that concerns the surrender of the Grail to the Spaniard, no mention is made of the act. From the house of Narsisus, Laurence goes to the Nepociana crypt in the neighborhood of Patricio where Justin is found in the company of 63 Christians, men and women. Unlike Donato's account, here Justin and Laurence try to kiss each other's feet for a time, and Laurence finally succeeds in washing them, as well as those of the others present. While this is taking place, Sixtus is led to the temple of the Earth goddess where Decius and Valerian order him to be taken once again to the temple of Mars with the ultimatum that if he doesn't sacrifice right there, he will be beheaded on the spot. The Pontiff cries out that the Son of the living God will destroy the idol, the Christians respond with "Amen!" and the temple falls. At this point, Laurence appears, and tells Sixtus that he has already distributed the treasures. As soon as the word "treasures" is uttered, Laurence is arrested and Sixtus is beheaded in front of the temple, along with his deacons Felicissimus and Agapitus. Again, the account is quite different from that of Donato: here, Laurence is not present during the destruction of the temple, and Sixtus is martyred right there, not outside the city as was customary. No mention is made of the other deacons who were martyred: Januarius, Magnus, Innocence and Stephen, as listed by Donato.

Laurence is taken into the custody of the Tribunal Partenius, who immediately informs Decius of his capture. Laurence is led to his presence, and ordered to surrender the treasures. Laurence says nothing, and is then taken to Valerian who tries to discover the secret of where they are hidden, threatening severe tortures if he does not sacrifice to the gods. Laurence is then entrusted to the custody of Hippolytus and taken to a jail in the company of many others, among them the blind man Lucillus, who is immediately converted, baptized, and restored with sight. As news of the miracle spreads, many other blind people come seeking cures, and Hippolytus is converted and baptized by Laurence who is then ordered to appear before Valerian. He negotiates the time period of three days to collect the treasures, but spends the time collecting the blind, infirm, lame and poor who are taken to the house of Hippolytus. He then appears before the prefect and declares that the poor are the eternal treasures of the Church, and that the Romans are sacrificing to the demons and to deaf and dumb idols rather than the true God.

Laurence is then scourged with whips with lead points and shown all the other instruments of torture that will be used if he does not sacrifice to the gods: hot sheets of lead, lead mallots, and the torture rack, among others. He is taken to the place of Tiberius where he once again refuses to yield the treasures and sacrifice to the gods, and is consequently scourged and then tortured with the hot metal sheets. A voice is heard announcing that Laurence still has much to suffer, which Decius calls the "consolation of the demons." He is then spread on the rack and beaten with the "scorpions." As Laurence gives thanks to God, Romanus sees a beautiful youth next to him, wiping his body with a linen cloth. Decius, convinced that they have been defeated by magic, orders Laurence taken from the rack. Romanus takes a jar full of water to Laurence, seeking baptism, and Laurence complies. Romanus is then beaten and condemned to death, which takes place outside the walls of the Salarian gate, beheaded on August 9 and buried by Justin at night in the Campo Verano. It is clear that the major events are repeated not only in Donato's account, but that of Nigel of Canterbury.

The other events are also all more or less similar to what is St. Donato describes, although the style and many details are different: the place of the final torture, Hippolytus' desire to reveal that he is now a Christian, the final demand to sacrifice in the sight of many other instruments of torture, and Laurence's mouth battered with stones after he proclaims that his night has no darkness, but is instead bathed with light. The gridiron is prepared, and Laurence dies after saying to Decius, *"Miserable one, one part of my body is already roasted; turn me over so that the other half is roasted, and eat me!"* Hippolytus and Justin take the body to the estate of the widow Cyriaca in the Via Tiburtina, where it was hid during the day, and then buried at night in a crypt in the Campo Verano on August 10.

It is clear that while the *Passio Polychronii* predates Donato's work, it could not have been the only source used, even without considering the early life history that here is totally absent. Although the major events of Laurence's passion are the same, many details are either missing or different, and when compared to Donato, the style is more concise, not as spiritual, and with far less concern for the accuracy manifested by the preoccupation with dates, years, names, and places that is so characteristic of Donato.

It is criticized for many of the same reasons that Rev. Patrick Healy has already presented: *1)* St. Laurence was martyred during the Valerian persecution, and Decius was already dead, but both are presented in the narration, a mistake that appears in all accounts, except that of Donato. The annotations of the Roman Martyrology, the Bollandists, and other hagiographers explain the error, however, as due to the proximity of the persecutions of Decius and Valerian, in the years 250 and 258, respectively, having always been spoken of as one single persecution rather than two, and others mention the Roman custom of an emperor carrying the name of his predecessor next to his own, as was the case with Augustus Caesar and Tiberius Augustus. According to Donato, Decius was coincidentally the name of the prefect in charge of the execution, which is not in conflict with history in any way. *2)* St. Hippolytus is often confused with another saint of the same name, a Roman priest of the early third century who was an important theological writer in the Roman church. He set himself up in opposition to Pope St. Pontian, was exiled to Sardinia during the persecution of Maximinus, and was later reconciled to the Church and martyred on that island and buried on the Via Tiburtina. Butler, for example, insists that the story of Hippolytus converted by Laurence was only a romance, and that he was probably in reality this other saint, citing his legendary death, according to which he was torn apart by horses, as evidence. Nevertheless, other hagiographers are certain that they were two distinct saints, and the legendary death does not invalidate the rest of the story that is given in all accounts of the jailer appointed to take custody of Laurence. *3)* Finally, some find objection to the manner of death by fire, which they insist would have been decapitation, citing that the imperial decree required an immediate death. Peñart argues that the Latin word *animadvertere* did not necessarily mean to decapitate, but rather to punish with death or execute, and that although decapitation was most common, other means were also used. The manner in which Laurence is reputed to have died is consistent with the fact that the saint, as administrator of the Church's possessions, refused to surrender them even after the martyrdom of Sixtus II. A crueler, prolonged, and more spectacular death was in order. Although this particular type of death was common by the persecution of Diocletian in 303-304, it was not new in the time of St. Laurence. According to Peñart, already in the year 177, during the persecution of Marcus Aurelius, the Christians Atalus and Blandina were martyred in Lyons on a type of iron chair placed over a fire, and during the Valerian persecution, only five months earlier, Sts. Fructuoso, Eulogio and Augurio were martyred by fire in Tarragona. The record of this martyrdom has been authenticated, and was probably written by an eyewitness. The fact that tradition has been constant and universal in insisting that Laurence was roasted on a gridiron is further evidence, impossible to explain if he were simply decapitated.

Evidence in favor of its authenticity and accuracy is the fact that ancient history offers testimony of the major characters, and these facts are provided by Peñart: *1)* Pope Sixtus II suffered martyrdom by decapitation on August 6 and was buried in the cemetery of St. Calixtus. *2)* Felicissimo and Agapitus, deacons and companions of Laurence, were martyred on the same day. Their sepulcher, along with an inscription with their two names, was found in the nineteenth century by De Rossi. *3)* De Rossi also discovered the crypt of Crescencius in the cemetery of Priscilla. *4)* Romanus' feast day is August 9 and according to an ancient itinerary his tomb was at the end of the gallery of the cemetery of Priscilla. The church of San Lorenzo in Fonte was built on the traditional site of his baptism. *5)* Hippolytus' feast day is celebrated on August 13, and although he is sometimes confused with other saints with the same name, he is mentioned in the Roman Martyrology as the saint who was martyred shortly after Laurence. *6)* Cyriaca, the woman who was cured of headaches by Laurence, appears to have been the owner of the Campo Verano where Laurence was martyred and the first Basilica in his honor was constructed, now St. Laurence Outside the Walls. Her remains are close to those of Romanus and Crescencio in the cemetery of Priscilla. *7)* Justin, the presbyter who helped bury the martyrs, is also considered to be a real person, and there is later evidence of his sepulcher.

The *Passio Polychronii* is today considered to be a historical novel, with a nucleus that is based on historical truth. In ancient times, it was read as history, and today many critics insist that it is pure legend, but the truth lies in between. Certainly the conversations are novelized, as are many of the events, such as the continual repetition of the demand to sacrifice, followed by additional torments, Laurence's apparent insensitivity to pain, the presence of both Decius and Valerian as participants in the passion, and many of the external signs. But that does not negate the historical nature of the document, and the fact that the characters were real people who were buried in the catacombs of Rome. For those who still doubt that Laurence was roasted, there is still the undeniable evidence of his mortal remains, still in their original resting place in the Campo Verano, now the church of St. Laurence Outside the Walls. As will be detailed later, the skull clearly shows signs of death by fire: the incorrupt skin is charred, the nose burnt, and the lips contracted in pain, an eternal and undeniable testimony of his torture.

Nigel of Canterbury's Passio

Nigel bequeathed eight volumes to Christ Church, one of which was the *Passio Sancti Laurencii, uersifice*, a book of Latin verse about the martyrdom of Laurence.

Many of the allusions in it suggest that Nigel knew at least two or three of the many versifications of the *Passio* by earlier Latin poets, including the hymn by Ambrose and the poem of Prudentius, although he never mentions them directly. His twelfth-century work does not show signs of having been influenced by later treatments of the passion, such as *De sancto Sixto papa et Laurentio* by the late tenth-century poet Flodoardus of Reims, and the *Oratio* of Rainier, a monk of St. Lawrence in Liège who died in 1182. According to Jan Ziolkowski, there are some small parallels with Marbod of Rennes's *Versus de sancto Laurentio*, written by a man of letters of the late eleventh and early twelfth century, who devoted much of his talent to versifications of the lives and passions of ancient martyrs, particularly verbal similarities of line openings and endings. There are significant similarities, however, with St. Donato's manuscript, an indication that both drew from the same common source, and in fact, Nigel adheres most closely to the narrative of the *Passio Polychronii*, which also appears to have influenced Donato far more than Ambrose's hymn and the poem of Prudentius, which are not nearly as detailed. It is certain that the *Passio Polychronii* was known in Anglo-Norman circles, and the Anglo-Norman poet who composed the rhymed *Vie de St. Laurent* in this same period of time, also followed it closely.

At the time Nigel wrote his Latin verse *passio* of Laurence, it was no longer in vogue to versify the legends of the saints as prose had already become the preferred medium. The exception was Anglo-Norman England, where verse legends of saints continued to be popular, and remained the main form of literary expression for both Benedictines and Canons. The norm was to write about local saints directly associated with the monasteries of England, those who had lived or died in the community of the monks. St. Laurence, however, was an exception. The cult to St. Laurence began in earnest in the seventh century, and by the time of the Reformation Laurence had been honored by at least 228 dedications in England. The saint's popularity is also evident in the occurrences of the name *Laurentius* in documents that survive from the latter part of the twelfth century. This is quite significant, indicating that this popularity ran parallel with that of the Holy Grail, reputed in medieval times to be hidden in the mountains of the Pyrenees after having been rescued by the martyr. The number of hagiographic treatments of Laurence is remarkable, especially in England where literary interest was primarily in local saints, indicating that not only the manner of death had been unique, but that he also was being remembered for the transcendent importance of what he had saved, the Holy Grail.

The events in Nigel's *Passio* can be summarized as follows, and it is clear that he has adhered to the events of the *Passio Polychronii*. During the pontificate of Sixtus II in Rome, Decius orders the Christians to offer pagan sacrifice under penalty of death.[49] Sixtus appears before Caesar, who tells him that he must either perish amid torments, or submit to the laws by sacrificing to the Roman gods, but Sixtus refuses and is imprisoned. At that time Laurence was the archdeacon, of noble stock, a saintly and just man who especially loved the poor and wretched. He visits Sixtus in prison and admonishes him for going to his martyrdom without his servant, but Sixtus promises that Laurence will follow him after three days. Laurence transfers the possessions of the Church that had been entrusted to him to Mount Caelius and distributes them among the poor. He then cures Cyriaca, the pious hostess, of her head pains, and finds the house of Narcissus, washing the feet of the Christians there. A blind man named Crescencio is present and Laurence restores his sight.

Laurence appears in the Nepotian crypt, where many Christians have hidden, cared for by Justin, and disperses some of the treasures. In the meantime, Sixtus is martyred. Laurence, present at his death, shouts to the Father to spend the treasures of the Church that have already been given to the children. At the word "treasure" the throng rushes in haste, and Laurence is imprisoned. Parthemius announces to Decius that the person who has the treasures, Laurence, is in custody. Laurence is brought before Decius and refuses to reveal the whereabouts of the treasures. Decius then orders Valerian to interrogate the prisoner. Hippolytus takes charge of Laurence in prison, where he is incarcerated with a man named Lucillus, who became blind through long weeping. Laurence promises to restore his sight if he is baptized, and then catechizes and baptizes the man, who regains his sight. Then many other blind people come to Laurence to receive the sign of the cross.

Hippolytus tries to convince Laurence to reveal the location of the treasures, but is instead converted by Laurence who baptizes him. Laurence is then summoned to appear before the king, and is accompanied by Hippolytus. The prefect, Valerian, acting on behalf of Decius, inquires about the treasure. Laurence asks for three days to produce it, distributes the remainder of the money during this time, and gathers together the poor and lame in the home of Hippolytus.

---

[49] This repeats the mistake of the Passio Polychronii, which is corrected in the work of St. Donato.

Laurence then goes to Decius. When asked about the funds, Laurence brings forth the poor to whom he had given the money. Decius demands that he sacrifice to the gods, but Laurence refuses, and is consequently stripped and beaten to no avail. The enraged Decius threatens him with various other tortures.

After many people convert, Decius changes the place of torture to the temple of Jove. Laurence reminds Decius that death and judgment day are inevitable. Valerian urges Laurence to repent and produce the riches while he still has the opportunity, but Laurence answers that he has faith in Christ. Decius has Laurence clubbed, and then orders Valerian to have him burned with hot metal plates, but Laurence remains unmoved. Decius becomes even more enraged, and threatens worse torments if Laurence does not deny Christ. As Laurence prays, a voice from heaven encourages him to persevere. This makes the crowd fearful, but Decius tells them that the voice was demonic and orders a grill to be prepared. Laurence still appears handsome and remains unbroken. The soldier Romanus sees a handsome youth standing next to Laurence, which prompts him to desire baptism. He brings water to Laurence, who baptizes him. Romanus is then martyred, and his body buried by Justin. Just before Laurence is martyred, Hippolytus comes to Laurence and expresses the hope that he will also be martyred. Laurence informs him that he will die in three days.

The number of tortures employed is listed, but none succeeds in disturbing the happiness of Laurence. Decius accuses him of surmounting them through magic tricks, and threatens worse punishment if he does not worship the gods. He orders him to reveal his lineage, and Laurence complies, answering that he is a Spaniard of noble lineage, raised from boyhood at Rome where he learned the doctrines of the divine law. Decius accuses him of blasphemy and has him stoned. After having been beaten for a long time, Laurence laughs and ridicules the king. As Laurence prays, the grill is heated, a punishment that had never before been seen. The deacon, lying on the fiery grill, declares that the more the emperor's rage kindles the flames, the more strongly the spiritual mind is intent on its purpose, and the flesh no longer holds dominion over the spirit but serves it. As the tormenters blaspheme, mocking and insulting Laurence, he is ordered once again to revere the gods. Laurence answers by affirming his faith in Christ, and says that the fire seems cold to him, taunting them by asking to be turned so that he will cook evenly on both sides. He finally calls upon Christ and ascends to heaven. Decius laments his defeat, and Hippolytus buries Laurence's body. After three days Hippolytus dies, torn apart by horses. After Valerian drops dead in front of Decius, the emperor falls from his throne, is beset by demons, and dies.

If we compare Nigel's *Passio* with the manuscript of St. Donato, the differences are considerable. The first is written in Latin verse, while the second was reportedly composed in Latin prose. Unlike Nigel, Donato provides unique facts surrounding the childhood of St. Laurence in Spain, as well as his adolescence in Rome, but it is clear that Nigel's *Passio* and Donato's version contain the same major events from the *Passio Polychronii*. Beginning, therefore, at the point where the two coincide, Nigel commences with a sermon about the "palm of triumph" that "excels all riches in worthy honor," unique to his work. He insists that the martyrdom took place in the reign of Decius, while Donato is explicit in saying that Valerian was emperor, and that having been perverted by an Egyptian magician, he began to persecute Christians, in line with the historical reality provided by Patrick Healy. Nigel adds considerable dialogue to the scene of Sixtus II before Decius, absent in Donato's narrative, although both contain a similar conversation between Laurence and the Pope. The next series of events coincide almost exactly with one notable exception: the mention of Laurence entrusting the Holy Grail to Precelius, the Spaniard from the city of Hippo in Carpentanea is not present in Nigel's *Passio*, and neither are the details surrounding the martyrdom of Sixtus II, who according to Donato was taken from the Temple of Mars, where the image of the false god was destroyed, to a place outside the city to be beheaded.

The cure of Lucillus, the assembly of the blind at the jail seeking cures, and the conversion of Hippolytus are essentially the same, although the conversations and style are quite different. It is evident that both are amplifications of the story with personal variations. In Nigel's account, Decius is ruler, and the prefect Valerian intervenes, granting Laurence the three-day time period, but this situation is the opposite in Donato's manuscript. Nigel's account is historically impossible, as the Emperor Decius died in 251 AD, but as mentioned, Donato clearly distinguishes between the Emperor Decius and the Prefect Decius who is responsible for Laurence's arrest.

Nigel then goes into a rather long discourse about the evil of gifts, which Laurence distributes to the poor lest they condemn the just and exalt the wicked, a rather strange addition, given that the poor congregate in the house of Hippolytus, assured of the hope of a gift. This passage is followed by another lengthy speech in praise of martyrdom and the virtues of Laurence that rambles and digresses considerably from the story and is rather difficult to follow.

The two accounts converge once again when Laurence returns to the authorities without the treasures, presenting instead the poor. The essentials appear in both, but Nigel's account is far more detailed, with a lengthy conversation between Laurence and Decius, who has now replaced Valerian in the task of condemning Laurence to death. In both, however, Laurence courageously mocks him by saying that the Roman gods are nothing but demons, enraging the Caesar to the point that he has the martyr scourged. Nigel again digresses with a hideous description of Decius frothing at the mouth and gnashing his teeth, followed by a lengthy sermon about the lethal venom of anger and the vice of pride, which ends when Laurence admonishes Decius for his rage, who responds by increasing his torments. While Donato follows the main events with a fairly concise and interesting narration, Nigel is continually sidetracked, this time moralizing about how flesh, when subject to the spirit, is obliged to serve, as a wife serves a husband. In both, however, Laurence is subjected to a multitude of tortures.

Before the conversion of Romanus, which immediately follows the torments of Laurence in Donato's account, Nigel again digresses for more than twenty pages, which includes a scene in the temple of Jupiter with a long speech in which the prefect pleads with Laurence to endure either death or the rites of the gods, followed by Laurence's condemnation of Roman vice and pride, and a discourse on the true meaning of the word "treasure," the cleansing power of the torments, and the certainty of death and the final judgment. Valerian accuses Laurence of practicing magical arts, and pleads with him to worship the gods. Laurence refuses, and the anger of the king is again ignited; Laurence is then beaten with cudgels. More pious digressions follow: a prayer of Laurence, Decius' meditation about how Christ cannot be a god because he was bound by the law of death, and Laurence's reply about the transitory nature of the world and lessons in Christianity. After more beatings, Laurence prays and a voice from the heavens responds that he still has more torments to endure. This event also appears in Donato's work, but Nigel embellishes it with a long account of how this voice terrified the people who were standing nearby, including Decius who tries to assure the bystanders that it is the voice of a demon.

The essential elements of Romanus' conversion and martyrdom coincide, but Nigel adds that Romanus was buried by Justin. Laurence is condemned to death by fire, and Hippolytus asks Laurence for permission to show himself as a Christian. Laurence, however, asks him to hide his faith for a short time, assuring him that he will soon be martyred. Nigel says that this will occur in three days' time, but Donato does not mention when the event will occur. Both accounts agree that Laurence was asked to declare his homeland and family. Laurence responds in a similar manner: He is Spanish, born of a noble lineage, a Christian from birth, and raised in Rome, but Donato adds that he was born in Valencia, close to Sagunto, of noble parents from Huesca, an important inclusion given his proximity to those places.

The tyrant promises to spend the entire night tormenting him if he does not sacrifice, and Laurence replies that his night will be filled with light. An iron grill is then brought in order to execute a torture never before seen, with live coals placed beneath the grating, in order to roast his flesh over a slow fire. Nigel's Laurence complains that the embers are too cool, while Donato emphasizes its penetrating voracity that nevertheless did not have an effect on his peaceful countenance. As previously mentioned, the saint's famous words are presented by Donato in a prayerful and pious manner, reminiscent of the Eucharistic celebration. Nigel's Laurence, however, speaks for a very long time. The passage is as grotesque as Prudentius' description, although greatly expanded as is so typical of Nigel. It seems to take delight in the cannibalistic nature of the remark, and is interlaced with insults:

> Therefore, king, that which has been given to the fires and yet has not been overcome by them has now been sufficiently roasted: turn it and devour what has been consumed by fire. This side has been sufficiently heated. Cut off a piece, so that our flesh may afford Decius an appealing taste. Why do you not turn the other side so that you may eat, for you know that this side has been roasted enough in the fire? Have this side turned swiftly and the other heated, so that the raw and cooked of the roast can be devoured. Therefore let the cooked be turned over and the raw be heated, so that as the raw part is grilled, the well-done part may be devoured. Turn and taste the raw, devour the cooked, and satisfy yourself with the taste of the flesh you have preferred. Without delay (lest the hour granted you pass by) turn and devour this side, scoundrel, substituting even graver torments for grave ones. Spare me nothing as if for a show of piety; ingrates, take freely from the roast flesh.

Donato ends his biography with the death of Laurence, followed by the burial of the body by Hippolytus and Justin in the Campo Verano of the Via Tiburtina. Nigel includes the legendary martyrdom of Hippolytus, who is torn apart by horses. Valerian is stricken by a sudden death at the feet of Decius; the whole earth trembles as Decius tumbles down from the seat of the throne, having been possessed for a long time by a demon. While dying, Decius shouts that Laurence has won, and accuses him of paying him back for the misdeeds he committed against the martyr, and also of being vengeful and cruel, with a menacing demeanor. Nigel ends his poem by asking Laurence to take pity on him, asking that forgiveness of sin, which he acknowledges not to have deserved, be granted him through his merits and prayers.

It is not difficult to see that in spite of the similarities – the major characters and events are essentially the same, and show signs of having a common source – the differences are enormous. Nigel is a monk who interjects long sermons, imaginary conversations, and pious discourses into the biography, while Donato is a saint who writes with simplicity, a love for accuracy, and tastefulness. Donato's account is surprisingly accurate historically, in spite of the minor errors, such as the presence of Valerian at Laurence's martyrdom, who Healy insists was not in Rome at the time, and the year of his death. Unlike Nigel, however, he avoids obscure classical references, difficult syntax and language that would make his account difficult to read or understand. His biography is written in common Latin from the point of view of someone who desires to set the record straight, especially concerning Laurence's origins in Spain and the role he played in saving the Holy Grail. It is more historical than literary, with many facts that are not included in any other existing written source. Therefore, although Nigel's *Passio* is equally detailed and draws on the same information, it sets itself apart as a work of literature that was written at the height of Laurence's popularity in the Middle Ages.

Gonzalo de Berceo: El martirio de San Lorenzo

Literary activity in Berceo's time was considerable, but educated poets preferred to write in the Portuguese dialect known as Galician rather than Castilian, the most notable example being King Alfonso X who composed the famous *Cantigas de Santa María* in lyric verse. Berceo, however, preferred the epic-type poetry known as the *mester de juglaría*, made popular in the famous *Cantar de Mio Cid*. This type of poetry was of irregular verses written in Castilian, predominantly of fourteen syllables with two hemistitchs of seven syllables divided by a *caesura* or pause, with assonant rhyme; it was already becoming out-dated, however, in Berceo's time. Berceo also read Latin, and it is believed that for the most part, all of his important works are translations or renditions of works written earlier in Latin, which he read in the archives of Santo Domingo de Silos and San Millán de la Cogolla.

All of Berceo's works are intimately related to the Monastery of San Millán de la Cogolla, for example, the biographies of San Millán, Santo Domingo de Silos, and Santa Oria are about saints related closely to San Millán de Suso. His Marian works, such as *Milagros de Nuestra Señora*, are related to the special veneration of the Virgin in San Millán de Yuso. Brian Dutton believes that there is also a connection between the *Martirio de San Lorenzo* and San Millán, because the great peak that dominates the valley of San Millán is called San Lorenzo, and is the highest peak in the entire sierra. In 1808 there was still a hermitage dedicated to the saint, where the people would go on St. Laurence's feast day for services. The peak is covered with snow almost the entire year. It is believed that in the time of the Romans there already existed veneration to St. Laurence, due to the hymn of Prudentius dedicated to the saint. There are numerous Visigoth references, such as the following from Mateo de Anguinao[50]:

> There are two caves where the Saint resided, with a distance of two leagues between the two: both are quite dark; but the one that is at the foot of the high hill or mountain of San Lorenzo is much darker and more humid that the other, two leagues in distance from the large monastery and one from the river. Here the Saint lived in seclusion for 40 years, and from it the bishop took him to ordain him as priest and put him in charge of the church of Berceo.

From this, one wonders if it could possibly be referring to St. Laurence. The tradition of Aragón that Pope Sixtus II came to Spain to take Vincent and Laurence with him to Rome is highly unlikely, as is the belief that he lived as a hermit for 40 years in local cave. This is denied by Donato's work, and we do know from all sources that Laurence was a young man when he was martyred. Atienza believes that the mystery of how this mountain came to be associated with St. Laurence may have its roots in the Grail legends of the Middle Ages, when it was rumored that the relic was hidden in a secret place in the mountains. Before Christianity the symbolism was centered in an all-powerful object, capable of providing nourishment, miraculously curing the most serious wounds, and even of bringing the dead back to life, a theme that already appeared in the pre-Celtic myths of Ireland. This sacred object, according to manuscripts still

---

[50] Compendio historial de la Rioja, 2.a ed. (Madrid, 1704), cap. 6, libro 2.

preserved, was a prodigious cauldron that was given to the Thuatha of Dana by their god, Lug, to help them obtain victory against their enemies, Fir Bolg. According to Atienza, the cult to this god was prolonged in time and became part of the peninsular pantheon under Roman domination, lending its name to minor divinities; from this god the names of many places in Spain were derived, such as Luco, Lugo, Luyego, Luchente, Lucena, Logroño, and many others. He believes that the mountain of St. Laurence was already known before Christ, under the protection of Lug, and that the pilgrimage to the peak took place in ancient times, for the purpose of thanking the mountain for watching the lands. Added to this is the fact that the peak dominates a sierra that is called the Quest, of great significance for the Holy Grail and its connection to Laurence.

Berceo was the first to compose Spanish verses about the martyrdom of Laurence, which he interprets with a colorful vocabulary, charming dialogue, idiomatic constructions, and other stylistic techniques characteristic of his poetry. He also uses the first person, which he preferred for its ability to bring the poetry to the cultural level of his audience, with whom he wished to form close ties. It begins with the typical medieval disdain for the world, exhorting people to live for God alone:

> Friends, let us hold this life in little esteem;
> Let us forget the world, let us think about our souls;
> Everything that we forfeit here we shall obtain in heaven;
> Let no fear encumber us, let us trust in God alone.

> Amigos esta vida mucho non la preçiemos,
> Olvidemos el mundo, de las almas pensemos,
> Quanto aquí dessaremos, todo lo cobraremos,
> Non nos embargue miedo, en Dios solo fiemos.

Again, like Prudentius and Nigel of Canterbury, no mention is made of Laurence's childhood, only of his life as a grown man. It differs considerably from Donato's version, however, in that Laurence and Vincent are both from Huesca, trained by Bishop Valerio, and leave for Rome together as young men in the company of the bishop, who was called to attend a conclave of clerics in Rome. Pope Sixtus II observes their simple Spanish virtues, which included wisdom, and the ability to speak straightforward words and excel in debate.

> Vincencio and Laurencio, men without flaw,
> Were both from Huesca, the documents say so;
> Both were Catholics, both of great wisdom,

Trained by Valerio and of his quality. (2)
At the time that Valerio occupied the bishopric
Of Huesca, which was a very noble position,
He trained these novitiates; he showed them the way
To love the Son of the Virgin Mary. (3)
He was delighted with these two priests,
Because they were as unsophisticated as cloistered monks:
They spoke with wisdom, they uttered straightforward words;
And in debates they spoke out strongly. (9)

The Pope is so impressed that he asks the bishop to command that both young men join him, but the bishop, alarmed, objects that he would rather lose his bishopric than his "tongue" and "counsellor," as he refers to them. They finally compromise, with the Pope agreeing to decide which of the two he wants to serve him. He chooses Laurence, who greatly succeeds his expectations, a "perfect man" who also "longed to be a martyr, to suffer passion for God's sake."

Berceo utilizes the common medieval "wheel of fortune" motif, which changes suddenly when a wicked emperor rises to power, an enemy of all Christianity, who begins to "inflict terrible cruelty upon the clergy." Pope Sixtus II defends the Church from the infamous deeds of the Emperor Decius, refusing to surrender the ecclesiastical treasury. After he refuses to sacrifice to the Roman idols, he is sentenced to death by decapitation. In the meantime, Laurence gives the possessions in his charge to the poor and works miracles, two of which are related: Laurence cures a widow who suffers from excruciating headaches, and restores sight to a blind man.

Before Sixtus is executed, Laurence speaks to him, expressing his desire to accompany him in martyrdom:

"I beseech you, Father, with all my heart,
That you do not desert me, for God's sake and charity's.
If you do not take me with you, Father, in your company,
I shall remain behind like an orphan in his poverty." (64)

Laurence assures the Pope that the treasure is safe from Decius. Sixtus tells him that being "a young man in full vigor," he will fight for them and gain a greater reward. After the Pope's martyrdom, Laurence is arrested and imprisoned where he cures a blind prisoner, a miracle that attracts a great number of people suffering from various illnesses, who are also cured. Decius then summons Laurence and gives him the ultimatum to either surrender the treasure or die. Laurence's reply shows Berceo's sense of humor:

> Said St. Laurence to him: "All your threats
> Are more tasty to me than spinach;
> Neither all your henchmen, nor you who beset me,
> Make me more fearful than would ring-neck doves." (87)

Laurence asks for a period of three days to yield the treasure, asking for a "truce." Berceo mocks Valerian's acceptance of the agreement, saying:

> The Duke Valeriano trusted this statement:
> He considered that he had everything in his hand;
> He praised himself to Decius and did a foolish thing,
> For he promised everything to the last mite. (95)

At the end of the three-day period, Laurence appears before the Romans, accompanied by a multitude of poor people – "all he could find" – and announces:

> "These are the treasures which never grow old;
> The more they are scattered, the more they always increase;
> Those who love these treasures and serve them,
> Will gain the kingdom where souls are honored." (97)

Valerian then sees that he was tricked and becomes furious and irate. He orders Laurence to either sacrifice to the gods or endure torture, and Laurence chooses the latter. In order to give him the most horrible death possible, an iron bed is prepared with slats set so that the flames could pass through. Laurence is bound to it by his hands and feet, and the tormentors fan the flames, which "burned fiercely without containment," so that the "holy body caught fire in the intense heat." Laurence's famous words are captured as follows:

> "Please turn me over on the other side," said St. Laurence;
> "Look for your best pepper, for I am roasted to a turn;
> Plan your lunch, for you have laboured much;
> And, my sons, may God forgive you, for you have sorely sinned!
> "You have afforded me a fine repast, have made me a fine bed;
> I am most grateful to you and quite rightly;
> Nor would I wish for you a sadder fortune for this;
> Nor would I hold more anger, nor have for you a greater animus."

The poem ends in medias res[51], with the words of Laurence as he is dying on the gridiron, not by design, but because the last quatrains were lost. It is not difficult to see that Gonzalo de Berceo's Martirio de San Lorenzo is a rather succinct, poeticized, and tongue-in-cheek version of the major events from the St. Laurence tradition, following the conviction of Aragón that Laurence was born in Huesca, and went to Rome with Vincent as an adult. John Esten Keller assumes that they were priests, but this is due to his interpretation of the Spanish word *compañeros*, which has nothing to do with their ordination.[52] In reality, both were deacons, and it is evident from historical documents that Vincent was considerably younger than Laurence, apprehended by the Romans under Dacian not long after he began to preach and instruct the people after his ordination as deacon, and martyred in 303 AD, nearly fifty years after Laurence's death. It is inconceivable that they could have travelled to Rome as companions.

The manner of death for Laurence also departs from the standard tradition. Instead of being slowly roasted to death over live coals, here the flames are so intense that the body catches fire, and it is, of course, highly unlikely that Laurence would have been able to speak at all in those circumstances. Nevertheless, the key elements appear here, as in all known versions of the tradition: During the Roman persecutions, Pope Sixtus II refuses to turn over the ecclesiastical treasury and sacrifice to the gods. He is martyred, but before his death he entrusts the goods to Laurence, predicting that he will follow him in death in three days' time. Laurence is arrested, and cures a blind man while in prison. The Romans demand that he yield the treasure, and Laurence asks for a grace period of three days. During this time he disperses the treasures among the poor, curing the blind and ill. He then appears at court with the poor, announcing to the Romans that they are the treasures of the Church. The Romans are so enraged that they prepare a special torture for him: he is roasted alive on a gridiron, and asks that his body be turned. Romanus and Hippolytus are converted during his passion, and also martyred.

The legend of St. Sixtus' visit to Spain appears in several documents, such as *Rationale Divinorum Officiorum*[53], written around 1175 and in the *Leyenda Aurea* of Vorágine, but this was rejected by Ambrosio de Morales[54], who says:

The martyrologies, the breviaries and calendars of saints' days make St. Laurence a

---

[51] A literary term meaning that the story ends in the midst of the plot.

[52] Gonzalo de Berceo (New York: Twayne Publishers, Inc., 1972), p.110.

[53] Chapter cxlv (Migne, PL CII), col. 148.

[54] Crónica general de España (Alcalá, 1576), volume I, book nine, chapter 46, p. 319 r-v.

native of the city of Huesca in Aragón, and the memory of this is preserved there, so complete that it takes away any doubt. His parents were named Orencio and Paciencia and of both that church prays...

Of the childhood or youth of this saint we do not know why or when he went to Rome...What some refer to, that Pope Sixtus came to Spain and took St. Laurence with him, I do not know where it has its foundation, nor have I seen any credible writer say that...And he who would like to say that before being Pope St. Sixtus could have come to Spain and taken St. Laurence at that time, he would probably not be able to cite a trustworthy author either...

All of these accounts, although interesting, certainly lack credibility as historical records of the events. In that respect, the seventeenth-century translation of Donato's biography, written in Latin at the end of the sixth century, stands out for its candor, accuracy, and apparent fidelity to what it claims to be: an honest endeavor by a saint to record the details of the life of the martyr Laurence. It is unique in that it provides details about the childhood and adolescence of the saint, along with explanations for traditional errors and contradictions, such as the Huesca/Valencia conflict. It names its sources as the presbyters of Valencia who were caretakers of the ancient monuments dedicated to Saints Orencio, Paciencia, Laurence, and Vincent. Laurence's childhood in Spain is historically plausible, with its facts supported by the historical annals, and is written with a simplicity, candor, and holiness that are not in conflict with its reputed authorship. Dates are given according to the old calendar, as well as the new, and the narration begins with the story of the flood. Even the biography written about Laurence's life in Italy contains details found in no other source, explaining such things as Laurence's relationship with Pope Sixtus II and the death of his parents. The account of his passion and death is very possibly the most tasteful of all versions, and is also more historically accurate, written to show the incredible suffering and courage of the young Spaniard, without unnecessary additions and devoid of artificial devices, classical references, and difficult syntax.

Concerning the life of St. Donato, the *Anales del Reyno de Valencia*, written by Francisco Diago, provide some details, which will be explained in the next chapter □

Chapter 8

AN EXAMINATION OF
ST. DONATO'S ACCOUNT

One of the problems with the account of the Abbot Donato, translated in 1636 by Fray Buenaventura Ausina (pseudonym of Fray Lorenzo Mateu y Sanz), is that it appears not to have been seriously analyzed by scholars. The reason for this oversight is unknown, because if it were considered counterfeit, meaning conceived by Fray Lorenzo Mateu y Sanz as an attempt to prove Laurence's origin in Valencia and the authenticity of the Holy Chalice, rather than a translation of a sixth-century work by St. Donato, a serious study of the work would exist, and as this appears not to be the case, it leads one to speculate that it has in fact never been analyzed. As a professor of Huesca, the Augustinian translator lacked motivation to disprove the tradition of that city, and although he appears to have been familiar with Francisco Diago's *Anales*, it was not his source of information. Although Diago's history provides support for the manuscript in question, the version of the *Anales* is presented very briefly, and furthermore, the two disagree on certain points, such as the relationship of Orencio, bishop of Aix, with Laurence. It is clear that only St. Donato, not Mateu y Sanz, would have had the basis and sources to question Huesca's popular belief that Laurence was born there: as a sixth-century resident of Valencia, he was familiar with the local shrines and was able to talk with clergy familiar with the family's history, preserved by oral tradition. As Donato's manuscript is the only known source that mentions the surrender of the Holy Grail to Laurence, it deserves examination and discussion for that reason alone, not to mention the unique details provided concerning Laurence's childhood.

One of the only references I have seen is that of Brian Dutton[55], who says in a footnote on the final page (the original is written in Spanish), "As a final note, let's look at the *later* [emphasis mine] development of the history of St. Laurence, precisely the *Vida y martirio del Glorioso Español San Lorenço…*(Valencia, 1710, second ed. of the book published in Salamanca, 1636) by Fray Buenaventura Ausina (pseudonym of Fray Lorenzo Mateu y Sanz). According to this author[56] the parents of the saint were nobility from Huesca, Orencio and Paciencia. Under the emperors Severus and Antoninus Caracala, Cornelius directed the persecution of the Christians. The parents of St. Laurence took refuge in Valencia where they began a new life. Paciencia gave birth to Laurence on the feast day of St. Stephen, 225, and he was baptized on the feast of the Epiphany, 226. The family decided to visit the Holy Land, but the boat shipwrecked in Campania, Italy. On this point the author[57] writes: 'The kinship of St. Laurence with St. Vincent was because St. Paciencia had a younger sister, named Enola, who was the mother of St. Vincent.' St. Vincent was martyred on January 22, 303. St. Sixtus met Laurence in Capua and took him to Rome, when he was fourteen years old. On the first of May, 246, Laurence's parents were martyred. St. Sixtus ordains Laurence as deacon. On August 6, 261, St. Sixtus, after entrusting the treasures of the Church to St. Laurence, suffered martyrdom. From this point the history follows more or less the version of the *Passio Polychronii*."

The author calls the work a *later* development of the Laurentine tradition, without explaining his reasons for that belief, and does not even mention the fact that the work is reputedly a translation of a Latin document from the second half of the sixth century, but rather credits the childhood information to the translator without even suggesting how he suddenly acquired this new data in the seventeenth century. All of this and the brevity of his comments suggest that he has not studied it extensively.

Donato's account agrees with the other sources in the fact that Laurence's parents were wealthy landowners from Huesca, of a noble family and Christians by birth. He relates that the persecution of Christians began during the reign of

---

[55] Estudio y edición crítica de *Obras Completas* V: *El Sacrificio de la Misa, La Vida de Santa Oria, El Martirio de San Lorenzo*, Gonzalo de Berceo (London: Tamesis Books Limited), p. 180. Damián Peñart y Peñart also briefly refers to Fr. Buenaventura's work in his book *San Lorenzo, santo español y oscense*, (Huesca, 1987), but as he sets out to prove that Huesca was Laurence's birthplace, it is not surprising that he devotes little attention to it and fails to mention that it is a translation of a much earlier work.

[56] Dutton attributes the authorship of the work to the translator, rather than the reputed author, St. Donato.

[57] Again, the quote is attributed to Mateu y Sanz, rather than St. Donato.

Severus (Lucius Septimius 146-211), whose reign marked a critical stage in the development of the absolute despotism for which the later Roman Empire was known. There is little historical information about the events that Donato describes in Spain at this time, although it is certain that the remains of Julita and her son Quirico are still venerated in Burgos in the hermitage *Puras de Villafranca*[58]. The cruel martyrdom of the widow's three-year-old son was the impetus for Orencio and Paciencia's flight to Valencia. Leonard A. Curchin attributes the lack of early references to Christianity in Spain partly to the 'underground' nature of the outlawed faith in the first three centuries, "which made advertisement perilous, and partly to the informality of its diffusion, which depended more on personal contacts with friends, neighbors and fellow workers than on bishops and clergy (who, given the illegality of the new religion, preached mostly to the converted in secret meeting rooms)"[59].

There is no doubt, however, according to the historians, that Christianity was firmly established in Baetica by the early second century because its churches are mentioned by Irenaeus, and Tertullian refers to the fact that 'all the boundaries of Spain know the name of Christ.'[60] Fructuosis was the only bishop martyred in Spain, which occurred during persecution of Valerian (258-9) when he was burned with two of his deacons in the amphitheatre of the city for refusing to take part in the state religion. Prudentius dedicates Book VI of his *Peristephanon* to Fructuosis and the deacons Augurius and Eulogius, who were imprisoned for six days before being judged by Aemilianus for refusing to worship at the Roman altars. Prudentius relates that as the three martyrs entered the flames, the "fastenings which kept their hands pulled back and tied behind them are burned and fall off, but the skin is unhurt. The torture dared not constrain the hands they purposed to lift up to the Father after the fashion of the cross; it set their arms free to pray to God."[61] Cyprian of Carthage was also executed during the persecution.

Donato places Laurence's birth in Valencia, which although traditionally disputed by those of Huesca, is firmly supported by Francisco Diago in the *Anales del Reyno de Valencia*, as he explains:

---

[58] Fray Valentín de la Cruz, *Burgos: Ermitas y Romerías* (Burgos: Caja de Ahorros Municipal, 1985).

[59] *Roman Spain: Conquest and Assimilation* (London and New York: Routledge, 1991).

[60] H. V. Livermore, *The Origins of Spain and Portugal* (London: George Allen & Unwin Ltd., 1971).

[61] *Crowns of Martyrdom* VI, p.211.

Saints Orencio and Paciencia were natives of the city of Huesca of Aragón, and there they had a house, that is now a Church; but to that I say, that some of the past persecutions of the Church… uprooted them from that land and they came to this pleasant garden, so that giving birth in it to Laurence it would not lack a laurel against the rays of the infernal furies. I myself know that the tradition favors greatly Huesca so that it can be taken as the native land of this saint, but I also know that much war is made concerning this tradition and it takes away a lot of its force, (the fact that there is) not to be found any ancient author that wrote to that effect, whether we speak of the foreigners, or of those of Spain, even if they might be from Aragón…[62]

Diago, unlike Donato, asserts that St. Orencio, the Bishop of Aix, France, was Laurence's brother, according to the common belief in Huesca, a mistake that Donato explains was clarified by the oldest Presbyters of Valencia, who told him that the French bishop was instead the grandson of one of Orencio's brothers, named Facundo. Escolano, another seventeenth-century historian, agrees that Valencia was the birthplace of Laurence, adding that Prudentius, a native of Zaragoza, who wrote of Laurence's martyrdom only 100 years after the fact, does not claim that Laurence was from Huesca in spite of the fact that he does celebrate and name many other martyrs from that region. The fact that Prudentius says nothing of Laurence's birthplace is quite significant in his opinion, and he adds that Saints Orencio and Paciencia were natives of Huesca, but came to Valencia for some unnamed reason. According to what he has written, the Church of St. Laurence in Huesca is commonly considered to be the birthplace of the saint, having been the house of his parents, but he explains that because the church was called St. Laurence, it was easy to persuade those of Huesca who were born in the following century that Laurence was born there.[63] Donato, however, is the only writer who provides a detailed account for his parents' unexpected move to Valencia, which was not intended to be their final destination. Diago also mentions the significant fact that Prudentius did not claim Huesca as the birthplace of Laurence, and both Diago and Escolano provide a list of the ancient writers who believed that Laurence was indeed born in Valencia.

---

[62] *Libro IIII de los Anales del Reyno de Valencia*, folios 165 and 166.

[63] *Libro Segundo de la historia de Valencia*, column 261.

There is no historical information that would seriously dispute Donato's facts, which, on the contrary, seem to clarify some of the misinformation, such as the popular belief that Pope Sixtus came to Spain and took Laurence with him back to Rome. Donato says:

> This is the reason for the mistake that some have made by saying that he was taken from a neighboring hamlet of Osca. I am not absolutely certain, but I don't believe that Sixtus came to Spain, nor that Orencio and Paciencia ever returned, but that those towns of Campania were formerly called Bolscos, and Capua Osca; those who heard that he was taken by Sixtus from a hamlet of Osca (not realizing that there was another, other than that of Spain) were convinced that he took him from there, so that it was necessary to conclude that Sixtus came to these Provinces. But I understand this, and believe that it is the truth.

Laurence, at the age of fourteen, thus came to Rome in the company of Sixtus from the town of Capua in Italy where his parents had settled after the shipwreck, which makes far more sense than the Pope making the difficult trip to Spain and attempting to bring both Laurence and Vincent to Rome, in spite of the fact that they were so far apart in age. Both were relatively young when they were martyred, with Laurence's execution traditionally placed in 258 AD (261 by some writers) and Vincent's taking place in the year 303 or 304.

Brian Dutton mentions that the genealogy of the martyr appears for the first time in *De translatione Sancti Vincentii* by the French priest Aymón, in the year 854 [64], which is later than Donato's manuscript based on verbal information from Church presbyters of Valencia. It was repeated in the Actas of the martyr, and lists his mother as Enola, native of Huesca.

> Exititit (Vincentius) enim patre Euticio progenitus, qui fuit Agresti nobilissimi Consulis filius: **mater vero ejus Enola ex Osca urbi noscitur procreata.** (ES, VII, p.231). [65]

Donato's claim that Enola was the younger sister of Paciencia is thus strengthened with later historical documentation.

St. Donato in the time of Leovigild

Donato is an obscure saint, and in fact, the only information I have been able to uncover appears in Francisco Diago's *Anales del Reyno de Valencia*. It is significant, however, that this information corresponds exactly with the manuscript in question. In *Libro V, capítulo VIII, IX,* and *X,* Diago relates how in the time of the Visigoth King Leovigild, St. Donato the miracle worker came from Africa and founded the Servitano Monastery in Valencia. He also tells of the martyrdom of Hermenegild, killed by his own father, Leovigild, for refusing to convert to Arianism, and how Leovigild's army sacked Donato's monastery, also known as San Martín.

In the year 570 AD, Diago says that St. Donato, Abbot of the Servitano Monastery was flourishing in holiness, already working miracles. As so many years had already passed since St. Ildefonso (d. 667) had explained the reasons for the foundation of the monastery, Diago repeats the story. It is said, according to St. Ildefonso, that Donato, a monk by profession and works, was the disciple of a certain hermitage in Africa. Seeing that the violence of the barbarian Gentiles was approaching, and fearing destruction and danger for the congregation of monks, he migrated to Spain with almost seventy of them, bringing many books along in the boat. With the help of the renowned and religious woman Minicea, he founded and built the Servitano Monastery. Of Donato, who was as noble in virtue when he first came to Spain as when he died, it is recorded that he was the first who brought to Spain the monastic life and rule. In life as well as in death, when he lay in repose in the sepulcher, he appeared radiant with health.

St. Ildefonso's account stops at this point, and Diago explains that from what St. Ildefonso said about Donato being the disciple of a certain hermitage in Africa, recording that the monks of St. Augustine flourished in it from the moment of its foundation because the saint had founded it there, one can deduce that it was an Augustinian hermitage, and that there were close to seventy monks from this order that he brought with him to Spain. According to Diago, neither the abbot of Valclara, who also wrote about Donato, nor St. Ildefonso say exactly where he founded the monastery, but it is clear that it was in the Kingdom of Valencia, because all agree on this point, some saying that it was on the Promontory of Ferraria, and others in Xatiua, a population in the countryside. Shortly after Leovigild's reign, Diago says that the *Anales* begin to speak of the Monastery of San Martín, that one author, Gregorio Turonense, situates between Cartagena and

---

[64] (Migne, PL, CCSSVI, col. 1.013).

[65] *Vincent's father was Euticius, the son of a noble consul from Agreste: his mother was called Enola and is known to have been born in Huesca.* Translation by Mark Guscin.

Sagunto, saying that it was no longer known exactly when this monastery was founded in the Kingdom of Valencia. But because Donato, who according to St. Ildefonso was its founder, was already flourishing in Spain as a miracle worker in the year 570, according to the Abbot of Valclara, from all of this information one can deduce the time in which, more or less, he founded the monastery, which Diago says was neither in the first year of Leovigild's reign (572), nor even in the only year of the reign of his predecessor and brother Liuva. In agreement with what Ambrosio de Morales says, that although Donato, the founder of this monastery, was celebrated and renowned and very well known in the time of King Liuva, he had come to Spain prior to that.[66]

Diago adds that Donato, with his sanctity, wonders, and doctrine, was the light that heaven sent to the Kingdom of Valencia in the time of the dark night of the Arian heresy, that was being spread by Leovigild, so that the faithful of Valencia could see its hidden poison, and that seeing it, they would die before submitting to Arianism due to the threats and favors of Leovigild. His brother Liuva died in 572, and from then on Leovigild had absolute control over Spain and the city of Narbonne in France.

Diago also relates how King Leovigild came to Valencia against his son, because those people who had refused to convert to Arianism had liberated Hermenegild and raised him as their king, a fascinating account. According to Gregorio Turonense, the author of that time, the uprising was quite significant, writing that Leovigild's army sacked the Monastery of San Martín, one and the same as the Servitano, situated between Cartagena and Sagunto, in search of Leovigild's son who had managed to flee there. When the monks heard that the army was approaching, they fled and hid on an island in the Mediterranean, leaving their ancient Abbot Donato in the Monastery. The Visigoths arrived and took his belongings, which had been left unguarded, and found the Abbot, although stooped with age, levitated due to his sanctity. One of the soldiers drew his sword, desiring to cut his neck, but instead fell face down on the ground and died. The others, seeing this, fled in fear.

When the Leovigild heard the news, he ordered with great seriousness that they return to the Monastery everything they had stolen. Seeing that so many great

---

[66] Although this is not always a direct translation, I have attempted to preserve the language and style of the *Anales* as much as possible so that one can understand how this typical ancient historian liked to ramble and digress.

miracles were being done by the servants of God, who were Catholics, he called one of his Bishops, and told him secretly, "Because all of you do not show signs of your faith to the people, how do those who call themselves Christians do it? The bishop answered, "I have restored sight to the blind many times, and hearing to the deaf, and I can do what you say now. And calling one of the heretics, he told him secretly, "Take forty ducats, and put yourself, with your eyes closed, in the place where they have to pass; and when I go by with the King, say loudly that I am restoring your lost sight. And having taken the money, the man did what he had been commanded, and passed to the right of the King, surrounded by a crowd of heretics. Then this man, who had been blinded by money, said loudly that his sight was being restored through the faith of the Bishop. And putting his hands over his eyes, with more than a little arrogance, said to him, "Grant it to me according to my faith. And as he said this, the eyes of the pretend blind man closed in pain, and he not only lost his sight, but the scheme that he had feigned was also publicized.

Diago concludes that the Servitano Monastery was the same as that of San Martín for several reasons: 1) that it would not have been likely to find two principal monasteries in such close proximity to one another in those ancient times when the Visigoths dominated Spain, and were enemies of the Catholic faith, as men who professed the Arian heresy, 2) The two names, San Martín and Servitano, would have been given for different reasons, with San Martin as the name of its patron saint, and the other of the territory where it was founded, and 3) the two appear to be one and the same in all respects: what St. Ildefonsus wrote about the Servitano and the information given by Gregorio Turonense about San Martín coincide. Both say that the Abbot was a saint, that he worked miracles, and that he was already very old when Leovigild came to the monastery against his son, which is in agreement with the historical fact that Donato had previously been an Abbot in Africa with great authority, and that he had been in Spain at least seventeen years when this event occurred.

Diago explains that the Abbot of Valclara indicates that Donato survived until his time, and refers to events of his successor, Eutropio, the Abbot of the Monastery who was Donato's disciple. Diago insists that the Monastery was not situated in Xatiua[67], but rather on the Promontory of Ferraria that divides the two bays Illicitano and Sucronente, in accordance with Gregorio Turonense's assertion that it was between Sagunto and Cartagena on the coast. The Promontory is located almost exactly between the two cities, while Xatiua isn't even on the coast.

If it is on the Promontory of Ferraria, Diago reasons, it could very well have the name of Servitano, although this could be that of Setabitano with a little alteration. Xabea, ancient Setabicula, is located there, referred to by Claudio Prolomeo as one of the cities of Contestania. There was also a river called Serabis, according to this same author, now called Altea, a distance of two leagues from the Promontory. Diago believes that there was no doubt that from Setabicula the Monastery came to be called Setabiculitano and the river Setabis, Setabitano, until by altering the two names it came to have the name of Servitano.[68]

Diago goes on to say that Minicea is the one who aided Donato in the foundation of this Monastery, being a descendent of those of her family who lived in the Kingdom of Valencia, close to the Promontory of Ferraria, from the time of the Romans, known as Minicea[69] Elfa in that century, who in the company of the Republic made a sepulcher for Cayo Sempronio Severino, son of Cayo, of the Galeria Tribe, in an ancient population called Elca, that is no longer standing. Its ruins were discovered a quarter of a league from Oliva in the direction of Denia, on the right hand side, at the foot of the mountain, at least four leagues from the Promontory. The Epitaph that she ordered placed on the stone of the sepulcher says: *C. SEMPRONIVS C.F. GAL. SEVERINVS. H. S. E. MINICIA ELFI ET R. P. M. VNA F.*, which means: Here is interred Cayo Sempronio Severino, son of Cayo, of the Galeria Tribe. Minicia Elfa and the Republic raised together this sepulcher with reason. Diago believes that because Minicia Elfa and the Republic of the population carried this out together, that she was its first lady, and that it came to be called Elfa out of respect for her, and later Elca. This stone was first in the ruins of Elca in the Hermitage of San Alberto, and later when Oliva rebuilt the Hermitage farther down on the ruins of Benifarès, located on the plain in the middle of the olive groves, the stone was ordered placed in his walls, where Diago saw it. He believes that it proves that Minicea was from Elca, and consequently was renowned and rich, with the financial means to found the Servitano Monastery on

---

[67] Today spelled Xàtiva, located to the west of Gandía and to the north of Alcoy.

[68] While this is a rather tedius discussion on ancient names, it authenticates Donato's account of the life of St. Laurence. The Monastery was situated near Xàbia/Jávea. Altea is a town on the coast to the south, next to a river.

[69] Donato mentions that Minicea is his benefactress, a statement that is well supported in the *Anales*.

the Promontory of Ferraria, not far from where she lived, which would have made it possible for her to aid the Augustinian monks who lived there, who being of the Order of St. Augustine, would have preferred that isolated piece of land to the city of Xatiua. A further proof is that the teacher Maluenda says that the monks were able to go down to the sea in boats, which would have been possible on the river Xucar[70].

The island where they hid was Colubraria, which is now called either Moncolobrer, Yuiça or Santa Pola, according to Maluenda, but Diago disagrees, believing that is was the island that the ancients called Planefia, which now has the name of Benidorm, because this one was in front of a town that had the same name[71], and is the closest to the Promontory, only a distance of three leagues, which would have made it possible for them to return to the Monastery in three hours time, as it is written they did. The Abbot Donato died several days after the monks returned to the monastery, and they then named Eutropio as his successor; this was in the year 583 AD. Eutropio was later named Bishop of Valencia. Valencia was thus blessed to have the Servitano Monastery within its territory, being the first Monastery in all of Spain, or at least the first that followed the rules of monastic life, because as St. Ildefonso wrote concerning St. Donato, this saint was the "first who brought to Spain the use and rule of the monastic observance," in an epoch when, according to Donato, idolatry was being practiced, with Greek ceremonies and sacrifices, and with Temples for the Idols, such as the Temple to Diana in Sagunto.

That is the extent of Diago's information on St. Donato, which agrees exactly with the manuscript in question, which says, "Until now (says Donato) I am able to have written with exactness that I discovered, because although I am African, I have lived for many years around Valencia, having gone to Spain with many companions from my order. And because of the generosity of the renowned Matron Minicea, adorned with Christian virtue, I settled on the side of the Promontory of Ferratia, between Setabicula and Dianio, and founded the Monastery Servitano, dedicated to St. Martín, an Augustinian Hermitage, instituting in these parts the monastic discipline, which had been lacking in Spain until now."

---

[70] It seems that this would be the River Gorgos, located next to the modern Parador of Jávea.

[71] Benidorm has a small island and is located 50 km to the south of Jávea.

The story of King Leovigild's turning against his own son, Hermenegild, the motive for his trip to St. Donato's Monastery, is quite interesting and merits a digression. As can be seen from this discussion, the Arian heresy was prevalent in this epoch in Spain, having been started by an ascetic priest called Arius, who lived in Alexandria from about 250 to 336. Around 319 he became involved in a dispute with the bishop of Alexandria over the nature of Christ, because he could not understand how Christ could be the begotten Son of the Father and yet have been in existence before the creation of the world and time. He began to teach that only God the Father was "uncreated," and that the Son was created at some point and was therefore not eternal. He was soon excommunicated, and the bishop declared him a heretic equal to Simon Magus, the Gnostic magician of *Acts of the Apostles*. His teachings were officially condemned by the Council of Nicaea,[72] convened by Constantine in 325, but were supported by some of the hierarchy, causing a schism.

Hermenegild and his brother Reccared were the two sons of the Visigoth king of Spain, Leovigild, and were educated by their father in the Arian heresy, which was especially popular with the Goths. Hermenegild, however, married a Catholic, who was quite zealous and soon converted him to the true faith. When Leovigild heard of his son's conversion he was furious, and demanded that he renounce all of his privileges and possessions. Hermenegild refused, and sent St. Leander to Constantinople to obtain support and assistance for a revolt. This attempt failed, and Hermenegild then implored assistance from the Roman generals who still possessed a strip of land along the Mediterranean coast. They took his wife and son as hostages and reneged on their promises. Hermenegild was consequently besieged in Seville by his father's troops for over a year, and finally fled to the Roman camp where his friends, having been bribed by his father, betrayed him. Leovigild finally sent his younger son Reccared, who was still an Arian, to go to the church where his brother had taken refuge, offering forgiveness if Hermenegild would only ask for pardon. Leovigild and his son were reconciled, but the king's second wife soon managed to estrange them once again.

Hermenegild was then imprisoned at Tarragona, accused of heresy rather than treason, and promised liberty at the price of renouncing Catholicism. Leovigild sent an Arian bishop to the prison, offering his son forgiveness if he

---

[72] Nicaea is an ancient city in Bithynia, northwest Asia Minor; the Nicene Creed was formulated here in 325 AD.

would receive communion from the bishop's hands, but Hermenegild refused, igniting a rage in his father that impelled him to order his son put to death. Soldiers were dispatched to the prison, killing Hermenegild instantaneously by one blow from an axe. As a martyr, St. Gregory the Great credits St. Hermenegild with the conversion of all of Visigoth Spain. Leovigild himself never actually renounced Arianism, but was so filled with remorse for his crime that he commended Reccared to St. Leander on his deathbed, desiring that his other son would convert to Catholicism. His wish was soon fulfiled. There is a nearly life-size bust of St. Hermenegild in the Cathedral of Plasencia in the west of Spain, depicted with a axe in his neck, a rather graphic memorial to a little-known saint of the Church, whose conduct in taking up arms against his own father is condemned by Butler, who quickly adds that as St. Gregory of Tours has pointed out, his guilt was expiated by his heroic sufferings and death, and continues by mentioning that St. Gregory the Great wrote that Hermenegild only began to be truly a king when he became a martyr.

The great differences between Donato's work and the other versions of the life and passion of St. Laurence have already been pointed out. Donato wrote a historical piece that did not attempt in any way to poeticize or glorify Laurence's martyrdom in attempt to suit his own purposes. It is simple and straightforward, yet spiritual, with a sincere desire to clarify the facts and dispel the errors that were being disseminated by some who were confused by the similarity of some of the names of ancient populations. The language, tone, and detail all indicate that it was written far earlier than the seventeenth century when the translation was done; certainly, if the translator's intent was to falsify written documentation of the surrender of the Holy Grail to a Spaniard, he went far beyond what would have been necessary, and by that late date, the details of Laurence's childhood would have been long forgotten by those who lived in the area of Valencia. Due also to the oblivion from which this work appears to have suffered, it appears that it could not have been done for publicity or personal fame, but rather from the desire to preserve the remains of an ancient document for posterity.

The sincerity of both the author's and translator's intentions is most remarkable; in contrast to the pompous and inflated medieval versions, with their obvious manipulation of the events, Donato's manuscript stands out for its candor and verisimilitude. There appears to be nothing that might indicate fraud or manipulation; on the contrary, many of the details, such as the martyrdom of Julita and her son Quirico, are supported by historical reality, in this case the hermitage in Burgos dedicated to their memory. The location of the Monastery of San Martín, described so precisely in the manuscript with the ancient names, is argued in the seventeenth century *Anales*, with the author finally arriving at the conclusion that it could only have been in the place indicated by Donato. Finally, the long-standing Huesca/Valencia debate over the birthplace of St. Laurence is explained and supported by other historical documents, which insist that it could only have been in Valencia. Although Laurence's parents fled to the coastal city, the rest of the family remained in Huesca, which provides an explanation for why the Grail would have been sent there.

If St. Vincent was the son of Enola, Paciencia's younger sister, as Donato indicates, everything easily falls into place: the respective martyrdoms of Laurence and Vincent in 258 and 303, how Laurence ended up in Italy while the rest of the family continued to reside in the areas of Huesca and Zaragoza, and why the Grail would have been sent to the city of Huesca, in spite of the fact that Precelius, the Spaniard mentioned by Donato, was not from that region. It is quite likely that Vincent would have been involved with the custody of the Grail in the former home of Laurence's parents, and it is noteworthy that he was martyred in Valencia, becoming the patron saint of the city that has become the permanent residence for the holy relic, in a manner remarkably similar to Laurence's cruel death that continues to be contested by modern historians as contrary to the normal method of the time, yet so common by this time, less than fifty years later, that death by fire on a gridiron is now called by the acts *quaestio legitima*, "the legal torture." What, if not Laurence's famous defiance of Roman authority, could have instigated the sudden escalation in their barbarity?

Valencia, therefore, the home of the Holy Grail, has two saintly custodians for the precious relic: Laurence, born in the city, and responsible for saving the cup from destruction, and Vincent, patron of Valencia and Laurence's cousin, martyred there, and also very possibly one of the first guardians in Spain of the most precious relic known to Christianity. It is not difficult to see the workings of Divine Providence □

Part 4

LEGEND ARISES
FROM TRADITION

A light was in the crannies, and I heard,
'Glory and joy and honor to our Lord
And to the Holy Vessel of the Grail.'
Then in my madness I essay'd the door;
It gave; and thro' a stormy glare, a heat
As from a seventimes-heated furnace, I,
Blasted and burnt, and blinded as I was,
With such a fierceness that I swoon'd away —
O, yet methought I saw the Holy Grail,
All pall'd in crimson samite, and around
Great angels, awful shapes, and wings and eyes
And but for all my madness and my sin,
And then my swooning, I had sworn I saw
That which I saw; but what I saw was veil'd
And cover'd; and this Quest was not for me.

Alfred Lord Tennyson, Idylls of the King (1872)

Illustrations

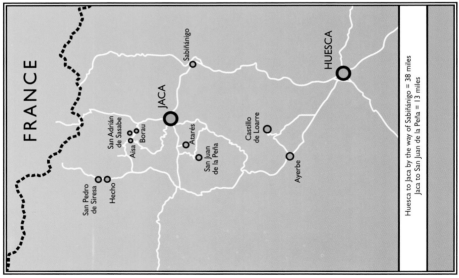

1: Map of Spain and detail of the area where the Holy Grail was hidden during the Middle Ages.

2: The Holy Chalice of Valencia as it appears today in the Cathedral. The upper agate cup is considered to be that used by Jesus at the Last Supper to institute the Sacrament of the Eucharist. Courtesy of The Spanish Center for Sindonology.

3: The Church of San Pedro de Siresa in the Spanish Pyrenees, where the Holy Grail was first sheltered under the protection of St. Peter after the invasion of the Moors in 711 AD.

4: Exterior and interior views of the Monastery of San Adrián de Sasabe, another monastery of the Pyrenees believed to have sheltered the Holy Grail.

5: The Last Supper, and two capitals from the eleventh-century Cathedral of Jaca, custodian of the Holy Grail until 1071 when the famous relic was replaced with the remains of St. Orosia.

6: The massive rocky outcroppings of San Juan de la Peña, believed to be Wolfram von Eschenbach's *Munsalvaesche*.

7: The unique cloister of San Juan de la Peña with its freestanding columns.

8: Capitals from the cloister, renowned for the enormous eyes of personages taken from the Old and New Testaments: The Last Supper, St. Joseph's dream, and the raising of Lazarus.

9: Chapel of Sts. Voto and Felix, hiding place for the Holy Grail during the religious fervor of the Middle Ages.

10: The central arches with a replica of the Holy Chalice, where it was exposed for the veneration of the monks during the Middle Ages.

11: The Eucharistic miracle of Daroca, associated with the Spanish Reconquest and impetus for the Corpus Christi celebration.

12: The Cathedral of Valencia, now gloriously restored after the desecration and burning of the Spanish Civil War.

13.a: The Cathedral of Valencia with the Chapel of the Holy Grail to the right of the entrance. **b.** The Door of the Apostles.

14: Interior of the Chapel of the Holy Grail.

15.a: Close-up of the Tabernacle of the Holy Grail. **b.** First Communicants listen as a priest narrates how St. Laurence saved the Holy Grail from the Romans.

16: Painting of the Last Supper by Juan de Juanes, depicting the Holy Chalice of Valencia. Museo del Prado, Madrid.

17: The *Roca del Santo Grial* and a photograph of Pope John Paul II blessing it in Rome in 1996. The Holy Father said Mass with the Holy Chalice during his visit to Spain in 1982.

18: Floral display of the Holy Chalice for the Corpus Christi procession of June 2001, and a detail of the
Roca del Santo Grial.

19: The Corpus Christi procession in Madrid, June of 2000, and Valencia, June of 2001.

20. a: Roman cups in the British Museum, dated 1-50 AD, made of chalcedony and sardonyx, similar in style to the original agate cup of the Holy Chalice. **b.** Roman fine-ware cup with a sanded surface, from Tharros, Sardinia, about 10 BC to 50 AD. British Museum, London.

21.a: "Roman fine-ware cups made in Italy about 1-70 AD. **b.** 'The Crawford Cup" of fluorspar, Roman, made about 50-100 AD. The emperor Nero (54-68 AD) is said to have paid a million sesterces for a fluorspar cup. **c.** Roman kotyle (drinking cup), made in Asia Minor in the 1st century AD. **d.** A pair of Roman silver cups from Asia Minor, about 1-30 AD. British Museum, London.

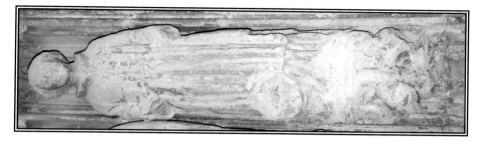

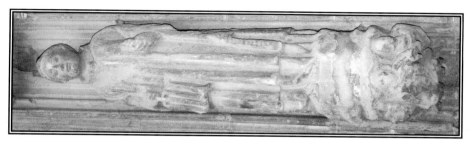

22: The Cathedral of Huesca, entryway and details of Sts. Laurence and Vincent, cousins martyred nearly fifty years apart, the first in Rome and the second in Spain.

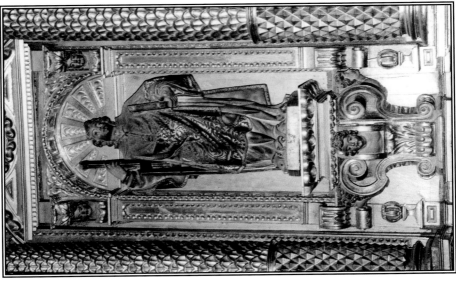

23: Representations of Sts. Laurence and Vincent in the Cathedral of Huesca.

24: The Hermitage of Loreto and detail of the façade depicting St. Laurence, constructed on the family farm of Sts. Orencio and Paciencia, his parents.

25.a: Cross at the site of the family farm. **b.** Road sign marking the spot where, according to Huesca's tradition, the parents of St. Laurence would greet their twin sons Laurence and Orencio as they returned home from school.

26: San Pedro el Viejo, the parish church of St. Laurence's parents and where St. Vincent was baptized, according to tradition. Detail of St. Peter, protector of the Holy Grail for so many centuries.

27: Altar in San Pedro el Viejo dedicated to Sts. Laurence and Vincent, with details showing the martyrdom of each saint.

28: Sculpture on the interior rail of San Pedro el Viejo, depicting its patron saints, Justus and Pastor, with St. Vincent in the center, sometimes confused with Sts. Laurence and Orencio in the company of their father, Orencio.

29: Basilica of St. Laurence in Huesca. Chapel of St. Hippolytus and representation of Jesus consecrating the wine.

30: Murals by Echevarría-Bermúdez in the Basilica of St. Laurence: St. Laurence sends the Holy Cup of the Last Supper to Huesca, St. Laurence before the Emperor, and St. Laurence tormented with red-hot steel plates.

AQUA BENEDICTA SIT NOBIS SALUS ET VITA

31: Chapel of St. Laurence in the Basilica of Huesca, and details of the gridiron theme prevalent throughout the church.

32.a: Church of St. Laurence Outside the Walls in Rome, built on the original burial spot of the saint on the Via Tiburtina. **b.** Representation of St. Laurence in the stone floor. **c.** The grave of the saint.

Chapter 9

FROM HUESCA TO SAN JUAN DE LA PEÑA

The manuscript of Donato is the only source that mentions the name of the person to whom St. Laurence entrusted the Holy Grail: Precelius, his co-disciple and fellow countryman from the city of Hippo in Carpentanea, whose capital was Toledo and included the area of La Mancha. It is believed that the Holy Cup was sent specifically to Huesca, along with a letter written by Laurence himself, because it was the town where his parents originated and where many of his relatives still resided. This has been a constant tradition in the kingdom of Aragón, corroborated by Spanish writers of all times, including the seventeenth-century historian and abbot of San Juan de la Peña, Juan Briz Martínez. Most modern writers believe that Laurence sent the Grail to his parents, due to the confusion concerning his origin, but it appears more likely that this was not the case. It is thought that the Cup first went to Loreto where his parents formerly had their house and farm, which might explain the error. The letter, however, has unfortunately disappeared, and although a record of it exists in the Cathedral Library of Huesca, this is not at all unusual since all third-century writings are missing. While we can assume that veneration of the relic quickly spread among the Christians, it was done in secret and with all of the precautions required by those times of persecution, until the Edict of Constantine declared the Christian religion legal in the middle of the next century.

Although little is known about the early history of the relic in Spain, it appears that only Divine Providence could have saved it from the terrible persecutions under Diocletian and Maximian, which began in 303 when they published their second and third edicts against the laity. Dacian was then governor of Spain. Donato's biography of Laurence and Diago's *Anales* both indicate that St. Vincent was the cousin of St. Laurence, as the son of Enola, his mother's younger sister. Dacian put to death eighteen martyrs at Zaragoza, a city not far from Huesca, and then apprehended its bishop, Valerius, along with his deacon Vincent, and both were soon transferred to Valencia where they suffered extreme famine and other miseries that did not shake their constancy in the faith. When they were brought before the proconsul, still vigorous and strong in body and spirit, he attempted to induce them to sacrifice with threats and promises, but they informed him that they were ready to suffer everything for the true God. Valerius was banished, but Vincent, like his cousin Laurence, was subjected to every torture possible. St. Augustine assures us that he suffered torments beyond what any man could have endured unless supported by supernatural strength, astonishing his persecutors with his peace and tranquility.

Like Laurence, he was first stretched on the rack by his hands and feet, and while he hung his flesh was torn with iron hooks. Vincent responded with smiles, calling the executioners weak and faint-hearted, which caused them to be beaten by Dacian because the emperor thought they were sparing Vincent from suffering too much pain. The more Vincent's body was tormented, the more he demonstrated the presence of God, so that the proconsul finally confessed that the courage of the young martyr had vanquished him. He ordered the torments to cease, and told Vincent that if he would not offer sacrifice to the gods, that he at least give up the sacred books to be burnt, according to the edicts. Vincent refused, and Dacian then condemned him to the cruelest torture, fire upon a gridiron, now a legal form of death.

According to Butler's account[1] of Vincent's torture, the flames seemed to give Vincent new strength and courage, for the more he suffered, the greater was his inward joy and consolation. Filled with rage and confusion, the tyrant threw

---

[1] Alban Butler has followed the narrative of the poet Prudentius (*Peristephanon*, 5). It is interesting that Francisco Diago, in the *Anales del Reyno de Valencia*, does not mention the torture by fire on a gridiron. In his account, Vincent, after suffering many torments, is hung on a cross, a punishment that pleased the saint so much that he was immediately lowered by the executioners and subjected to other tortures instead, among them iron hooks, whips, and large lit candles. As Vincent is generally depicted as having been martyred on a rack, rather than a gridiron, this part of his martyrdom appears to be questionable. It is also doubtful that he could have survived the flames. As has been explained, the *Peristephanon* is not a particularly reliable document historically speaking, and the reader should remember that Prudentius mistakenly believed that Pope Sixtus II was crucified rather than beheaded. Nevertheless, death on the gridiron was by this time a common form of martyrdom.

Vincent into a dungeon unto a floor strewn with potsherds that tore his flesh. His legs were stretched apart in wooden stocks, and orders were given that he should be left without food. It seemed that angels came to comfort him, because when the jailer gazed through the narrow openings, the prison was filled with light, and Vincent was seen walking and praising God. He immediately converted to Christianity. Dacian wept with rage, but nevertheless agreed to allow visits from the faithful, who dressed his wounds and dipped cloths in his blood to keep for themselves. They prepared a bed for him, and no sooner was he laid upon it than his soul was taken to God. The image of a deacon's dalmatic or robe and a palm-branch spread quickly in early art, but it is often impossible to determine whether it was intended for St. Vincent or St. Laurence, the martyrdoms are so similar. Laurence and Vincent appear side by side in the iconographic representations of Huesca, and it is often difficult to tell them apart, as both are young, educated deacons, generally depicted holding a book, palm-branch, or both. Laurence is more frequently shown holding a piece of grating, symbol of the gridiron.

After peace was restored in the middle of the fourth century, the Visigoths dominated Spain until the invasion of the Arabs in 711 AD. The Church suffered under the heresy of Arianism, but in the following three centuries did not undergo any further persecutions such as what had occurred during the Roman dominion. The only serious danger was that of the Holy Grail falling into the hands of Childebert I, the Frankish king of Paris who stole sixty golden chalices from the churches of Spain, in order to "restore" them to France to be used as models for French goldsmiths. Childebert invaded Visigoth Spain in 541-542, where his greatest exploit was the conquest of Pamplona. As Comenge Gabasa remarks, the "famous 'cleptomaniac' collector of expensive chalices either didn't pass through Huesca, or God did not allow him to find out about the Holy Grail," but he did manage to return to France with the tunic of St. Vincent, which he deposited in the monastery that is now St. Germain-des-Prés in Paris.

When the Muslims invaded Spain in 711 AD, after their victory in Guadalete, they quickly spread through the entire peninsula, overtaking the cities and towns they passed. Many Christians took refuge in the mountains, especially in those of the north, where they defended their land, giving rise to the Reconquest of Spain that lasted eight centuries. Just as happened with the Sudarium of the Lord that was hidden in the mountains near Oviedo, they took with them their most valuable belongings, especially the precious relics and treasures from the churches that the bishops tried to save in order to prevent them from being profaned by the invaders. The bishop of Huesca, taking with him the Holy Grail sent to Spain by St. Laurence, took refuge in the mountains. Tradition affirms that before the relic was placed in the cave monastery of San Juan de la Peña, it first went to several secluded places of the Pyrenees: the cave of Yebra, San Pedro de Siresa, and San Adrián de Sasabe.

By this time the Holy Grail had been in Rome for a little more than 200 years, and in Huesca for about 450 years. At this point in time, the history is still poorly documented, for the simple reason that the famous relic was in grave danger. It had been hidden in Jerusalem with the Apostles for fear of the Jews, was well guarded in Rome because of the persecutions of Christians, was concealed in Huesca until the Church was once again at peace, and then hidden in the Pyrenees of Aragón in the odyssey taken by the bishops and Christian faithful who became mountain fugitives, until it was secretly placed in the monastery of San Juan de la Peña where it was surrounded by the mysterious veneration of the monks, becoming the inspiration of medieval legends for four hundred years.

The Spanish writer Dr. Dámaso Sangorrín writes that in 712 AD, the year following the Muslim invasion, Bishop Acisclo, who at that time presided over the see of Huesca, and his niece and nephew, Orosia and Cornelius, formed an enormous caravan with a great number of faithful Christians, carrying with them *res sacras et Sanctorum reliquias*, or the sacred things and the relics of the saints, and fled toward the foothills of the Pyrenees, taking refuge in the Cave of Yebra, situated on a high plateau of Mt. Ontoria that is today the refuge of St. Orosia, where they were shortly reached by the Muslims. The enemy martyred the Bishop, as well as the youths Orosia, who was immolated for defending her faith and her virginity, and her brother Cornelius. The caravan of fugitives began to march once again, carrying with them the Holy Grail, and came to take shelter in San Pedro de Siresa, perhaps the most ancient and important of the monasteries of Aragón during the time of the Visigoths.

An interesting legend grew up around St. Orosia, whose body continues to be kept in a special chapel constructed for it next to the cloister of the Cathedral of Jaca. Until less than a century ago, the devotion for her remains constituted one of the most singular celebrations of that region, because the saint acquired a good part of her fame for her special powers to expel demons from the bodies of the possessed. Thus, in the days of her feast, entire families would come to Jaca, accompanying those unfortunate people who had suffered the disgrace of falling into diabolic possession, in order to invoke the favors of the relic. The ritual that was preceded by a procession during which the possessed were led to the Cathedral, consisted in tying colored ribbons to the fingers of those unfortunate people and leaving them there for the entire night in the Chapel of St. Orosia, in absolute darkness, turned over to their fears and hysterias. The following morning they would leave bruised after the experience, and the members of their families would count the ribbons that had been detached from their fingers. Each loose ribbon was, according to the reports, a devil that had abandoned the body. The legend of her martyrdom follows:

Orosia was, as they say, a princess from Aquitaine[2] who came to those mountains accompanied by a large entourage from Toledo, where she was to be married to a Gothic prince. Her long trip coincided with the Muslim invasion, of which she had no knowledge when she embarked on her journey. Thus, the entourage of the princess, when passing through the mountains close to Yebra, had the misfortune of encountering the party of Muslims who made them prisoners.

The head of that group, Aben Lupo, immediately felt enamored of the Christian princess and demanded love from her, but was rejected repeatedly by Orosia, who felt above all the incompatibility of her faith with the beliefs of that Moor who wanted to convert her to Islam and marry her in accordance with his religious beliefs. The enamored leader tried every trick imaginable in order to convince the Christian, and before her firm denials, found no other alternative than that of trying to persuade her through fear. Thus, in the presence of the virtuous princess, he beheaded her own uncle and brother, who were accompanying her. With that the only thing that he achieved was to make her even firmer in her convictions, and finally, furious from the horror that he had awakened in his beloved, had her decapitated along with all of the other members of her entourage, and threw their bodies in a nearby abyss.

Time passed and the few people who knew of that killing first searched fruitlessly for their remains and later forgot the event. But one fine day, while leading a flock of sheep, a shepherd from Yebra noticed lights that came from a small cave, and when he approached, noticed that an indefinable aroma was emanating from it. When he looked in, he found the remains of the martyrs, and among them, the decapitated and incorrupt body of the princess Orosia. The news spread throughout the region, and very soon the Chapter of the Cathedral of Jaca claimed the relic of the princess, who

---

[2] The lowland region of southwest France.

150

immediately after being found was proclaimed a saint and began to work prodigious miracles. The town of Yebra, in whose jurisdiction the finding had taken place, claimed for itself the right to keep their saint and only after long conversations with the religious authorities was a solution found: Yebra would keep the head of the martyred princess, but the body would be transported to the Cathedral of Jaca, where it would receive the appropriate veneration so that her sanctity would be known by the greatest number of faithful. And thus it happened. And, since then, the relics of St. Orosia continued to grant miraculous favors from her chapel of the Cathedral.[3]

At the cost of great personal sacrifice, the Holy Cup was then sheltered in San Pedro de Siresa, an ancient monastery in the valley of Hecho, next to the Roman road that leads to French territory through the Puerto de Palo, where it was venerated by monks and the faithful for approximately one hundred years, substituting its original name of San Zacarias of Siresa with San Pedro, a title that it was given for being the sanctuary and guardian of the Holy Cup. The valleys above Jaca, the Aragón river and Mt. Arbe were the principal asylums for the Christians who escaped the slavery of the Moors, and they armed themselves for their defense in the rugged terrain of the Pyrenees. Their possession of the mountain valleys was not pacific in the early years, because of the sudden attacks of the Muslims. The kings of Aragón formerly raised their sons there, so that with the rigorous cold that is felt in those parts, they would grow to be more robust and prepared for the work of the military. One of these was the son of Sancho Ramírez, Alfonso I, the future *Rey Batallador*, or fighter king.

The church is practically all that remains of the Monastery of San Pedro de Siresa, one of the oldest in all of Aragón, and the scene of the famous battle of Roncevalles in the year 778, when the emperor Charlemagne retreated to Zaragoza. The defeat, in which the mythical Roland died, awoke in Charlemagne the interest of conquering this territory. The present monastery is Romanesque, constructed in the second half of the eleventh century over a Carolingian abbey of the ninth century. Many scholars believe that the architecture preserves the fundamental character of the original church, constructed at a time when the monastery was referred to as the "light of the west," with approximately 150 monks who possessed an impressive library.

---

[3]As narrated in Spanish by Juan G. Atienza, *Leyendas del Camino de Santiago* (Madrid: Editorial EDAF, 1998), p.29-31.

Juan G. Atienza believes that the monastery has characteristics that suggest that the Holy Grail was present there. The oldest part at the west entrance has a gallery similar to a choir, situated over the long access passage to the nave. Two other galleries, constructed on both sides of this central one, were later covered, and the pointed arches that led to the main body of the church can still be seen. Scholars question the function of this gallery at the time the church was built, and have not been able to arrive at any conclusion. Atienza believes that this might have been the place that housed the precious relic in its custody and that was expressly conceived for that function, as a special chapel with difficult access that would preserve the Holy Cup from the Muslims.

Sanchez Navarrete point out that on the floor close to this principal entrance there is a star with five or six points, surrounded by the stones with which the church is paved. The point in front does not point exactly to the main altar but deviates a little. Following the direction of this point of the star, a cavity is found in the apse in which local tradition insists that the Holy Cup was hidden. The cavity is the size of a large tabernacle, and is dug into the stone. It was hidden there to hide it from the Muslim invaders, with a star used in order to find the exact place once the danger was over. When Juan Carlos, the present king of Spain, was prince, he visited this monastery and carried out the pretense of looking for, finding, and taking the Holy Cup out of the wall.[4]

When circumstances permitted because there was no longer fear of new invasions of the Moors from the lower lying lands, the Bishops came down with their Holy Relic to a more sheltered monastery, that of San Adrián de Sasabe, situated three kilometers from the town of Borau and fifteen kilometers north of Jaca. Access to this monastery is far from easy, along an unpaved road wide enough for only one vehicle. The road goes around Borau, and continues up through the valley in the direction of Aisa. After three kilometers, one must follow a dirt trail to the bank of the Lubierre brook, formed by the union of two ravines, the Calcil and Lupán. The monastery is situated on the other side of this brook, and can only be approached by crossing the water on rocks. It can hardly be seen from a short distance because it appears to have been built lower than the adjacent land, with a type of moat around it, in an area that is nearly abandoned.

---

[4] From Oliván Baile, *El Monasterio de San Pedro de Siresa*.

Roberto Benedicto, the architect who directed the work of restoration not long ago, believes that it is not where it is by chance. He says, "The edifice is situated next to the confluence of two ravines, the Calcil and Lupán. The technical difficulties of construction would have been more than considerable, especially at the end of the eleventh century. Any other choice of place would have been much easier. In the process of restoration we could prove that those who constructed the monastery found technically perfect solutions to surmount all of the inconveniences of the location. The filtration of water was the reason that until a short time ago one had to enter the church in a pneumatic boat. In spite of the centuries that have gone by since it was abandoned, we could not detect a single structural flaw in the foundation and walls. A drilling study of the terrain was even carried out, in which at a certain depth we detected a layer of beams and a compact, fine material; they seem to describe a foundation of floating slabs, with the beams as the framework and the rest of the material functioning as concrete."[5]

If one goes to the back of the construction, avoiding the slopes that lead to the foundation, the well-preserved apse can be seen, covered by ten small arches, in whose intersection are traditional symbolic figures, such as flowers, stars, and concentric circles. Among these are two unique representations: a feminine face and a hand holding a cross. It is said that the first represents St. Natalia and the hand, St. Adrián, the two patron saints of the primitive Visigoth monastery.

Legend relates that Adrián was a centurion of the imperial military during the reign of Maximian, converted to Christianity while he was guarding 33 Christian captives on their way to martyrdom. Adrián asked the Christians what recompense they were hoping to obtain for their martyrdom, and they answered that they only hoped to obtain the glory that God had promised them. The centurion was immediately converted, and embracing their faith, set them free. He was then arrested by direct order of the emperor, but when questioned, refused to reveal where the Christians were hidden. To force him to confess, he was submitted to atrocious torments in the presence of his wife Natalia, who instead of encouraging him to confess as they had hoped, inspired him to resist the torments and think only of the celestial joys that awaited him. The torturers

---

[5] Alberto Serrano Dolader, *Historias fantásticas del viejo Aragón* (Zaragoza: Mira, 1994), p.58.

finally cut off Adrián's hands, and as he died Natalia took one of them and hid it in her clothing.

To avoid arrest she was forced to flee with other Christians, and embarked on a ship that soon had to face a terrible storm. Legend relates that they were saved through the celestial intervention of Adrián, who took command of the ship and guided the seamen until they reached safety. Natalia then returned to the place where the body of her husband had been placed, put the severed hand next to him, and saying goodbye to those who had accompanied her, embraced the corpse and entrusted her soul to God in silence. Her companions buried them together, and the Church proclaimed the faithful wife a martyr.[6]

It is believed that from the Monastery of San Adrián de Sasabe, the Holy Grail went to the church of San Pedro of Bailo for a short period. For reasons imposed by the fight against the invading Moors, the bishops changed residence frequently, and this transferal of the relic took place in the time of Bishop Mancio II (1014-1033), when Sancho Garcés II was residing there.

Don Ramiro I inherited the Kingdom of Aragón at the death of his father Don Sancho II in the year 1035. Feeling the necessity of establishing his capital in a strategic point, since Bailo and the entire region had become the fief of San Juan de la Peña through the donation of his father, he chose Jaca, dedicating himself to restore or rebuild the city that had been the historic capital of the area prior to the time of the Romans. Filled with fervor for the Holy Grail, he decided to build a Cathedral there to be the custodian of the relic, far more worthy than its two previous resting places. This was accomplished in 1063 with the donations of King Ramiro and his son, Sancho Ramírez, added to tithes from Jaca's markets, customs tax on imported merchandise, and other sources, to become the very first Cathedral of Spain. The Holy Grail was exposed for public veneration and kept in an expensive sacrarium that was surrounded by statues of the twelve apostles and other magnificent sculptures. The Council of Jaca, held to celebrate the great event, was attended by nine bishops who signed the document of consecration, dated in the month of April, 1063.

Atienza points out the symbolism that points to the transcendent mystery of the sacred relic that the Cathedral of Jaca safeguarded. Several can be found at the west entrance, underneath the great atrium through which the pilgrims passed.

---

[6] *Op. cit.*, Juan G. Atienza, p.26-27.

At the tympanum of this doorway there is a magnificent monogram of Christ with eight arms, containing orthodox signs with a profound message, whose mysterious symbolism explains that he who knows how to read it can extract from it the lesson that it contains. Written in Latin, the first is inscribed in the circle of the monogram, meaning: "In this sculpture, reader, try to recognize the following: P (is) the Father, A the Son, the double O, the Holy Spirit. The three are, by law, a one and only Lord." The message, directed toward "he who knows how to read," gives the spiritual key of the unity of the opposites: the alpha and the omega. At the foot of the tympanum is another message that when translated, means, "If you wish to live, you who are subject to the law of death, come supplicant, leaving behind venomous pleasures. Cleanse your heart from sin, in order not to die a second death."

The Cathedral was a great attraction for pilgrims on their way to Santiago de Compostela, but shortly thereafter lost the purpose for which it had been constructed: that of giving refuge to the Holy Grail. The sacred relic was transported to the Monastery of San Juan de la Peña, and the Cathedral substituted it with the body of St. Orosia, who immediately attracted the devotion of the faithful and replaced the Holy Cup as object of veneration for the numerous pilgrims. The route taken by her remains paralleled that of the Grail, and Atienza sees a connection between the two, because if the Grail was considered as a golden recipient of wisdom, St. Orosia alludes to gold through her name, besides being a woman, the recipient of life. He believes that the veneration of the Saint was a substitute for that of the Holy Grail □

Chapter 10

SAN JUAN DE LA PEÑA:
WOLFRAM'S *MUNSALVAESCHE*[8]

S
an Juan de la Peña is the jewel of all the monasteries of the Pyrenees, unique because of its placement in a large cave in a site that offers itself as a worthy ambient for the exultation of the spirit toward the ideal of freedom, raised high in the mountains as a symbol of strength against the Moorish invaders. It is situated in the valley of Atarés, only 16 kilometres from the French border, in a hidden corner of the sierra of San Juan. It was declared a National Monument in 1889 for its artistic merits, and honored in 1920 with the title of National Site, because of its glorious past. It has recently undergone restoration, with studies published as *San Juan de la Peña: Suma de estudios, I*[9], and its own website: www.monasteriosanjuan.com.

Legend relates that a noble Mozarabic youth named Voto, from Caesaraugusta, today Zaragoza, was hunting alone on horseback through the forests of the plateau of San Indalecio in the Pyrenees, in pursuit of a deer. As he crossed the summit of Mt. Pano, the deer was unexpectedly hurled down from the vertical drop of the immense rock that today serves as the vault of the old monastery. To avoid the same fate, the frightened youth managed to invoke the name of St. John the Baptist. It then seemed that a supernatural force suddenly stopped the horse suspended over the chasm, leaving the marks of its hooves engraved in the stone.[10] Voto dismounted and began to walk through the surrounding area in search of the deer, setting off along an almost invisible path that snaked along the thick undergrowth. Little by little, almost without perceiving it at first, a sweet and

---

[8] In Wolfram von Eschenbach's *Parzival*, the Grail is kept in the castle of *Munsalvaesche*, which is surrounded by a wild forest. *Salvaesche* is from the Old French form of *sauvage*, meaning "wild" (in Latin *silvaticus*).

[9] (Zaragoza: Mira Editores S.A., 2001).

celestial aroma led him to the mouth of a deep cave, half hidden among the foliage, with a crystalline fountain in its depths next to a church dedicated to the saint that had protected him.

Lying on the floor in deep mortal repose was the incorrupt body of a man whose venerable age and holy appearance inspired consolation rather than horror, and whose head was resting on a triangular stone, where an inscription revealed his name as Juan de Atarés[11], a hermit who had died embracing the cross against his heart. Although the fame of his sanctity had spread throughout the entire region, no one had ever dared disturb his solitude, and practically no one knew the place where he had spent his life in seclusion.

Touched by the sanctity of that man, Voto felt the call of God and greatly desired to follow his footsteps by entering into the seclusion of the cave, but not before easing the anxiety of his parents, selling his belongings, and bringing along his brother Félix. The two abandoned their home, family, and the comfortable life they had shared, and retired to the labyrinth of the cave, for the purpose of turning their lives over to God and contemplation. Before dying, they entrusted the cave and church to two virtuous disciples, Benito and Marcel, who built other chapels and formed the first nucleus of monks at San Juan de la Peña, extending its fame throughout the neighboring communities.

It is related in ancient histories that Juan de Atarés, the penitent and holy hermit whose body was found in the cave, lived there at the time of the invasion of the Moors, and had already built the hermitage in honor of St. John the Baptist during the reign of the Visigoths. Legend relates that he was a Christian knight from a prestigious and noble family of Atarés, dedicated to agriculture and livestock. One day, at the end of the seventh century, motivated by a profound religious vocation, he decided to renounce his belongings and leave his family, and became a penitent in the isolated cave of Mt. Pano, where he spent his time praying. One day, without knowing from where he came, a well-dressed knight happened to visit him (who was in reality the devil in disguise), and they both went to the exterior of the cave to talk. Suddenly a great noise like thunder was heard and the stones of the mountain began to move until they formed a beautiful

---

[10] According to other versions, Voto's horse landed gently on the ground at the bottom of the ravine where Voto immediately saw the small cave with the corpse of Juan de Atarés.

[11] Atarés is a small town close to the Monastery of San Juan de la Peña.

palace. Thus Satan showed Juan his immense power and urged him to renounce God and return to the things of the world. The hermit began to pray and fell senseless to the ground. When he recovered, he found himself in the presence of an angel and saw that the palace was being lowered with another great noise. "You see what remains of the power of the enemy of God who came to tempt you," the angel told him, and asked that he move to a great cave on Mt. Uruel and make an altar there under the advocacy and protection of St. John the Baptist, to whom he should commend his life and his soul. The angel disappeared, and Juan set out to fulfill the command. He wandered along the mountain and found a hollow with an immense grotto in the interior. He prepared a small living space as protection from inclement weather and improvised an altar, thus founding a church in honor of St. John, that with time would become the famous monastery of monks known as San Juan de la Peña.

In the year 713 many Christian fugitives came to the area opposite the cave, in a delightful plain close to Mt. Pano, where they began to form a small community that was given the name of the mountain. When the king of Córdoba, Abderramán Iben Mohabia, discovered its existence, he sent a formidable army that battered its walls, and demolished the population. Nevertheless, the army never even saw the holy cave of St. John opposite this community, believing it inaccessible. The Christian fugitives then banded together, electing Garcí Ximénez as their king, becoming a force that was capable of resisting any attack. They were soon joined by Christians from many parts, who came to enlist in order to overcome the heavy yoke of the barbarians, aided also by the strength of that mountainous region, just as the Asturians under Pelayo defended religious freedom at the same time in Covadonga. Garcí Ximénez converted the hermitage into a church, placing the stone on which the head of Juan de Atarés came to rest.

The Holy Grail was transferred from the Cathedral of Jaca to the Monastery of San Juan de la Peña in the reign of Sancho IV Ramírez, who decided to take advantage of the magnificent opportunity offered by the visit of Cardinal Hugo Cándido, a legate of Pope Alexander II in the year 1071. The trip of this papal nuncio is celebrated in the history of Aragón for being the first that ever came to the kingdom, and for the importance of the event in which solemn ceremonies were held to receive the legate who came to meet with the king, the bishops of Jaca and Roda, various abbots, eminent persons from the kingdom, and the monks of the now famous monastery.

One of these ceremonies was the inauguration of the Roman rite on March

1724 engraving with representations of St. John the Baptist and the upper and lower monasteries of San Juan de la Peña.

22 in the second week of Lent, admitted only days later by the Cathedral of Jaca, the first in Spain to adopt the new liturgy, five years before this took place in Castile and the other reconquered regions. The Roman rite would substitute and replace the ancient Hispanic-Visigoth or Mozarabic rite that was followed until then in the churches, inaugurated at San Juan de la Peña for having been the departure point for warlike enterprises, as well as the meeting place for the nobility of the kingdom, who came to this monastery to implore the benediction of the Abbot before undertaking any important action. For that reason the Abbot of San Juan came to occupy a preeminent place in the Courts of Aragón. He voted in the Councils, and did not recognize any hierarchy other than that of the Pope. During this momentous occasion, the cardinal used the Holy Cup of the Last Supper in the celebration of the Holy Sacrifice of the Mass, thus converting the monastery into the most appropriate refuge for the famous relic, in the custody of the holy monks who later copied and archived the entire history of Aragón, including the *Crónica Pinatense*, dedicated to the study of the origins of the ancient Pyrenean kingdoms.

From the moment in which the Holy Grail arrived in San Juan de la Peña in the eleventh century, until it left for the Palace of the Aljafería in Zaragoza at the end of the fifteenth century, in the possession of King Martín el Humano of Aragón, there is perhaps no more interesting moment in its history, in spite of the fact that it is not any better documented historically than in other chapters. The reason is that news of its existence continually reached the ears of the pilgrims, inspiring the famous legends of the Holy Grail, thus converting it into the relic par excellence and symbol of eternal life. Hidden in its secluded monastic refuge, venerated by holy monks, it became shrouded in a mystery that still conceals its physical reality and existence for those who cannot separate legend from tradition and history.

San Juan de la Peña, reputed from the first days of its existence to be a sacred place and symbol of Spain's resistance against its enemy, became the custodian of some of the most important relics and documents in existence. The Holy Grail was there in 1134, enclosed in a very expensive marble box, as is read in a Latin manuscript dated December 14 of that year which testifies: "In a marble chest is the Cup in which Christ our Lord consecrated his blood, which St. Laurence sent to his homeland Huesca." The document is preserved in the archives of the monastery, translated and copied by the Juan Agustín Ramírez, the canon of Zaragoza, in his work about the life of St. Laurence.[12]

As Atienza points out, this was the first time that the Grail was kept in custody under the protection of St. John, because in all of the previous years it was under that of St. Peter, the first Pope who founded the Church of Rome. John, associated with the Mystic Lamb, is present throughout the entire history of the monastery and its iconography, from the central figure of the capital of the cloister that represents the Last Supper, resting his head on the shoulder of the Savior, to the engraving of the seventeenth century in which, between two representations of the monastery – the old and the new – the Baptist appears with the inscription *Ecce Agnus Dei*. He believes that both the Mystic Lamb and the Holy Grail represent fundamental ideograms: the Lamb as the ancient victim of sacrificial rites, converted into the symbol of the Lamb of God who takes away the sin of the world, and the Grail, as divine receptacle that contained the sacrificed divine blood, and therefore, receptacle of the vital essence that leads to eternal life.

One of the keys to the history of the Holy Grail, according to Antonio Beltrán, is the document *Pergamino 136* of the archives of the Crown of Aragón, dated September 26, 1399, and cited by Briz Martínez, the seventeenth century abbot and historian of San Juan de la Peña. This important historical document records all of the details of the surrender of the Holy Grail. Beltrán reproduced the narration in Latin and Spanish, and it merits being translated into English:

In the name of God. Let it be known to all that as the most excellent prince and lord, Don Martín, by the grace of God king of Aragón, Valencia, Mallorca, Sardinia and Corsica, and count of Barcelona, Rosellón and Sardinia, has earnestly desired and procured to have in his royal chapel that stone Cup in which our Lord Jesus Christ, at his holy Supper, consecrated his precious blood, and that the blessed Laurence, who received it from St. Sixtus, then High Pontiff, whose disciple he was, and deacon of Santa María in dominit, sent and gave it with a letter of his to the monastery and convent of San Juan de la Peña, situated in the mountains of Jaca, of the kingdom of Aragón, with whose Cup the abbots, priors, and priests of the monastery were later accustomed to consecrate; and to have this Cup the above-mentioned king sent the reverend in Christ Father Antonio, Archbishop of the Athenians, his minister, to this same monastery. Finally, on the Friday that was September 16 of the year of the birth of the Lord 1399, that reverend archbishop and the religious Fr. Bernardo, prior of that

---

[12] *Vida de San Lorenzo*, tomo 1.°, p.101.

monastery, declared to the King, in his minor chapel of the Palace of the Aljafería of the city of Zaragoza, that when the document from him was explained to the priests of the monastery, all of the priors and religious who were gathered in chapter concerning the surrender of the sacred Cup, unanimously decided to give it to the King, and surrendered into his hands the stone Cup; and the King, who received in his hands the Cup, wanting to give some thanks for it to the monastery, gave and put in the hands of the prior, for the service of the monastery, a golden cup from his chapel, of five marks of Zaragoza plus one ounce in weight, in which are found the following marks, namely: three emeralds, two emblems, and a crucified Christ, and on the handle, that is in the middle, six emeralds, two with the arms of Aragón, two with the emblems of the kings and two images of St. George with a cross, and on the paten it is enamelled to the Eternal Father. The King donated this golden chalice to the monastery, with the condition that the elder abbot and the priors of this same monastery can neither sell nor pawn that cup for any amount of time, so that it would serve the monastery and be destined for its service alone. And the present abbot and priors, as well as those of the future, must swear not to sell or pawn that chalice. The prior, having received from the King the golden cup with the paten, promised, with thanks rendered, the mentioned pact of not selling or pawning it, and to preserve the chalice, as long as it was in his possession, and in the surrender that he was to make to the monastery, to obligate the observation of that act, as is described above.

It ends with the signature of Berenguer de Sarta, secretary of the king, with Berenguer de Cruilles, Roger de Moncada and Olfo de Prócida serving as witnesses.

This document describes the transaction by means of which King Martín el Humano receives the stone cup used for the Consecration at the Last Supper from San Juan de la Peña, giving in exchange a golden cup, with a paten, adorned with emeralds and with an approximate weight of 1,298 grams. Although this last cup is described in detail, very little is said about the first, identified only as that of the Last Supper.

The golden cup donated to the monastery by King Martín in exchange for the Holy Grail has unfortunately disappeared, melted in a fire at San Juan de la Peña on November 17, 1494. The fire began in the upper part of the monastery, above the kitchens, and rapidly spread throughout the premises. Sánchez Navarrete explains that "in all the monastery there did not remain a fistful of twigs, and the fire even melted most of the bells, and the others cracked, just as a good number of religious books were burned, some of which there were none more beautiful nor perfect in most of Spain." Another fire took place on February

24, 1675, of three days duration, that affected the refectory, guest quarters, and archives of the monastery, and that left it in such a lamentable state that the monks felt obligated to build another on the plateau of San Indalecio, celebrating the abandonment and definitive decline of the once important and powerful monastery of San Juan de la Peña, in the month of September of 1682. Even the new monastery seemed to suffer a curse with the departure of the Holy Grail. In August of 1809 the Napoleonic troops, under the orders of General Suchet, came to the monastery and ransacked it. By 1835, with the sale of Church property under Mendizábal,[13] the history of the glorious monastery was definitively closed.

At the death of King Martín el Humano, the Holy Grail was temporarily in Barcelona, recorded and described in the inventory of personal possessions that was made in September of 1410 as a chalcedony cup in which Jesus Christ consecrated his holy and precious blood.

The lack of documentation concerning the events that took place during these years is notable, and very likely intentional, in order to silence the existence of the Holy Grail in the Monastery of San Juan de la Peña. In spite of the fires that left it devastated so many years ago, it has been recently renovated and is still quite impressive, particularly the eleventh century Council Chamber, a dark and irregular dormitory covered with a vault and great arches, that is the oldest and most venerable part of the monastery, along with the lower church and crypt. It is constructed of living rock, with window-like loopholes providing the scarce illumination that makes it seem more like a castle than a sanctuary, but which proclaim the war-like nature of those times when danger demanded secrecy and silence. Its flooring, especially in the area closest to the rock, encloses many bones from the graves that were removed during recent renovations. Popular legend situates in one of its corners the legendary torment of the drop, which consisted of a constant dripping of water from a trapezoidal enclosure of storage water emanating from a gargoyle in the upper part of the cloister, which supposedly

---

[13] As Mark Williams explains, "During the height of the Carlist War and anti-clerical frenzy, the regent called on a Basque financial wizard named Mendizabal to head the government. A decree in 1835 closed all religious orders; in Madrid alone 44 churches and monasteries were shut down. Then, in an act of vast impact, this radical banker launched a program of land reform that confiscated church property and offered it for sale. About one-quarter of all church lands went on the block in the first two years." *The Story of Spain* (Málaga: Satana Books, 4th edition, 2000), p.167.

fell incessantly on the stones. Many believed that it was a special torture for the monks being punished, who found themselves unable to flee from the rhythmic sound.

The Church of San Juan, also known as the Upper Church for having been built on the ancient Mozarabic church, was constructed by King Sancho Ramírez and consecrated in 1094 by the Archbishop of Burdeo. It consists of a single nave that is crowned by three semicircular apses attached to the rock that serves as a vault, with three triumphal arches sustained by cylindrical semi-detached columns. It is here where the Holy Grail was exposed to the veneration of the faithful. The central altar is dedicated to St. John, patron of the monastery, and the two side altars to St. Michael and Pope St. Clement. Every year in the month of July, when it doesn't coincide with the festivity of St. John the Baptist in June, Mass is celebrated in this church, attended by the General Chapter of the *Hermandad de Caballeros*, or Brotherhood of Knights of San Juan de la Peña, created in 1949 and presided over by the King of Spain, its *Hermano Mayor*.

The Cloister is located on the other side of the church, entered through a Mozarabic door from the lower church, and unlike any other in the world. In the keystones of the entry arch is a twelfth-century inscription engraved in Latin, which translated, says: "The door of Heaven is opened, by means of this, to any of the faithful who applies himself in joining the commandments of God to Faith." The plan of the cloister is unique because of its impressive majesty, beauty and artistic originality, with four beautiful galleries, arches of varying types with twin columns, and precious capitals, meticulously sculpted by an anonymous man known only as the *Maestro* of San Juan de la Peña, who lived at the end of the twelfth century. The capitals have reliefs of the Old and New Testaments that are surprising for their movement and realism, and whose superb carving is characterized by oversized eyes that give a peaceful expression to their faces. Represented are scenes from the creation of the world to the coming of the evangelists, and the life of Christ from his infancy through public ministry, death, and resurrection. The columns are uniquely freestanding and extraordinarily designed.

The Chapel of Sts. Voto and Félix is located in the southeast angle of the cloister, constructed in the Neoclassical style. Its entrance is covered with the shield of the Abbot Briz Martínez, historian of the monastery, who decided to build the chapel after a miraculous event occurred: One day as he was passing through the cloister two large pieces of stone fell from the rocky vault of the cloister, one barely scraping his shoulder and the other falling to the floor. Unharmed, he ordered its construction, finished in 1631, which he dedicated to the holy hermits Voto and Félix, the successors of the first hermit Juan de Atarés. This was the obscure and marvellous place where the Holy Grail was kept for nearly three centuries, secure and far removed from the territories battling against the invading Arabs. Next to the shield of the Abbot is the pennant and lamb of St. John, which were the arms of the monastery, and in the interior is an altar dedicated to the saints, who are represented at the moment when they discovered the cave that preserved the body of the holy hermit Juan de Atarés, in a painting completed in 1631 by the painter Juan Pérez Galván of Zaragoza.

The site is astonishing, with a winding road surrounded by thick vegetation and the sounds of singing birds and gurgling streams. As the visitor descends toward the monastery, the rose-colored boulder or *peña* appears quite suddenly, with the massive rocky overhang that encloses the cave. It would be impossible for the visitor not to recognize that this natural phenomenon in which the monastery is sheltered from view is a totally unique, a grandiose and awesome marvel of the landscape that seems to have been conceived by providence eons ago with a special purpose in mind. Before it humanity seems small and insignificant, unable to find an adequate explanation for the mystery that permeates the enclosure, transporting the spectator into a world populated by knights, where the quest for the eternal is what causes the mere mortal to rise above the purely mundane. It is said and has been recorded in the chronicles that no one, in spite of the danger of falling rocks that sometimes detach because of the erosion produced by wind, water, and winter cold, has ever been hurt, not even the wild boars or fawns that at times come to the doors of the monastery in search of food. As Briz Martínez wrote in his history of San Juan de la Peña, a stone has never touched a single priest or monk, knight or pilgrim, king or beggar, of all those who ever came to the monastery throughout the centuries. The rocky cupola served as more than camouflage for the Holy Grail, therefore; its massive cupola was a mysterious guardian ordained by nature for the extraordinary and momentous occasion when mortal beings sought protection for the relic of relics, the Holy Grail, an event that inspired the wondrous and enduring legends and poems that arose in the Middle Ages, composed by a humanity that wished to sing the eternal praises of the holy relic whose fame emanated from the mysterious rocky cave, in spite of all attempts to stop it □

Engraving in a work of 1724 with scenes from the tradition of Sts. Voto, Félix and Juan de Atarés.

18th-century engravings of the Sacred Corporals and the west side of the city of Daroca. From the *Compendio Sagrado* by Tomás Orrios de la Torre (First Edition Francisco Moreno. Zaragoza, 1759).

167

Chapter 11

THE MIRACLE OF DAROCA

A singular event took place in the city of Daroca in the year 1239 that initiated the reconquest of Aragón and ultimately led to the Holy Grail being surrendered to Valencia in the year 1399. This occurrence was the famous Miracle of Daroca, a city located in northeastern Spain, whose past is still alive in its Roman, Moorish, and medieval edifices, walls and plazas. This historic city, however, owes its fame not to its architecture, but to its most priceless possession: the relic of the *Sagrados Corporales*, a cloth containing the bloodstains that were left when six Hosts disappeared on Sunday, February 23, as the chaplain was saying Mass in the town of Luchente. The Holy Grail and the Eucharistic miracle are sometimes represented together, both symbols of the Divine Presence that contributed to the establishment of Corpus Christi as a monumental celebration in Spain.

On that memorable day in 1239, the regiments from Calatayud, Teruel, and Daroca were in the territory of Valencia to defend the region from the attack of the Moors. The Catholic King Jaime II, who took succession over the kingdom of Aragón and the principality of Cataluña in the year 1213, had already made rapid progress in the plan to expel the infidels from Spain, surpassing the zeal and valor of his predecessors. With the desire to spread the Catholic faith and free the Christians from the sacrilegious abominations that were staining their laws and churches, he went to the Balearic Islands where he repossessed Mallorca and Menorca. He then returned to the kingdom of Valencia, an extremely amenable territory that was dominated by the Sarracens, planning to undertake a new conquest in order to restore the former glory of Spain. In only a few days a castle was built on the hill of Codól, which greatly dismayed the Saracen King Zaen Moro. Zaen became determined to demolish the castle and approached it with his numerous troops; at the time Berenguer de Entenza, the uncle of King

Jaime, was guarding it. A bloody battle ensued, but according to Spanish historians, those who fought for the cause of God were visibly aided by their patron, St. George. The enemy withdrew, and the victory was followed by the taking of Valencia in the year 1238.

The following year King Jaime went to Mompeller, leaving his army once again in the command of Berenguer de Entenza, whose regiments occupied the castle of Codól, hoping to tackle the castle of Chío, in which the Moors had their greatest resistance and power. King Zaen decided to recapture the city of Valencia with fresh troops brought from northern Africa, and multitudes of the barbarians quickly surrounded the hill of Codól with its few regiments of Christians, outnumbering them by one hundred to one. Having occupied and reinforced all of the ravines through which the Catholics might be able to flee, the Saracen troops prepared to attack. Knowing that his troops were in grave danger, and fearing that his soldiers would despair due to the absence of the Catholic King Jaime, Berenguer exhorted them to place themselves in the grace of the Lord through an act of fervent contrition, with the troops hearing the holy Sacrifice of the Mass, and with the six captains taking Communion in the name and presence of the combatants. He assured them that by meditating on the mysteries of the Mass they would have the grace to enter the battle with confidence and courage.

On that Sunday, February 23, Berenguer left camp to meditate piously on the impression he had made on his men. The priest had already finished the Consecration of the Hosts, and in the brief time that elapsed between consecrating the Hosts and consuming them, the shrieks of the Moors were heard, forcing the army to leave Mass in order to take up their arms. The priest, who was quite disturbed, swallowed the Host that was used for the Sacrifice, but rather than consume the remaining six that were intended for the captains, he placed them between the corporals and hid them in a secluded cave so that they would not be profaned by the barbarians.

The combat that ensued lasted three hours and is considered to be one of the bloodiest and most miraculous conflicts ever seen. Each Christian soldier carried a palm in his left hand, according to some so that they could be distinguished easily among the innumerable Saracens, but believed by others to be a sign of victory before they even entered the fight. It seemed as though the brutal attacks of the Moors came back to them rather than the Christians, because the Christian troops did not lose an inch of land and won their victory with little effort.

The regiments gave thanks to the Lord and returned anxiously to the cave where the Hosts had been deposited. Returning devoutly in procession to the tent where the Mass had been celebrated, the captains prostrated themselves humbly with their general in order to receive Holy Communion. The priest was surprised when he unfolded the corporals containing the Hosts, because he found that they were stained with blood and were so fused to the linen that they penetrate the weave even to the present day. The entire army was overcome with gratitude, not so much for the victory that they had won against the infidels, as for the singular fortune of having been able to adore the Sacrament that was stained with the visible blood of Christ.

The army spent so much time in contemplation and thanksgiving that they gave the enemy the opportunity to once again approach the Christians. The Saracens came to the top of the hill, but were put into such disarray that they began to kill their own men, with their armies turning against themselves. The priest hoisted the cloth as a miraculous standard of the Faith at the top of the hill, whose splendor seemed to dazzle the barbarians. The few who survived fled as cowards, verifying to the letter the verse of King David that seemed to be a literal prophecy of the victory: *Exurgat Deus, et dissipentur inimici ejus, et fugiant qui oderunt eum á facie ejus.*[14] The Saracens never again returned to this area; those who fled either returned to Africa or took refuge in the neighboring regions of Murcia and Granada.

There were disputes afterwards to decide which city would be the custodian of the sacred corporals. Since the battle had taken place outside of the city of Valencia, three towns – Teruel, Catalayud and Daroca – all claimed rights of ownership. They finally agreed to place the cloths in a metallic box that was fastened to the back of a small blind mule that had been seized from the Arabs. The animal was then allowed to wander to wherever Providence would direct it. The mule headed through the territory of Valencia, passed that of Teruel, appeared to turn toward the lands of Calatayud, and finally returned to Daroca where it collapsed at the town gates on March 7, 1239. Everyone agreed that Daroca would be the permanent custodian of the Eucharistic miracle, and the cloths were first placed in the Hospital of San Marcos before they finally came to rest in the Basilica of the Sacred Corporals.

---

[14] God rose up and his enemies were put to flight – those who hated him fled from his face. Translation by Mark Guscin.

The walk taken by the mule from Valencia to Daroca lasted about fourteen days, and was accompanied by crowds of people who witnessed several miracles. The mule was followed by all of the Christian soldiers, carrying in their hands lit torches, and it is said that celestial music from choruses of angels attracted more and more people along the route, who piously joined the procession behind the sacred ark carrying the visible blood of Christ. As they passed through Puebla de Artiaza, a small town next to Algecira, a demonic spirit, speaking from the mouth of a possessed man, repeated the same words that were directed to Jesus so long ago, as related in the Gospels. "Jesus Christ, Son of God, why did you come to torment us before the appointed time? Wasn't it enough that the Blood shed on the Cross destroyed us, taking away the power and dominion that you carried on your shoulders, but is what you use again now to torment us with the infinite power of that visible Blood of the Creator?" The words had hardly been uttered when the man was freed from the unclean spirit, who was filled with joy for having been the subject of the first miracle that resulted from the Divine Mystery on the cloth.

The second miracle took place as the procession passed the ancient village of Jerica. In the mountains bordering Aragón two criminals robbed a rich merchant of his money and possessions and were about to assassinate him. As they put the knife to his throat, the man had a revelation that the Eucharistic Miracle was not far away, approaching along the road and followed by the army and a large crowd of people. The merchant asked the thieves to grant him the opportunity to say something to them, and told them the following: *"I know that the fear that your crime not be discovered is what is driving you to take my life after having robbed me of my possessions, and although the promise that I made to you to keep silent did not make an impression on your hard hearts, I beg you once again to have pity on me and hear me before your fury bloodies itself in the execution of this crime. Know that I have had at this moment a revelation from Heaven, advising me that the Sovereign Mystery, that you have already heard occurred in Codól at the time of the battle in which the Moors were destroyed by the Christians, is approaching along the road, accompanied by innumerable people, among whom is the venerable priest who had the joy of consecrating the six Hosts. Strengthened by this revelation, I dare to beg you, with the most humble submission, that you give me the opportunity to confess my sins at the feet of this venerable priest, and I promise and swear to you, on behalf of the God that I adore in such a wondrous Miracle, to keep your crime hidden in my heart."* As the merchant articulated these words, the royal flags of the soldiers of Daroca could be seen from afar, soon followed by the other standards and the crowds of people, with the lit torches shining. All of this gave credit to the merchant's revelation, and the thieves fled, most likely threatened, and not repentant, because they did not make restitution to the man. The merchant, now free, climbed down the mountain, full of joy and happiness. He went to meet the procession and prostrated himself before the Divine Mystery, giving thanks with tears streaming down his face. He asked the priest to hear his confession, informing him of the marvels that he had seen, and of the revelation from Heaven and how he had been freed from the criminals as they held the knife to his throat.

As the priest and the others in the procession listened with surprise to the merchant's story, two men overwhelmed with tears and sobbing came down from the sierra to the road, and adored the Sacred Hosts with the greatest devotion, desiring to alleviate their anxieties. It was the two thieves, who only a short time earlier had robbed the merchant and tried to kill him. Converted by the virtue of the Most High, they felt such grace in their hearts that they were transformed from treacherous wolves into innocent lambs. The change, which made these men so different that they no longer resembled what they had been before, had its origin in the sweet celestial music that the thieves had heard from the mountain. They saw the field adorned with brilliant lights that were accompanied by spectacular squadrons of angels, who in beautiful carriages of transparent clouds, were singing in honor of the Lord. They also perceived the extremely sweet fragrance of aromas and incense, and attracted by such marvellous wonders, the hardness of their hearts was turned into wax. They confessed their sins, bathed in tears, and returned the money to the merchant after having made a general confession. Renouncing the vanities of the world, they left to do penance in the desert, followed by the merchant, who left behind his money and possessions to be distributed among the poor.

These were the three miracles that occurred. The procession then continued along the road through the cities of Segorbe and Teruel. In every town the procession was greeted with the greatest pomp, and the mule continued the journey without hesitation, until it finally arrived at Daroca. The townspeople received it with tears and devotion, praying to the Divine Mystery that their town would be worthy enough to be chosen as the throne of its glory. It arrived at the gates of the city in the same way that Jesus entered Jerusalem on the back of a donkey. But instead of entering through the gates, the mule turned from the city walls, taking the road that led to Calatayud. The people, fearing that they had lost the happiness, fortune and glory that they believed was theirs, were filled with great sorrow, and tearfully pleaded that its destiny would be changed. The mule suddenly turned right and entered a poor hostel that was then the Hospital of San Marcos, knelt down and gave its last breath, leaving his immense and marvellous treasure in the blessed city of Daroca.[15]

This primitive journey of an animal carrying a Eucharistic miracle on its back is considered to be the first Corpus Christi procession in Spain. Until then the reception of Communion was infrequent, but after the Miracle of Daroca a religious fervor was born which manifested itself in Marian devotion, the birth of Holy Week, and an awakening of the Eucharist. Unlike other Eucharistic miracles, which were considered to be signs to restore lost faith, this event was singular in nature. Years later, under Pope Urban IV, the Feast of Corpus Christi was instituted in the universal Church, and in Spain, the first processions of the Corpus were born: that of Toledo, in 1280; that of Seville, in 1282; that of Gerona, in 1314; that of Barcelona, in 1319; and that of Valencia, in 1355. The Miracle of Daroca became the seed of the meaning of Corpus Christi in Spain: a procession that goes out to everyone, believers or not, exhibiting the external presence of the Eucharist in order to express the love and peace of Jesus in the Holy Sacrament outside of the confines of the church. This is depicted in the two great murals that exist in the Cathedral of Orvieto, Italy, in which Pope Urban IV appears exhibiting the sacred corporals to the people, spreading the Eucharistic faith to all in the name of Jesus.

With that miracle, Daroca was converted into a pilgrimage center for the entire world, adjacent to the Road of Santiago, which was already beginning to attract multitudes of faithful from many countries. As security was restored to the Kingdom of Aragon, it was no longer necessary to keep the Holy Grail hidden in San Juan de la Peña. In fact, there is evidence that especially in these later years the Monastery of San Juan de la Peña attracted those pilgrims who were able to make the difficult trip to the mountain cave where the monastery had been constructed for privacy and protection. It is certain that with increased devotion for Eucharist, the fame of the miracle of Daroca and the Holy Grail spread rapidly, igniting a worldwide interest in the sacred vessel that was used by Christ to institute the Blessed Sacrament ☐

---

[15] As narrated by Tomás Orrios de la Torre in 1759.

Chapter 12

THE LEGENDARY GRAIL QUEST

A body of stories and medieval romances centered on the legendary king Arthur became quite popular in Europe after the late twelfth century, inspired by classical and Celtic mythologies that abound in horns of plenty, magic life-restoring cauldrons, and similar fantastic elements. The Arthurian legends began in Wales before the eleventh century, but became famous in the rest of Europe with Geoffrey of Monmouth's *Historia Regum Britannicae* (1135-1139). Using Celtic sources, Chrétien de Troyes introduced the theme of the Grail into Arthurian legend, initiating a new trend in prose romances of the thirteenth century, which began to treat the subject of the Grail as the object of legendary quest. In his late twelfth-century unfinished romance *Perceval, ou Le Conte du Graal*, Chrétien united the religious theme of the Grail with fantastic adventure, a combination that was immediately copied by other French poets. They were translated and adapted frequently as the romance continued to develop as a narrative form, with the Lancelot theme predominating. In these romances, Lancelot's son, the pure knight Sir Galahad, achieved the vision of God through the Grail as fully as is possible in this life, while Sir Lancelot was impeded in his progress because of his adulterous affair with Guinevere. Other branches of the same Vulgate cycle told of Arthur's birth and childhood, and his winning of the crown by drawing a magic sword from a stone, and the account of Arthur's Roman campaign and war with Mordred, which included the story of Lancelot's renewed adultery with Guinevere and the disastrous war between Lancelot and Sir Gawain that ensued as a result.

Perceval was one of the knights in Arthur's company, a hero known for his childlike innocence that set him apart from the others, linked with the primitive folktale theme of a great fool or simple hero. In Chrétien's poem, Perceval's great adventure is a visit to the castle of the wounded king, where he sees a damsel carrying a silver cup that gives off a great light, the mysterious grail, in a procession headed by a squire carrying a bleeding lance, followed by two more with ten-branched candlesticks. Having previously been scolded for asking too many questions, Perceval keeps silent, and awakes the next day to find the castle deserted. A damsel informs him that his host had been the Fisher King, who would have been cured of a wound caused by a spear thrust through both thighs if only Perceval had asked about the Grail. This inspires the knight to set off on a fruitless quest for the Grail, and he learns from a hermit that it had contained the Host, Christ's body.

Early in the thirteenth century, Robert de Boron's French poem *Joseph d'Arimathie, ou le roman de l'estoire dou Graal* linked this Grail with the cup used by Christ at the Last Supper and afterward by Joseph of Arimathea to catch the blood flowing from Christ's wounds as he hung upon the Cross. The work is part of a trilogy that also includes *Merlin and Perceval*, narrating the early history of the Grail by using the figure of Merlin, with his knowledge of past and future, to link this legend with the earlier Arthurian legendary cycle. Another early thirteenth-century romance, *Diu Krône*, turns Sir Galahad into the hero of the Grail quest. It was the German poet Wolfram von Eschenbach, however, who composed the epic masterpiece of medieval times: *Parzival*, a 16-book, 25,000-line poem based on the unfinished work by Chrétien de Troyes. Written in Middle High German between 1200 and 1210, the poem is a religious allegory describing Parzival's painful journey from utter ignorance and naiveté to spiritual awareness.

Another work, the *Queste del Saint Graal*, introduced a new hero, Sir Galahad, and had wide significance; it was translated for English-speaking readers through Thomas Malory's late fifteenth-century prose *Le Morte D'Arthur*. In the original *Queste*, the quest for the Grail became a search for mystical union with God, and those knights, such as Gawain, who did not seek the help of divine grace in this quest failed. Lancelot, because of his adulterous love for Queen Guinevere, was only able to see the Grail in a dream. Galahad, on the other hand, could look into the Grail and contemplate the indescribable divine mysteries. The work shows the influence of the mystical teachings of St. Bernard of Clairvaux, who explained man's rise toward perfection in the mystical life as stages corresponding to states of grace. In the final states of the French Vulgate cycle, the Grail, symbol of grace, was withdrawn, never to be seen again by human eyes.

Malory subdues this mystical approach, endowing his work instead with a content that is far more human than spiritual, emphasizing weakness, vulnerability, and the failings of the flesh. His Lancelot, being a sinner, fails to see the Grail, but this is not presented as a disgrace; in fact, Lancelot expresses satisfaction that he has come as near to the Grail as he has, saying: "for as I suppose no man in this world hath lived better than I have done to achieve what I have done." The Holy Grail appears to the Round Table at the Pentecost celebration. After all are seated the doors and windows close automatically, and after the "cracking and crying of thunder" the relic comes as if it were summoning its predestined knight. The hall is pierced with a sunbeam seven times brighter than day, and all are "alighted of the grace of the Holy Ghost." The Holy Grail enters the hall covered with white samite[16], but none could see it. First Gawain, and then the one hundred and fifty knights of the Round Table swear that they will lay aside all earthly goals and follow this quest until they can finally behold the Grail more openly.

Based on Malory's *Le Morte D'Arthur*, Alfred Lord Tennyson composed twelve poems published in various combinations between 1842 and 1888; these were published as *Idylls of the King* in 1859. This later work covers Arthur's entire life, from the moment he met Guinevere to his final battle with Mordred, and is a commentary on an idealistic community in decline, attributed in part to Guinevere's betrayal of Arthur with the knight Lancelot. It includes an Idyll called *The Holy Grail* that describes the knights departing on a quest for the vision of the Holy Grail, which only a few of them are privileged enough to see. Three of them retire from the world to a life of contemplation after seeing the vision, but those who do not see abandon the quest, and many of them are killed. As in Malory's version, Lancelot is not allowed to see the Grail because of his love for Queen Guinevere.

Wolfram's Story of the Grail

Of all these legends, Wolfram von Eschenbach's version stands out for one important reason: unlike the others, *Parzival* appears to give clues that link the legendary Grail with that being venerated in San Juan de la Peña. *1)* He first refers

---

[16] Samite is a heavy silk fabric worn in the Middle Ages; it was sometimes interwoven with gold or silver.

to his grail as a "thing called the Gral," and later a "stone." *2)* This stone has a name: *"Lapsit exillis,"* and by virtue of this stone the Phoenix is burned to ashes and then reborn. *3)* Its origin is uncertain, but it was already on the earth when God sent the neutral angels to it. *4)* The grail family, headed by Titurel, was later appointed to guard the grail. *5)* The grail provides food and drink for the people at the grail castle, *Munsalvaesche*, in the land of *Terre de Salvaesche. 6)* Anyone who is ill will be healed by seeing the grail. *7)* A dove comes down from heaven every Good Friday with a communion wafer and renews the powers of the grail. *8)* Only baptized Christians can see the grail; it is invisible to all others. *9)* Occasionally a written message appears on the grail, presumably from God. *10)* The grail is protected by the grail king and his family and by others who are summoned to serve the grail. The knights must observe the rule of chastity, and are called *templeise,* (or Knights Templar). By defending the stone they atone for any sins they may have committed. Normally they are called to the grail as small children of noble birth, both boys and girls, from many countries. *11)* It is generally believed that no one can find the grail without having been called.[17]

> *The Grail is described in Book IX, entitled "Prevrezent":*
> *'And this brotherhood so gallant, dost thou know what to them shall give*
> *Their life, and their strength and their valour – then know, by a stone they live,*
> *And that stone is both pure and precious – Its name has thou never heard?*
> *Men call it Lapis Exilis – by its magic the wondrous bird,*
> *The Phoenix, becometh ashes, and yet doth such virtue flow*
> *From the stone, that afresh it riseth renewed from the ashes glow,*
> *And the plumes that erewhile it moulted spring forth yet more fair and*
> *bright – And tho' faint be the man and feeble, yet the day that his failing sight*
> *Beholdeth the stone, he dies not, nor can, till eight days be gone,*
> *Nor his countenance wax less youthful – If one daily behold that stone,*
> *(If a man it shall be, or a maiden 'til the same,) for a hundred years,*
> *If they look on its power, their hair groweth not grey, and their face appears*
> *The same as when first they saw it, nor their flesh nor their bone shall fail*
> *But young they abide for ever – And this stone all men call the Grail.'*[18]

---

[17] Sidney Johnson, *A Companion to Wolfram's* Parzival (Camden House, 1999), p. 78-79.

[18] *Parzival: A Knightly Epic by Wolfram von Eschenbach.* Translated by Jessie L. Weston. (London: David Nutt in the Strand, 1894), p.270.

First of all, Wolfram's Grail is definitely a stone, referred to in the original German by the word *grâl*, which is not only close to Chrétien's *graal*, meaning cup, but also to the Hebrew word for precious stone, *goral*. It would be unusual for the author to radically change the nature of the grail from a cup to a stone unless he knew that the Holy Chalice in San Juan de la Peña was actually a cup made of precious stone, or agate. Chrétien refers to it as "*the* Grail," and it is made "de fin or esmeré" or of fine pure gold, a kind of bowl decorated with precious stones, with light emanating from it, a rather accurate description of the relic now in Valencia, with the light suggested by its fiery bands of gold. Wolfram goes one step further: by combining the words, he is also able to combine the meanings of "cup" and "stone," so that the reader now has a further clue to its identity. The Grail is not only decorated with precious stones, it is *made* from stone. He gives his grail a name, *lapsit exillis*, or the possible alternate spelling, *lapis exilis*, which some scholars suggest may be the stone Alexander found at the gate of Paradise: *lapis exilis*, the insignificant stone or stone of humility. Margaret Fitzgerald Richey suggests that the *lapis* form of the word "has the advantage of being the exact correspondence in Latin to the German *stein*," both meaning "stone" or "gem."

Wolfram goes on to say that the phoenix is burned to ashes by the power of the stone and then is regenerated from the ashes. The symbolism is significant: agate has been symbolically associated with the moon and the constellation Libra, and was believed to possess magical powers. Origen (184-254 AD) interpreted the moon as a symbol of the church, and in the Christian tradition, Libra's scales symbolize most importantly Christ as the great judge who will decide our fate on the Last Day. The legendary phoenix is a heron-like bird, widely associated with immortality and resurrection. Its name comes from the Greek word for red, the color of fire, because the bird was thought to arise again from its ashes after a purifying fire had consumed it, after three days' time. It was therefore seen by the fathers of the Church as a symbol of the immortal soul and the resurrection of Christ "on the third day," and as stated in the second-century text *Physiologus*, "If it is granted even to this unreasoning creature, who does not know the Creator of all things, to be raised from the dead, will we not be raised, who praise God and keep His commandments?" The carmine and golden color of its plumage suggests the multi-colored stripes of the upper cup of the Holy Chalice, which have been described as glowing embers. The ashes are also symbolically significant as a symbol of the transitory nature of all earthly form, and were believed to contain the concentrated powers of that which was burned.

They are a symbol of humility, mourning, and penitence, as well as hope for new life.

That Wolfram's grail is connected with Christianity is also evident in the fact that the consecrated wafer is brought by a dove every Good Friday, renewing the power of the grail, suggestive of the saving power of the Crucifixion and its close association with the Eucharistic feast. The dove, of course, is a symbol of the Holy Spirit, as well as love, peace, and hope, and is often depicted leading the way to paradise.

Wolfram claims that his source was Kyot, the Provençal. Some have suggested that Kyot might in reality have been the *trouvère* Guiot de Provins, who lived southeast of Paris around the year 1200, but this would only be possible if Wolfram had confused the city of Provins with Provence, and there is no record that Guiot ever wrote anything very important. Another possibility, however, would be William of Tudela, a town in Navarre near the Aragonese border in Spain, about halfway between Logroño and Zaragoza, and not far from San Juan de la Peña. Sidney Johnson believes that his name could correspond to the Catalan-Aragonese *Guillot*, a diminutive form of *Guillem*, and *Tudela* might be identified with *Dôlet*, thought to be Toledo by some scholars. As there is no record that this particular William ever wrote about the grail, it would have to have been through personal acquaintance with Wolfram. It is also possible that Wolfram was referring to a relatively unknown source, which appears likely given that the names are encoded. Taken at face value, the account is rather fantastic, considering that Wolfram adds that Kyot gained his knowledge from the book of the Saracen astrologer Flegetanis, and where this fell short, from the chronicle of the kings of Anjou.

It is significant, however, that Tudela was a city of Al-Andalus, under the caliphate of Córdoba whose territory also included the cities of Sevilla, Zaragoza, Toledo, and Algeciras. The tenth century was the Golden Age of Muslim culture in Spain, and medicine, physics, astrology, art and other disciplines were so developed and renowned that they became a magnet for many emigrants to Al-Andalus. The caliph's library came to contain more than 40,000 volumes, and the caliph Al-Hakam, successor to Abd al Rahman III (912-961), attracted great numbers of the wise and educated to his court from the Middle East, creating in Córdoba a cultural center comparable to Baghdad in its moment of greatest splendor. It is likely then that the base of the Holy Chalice with its Arabic inscription, could indeed be the product of tenth-century Córdoba, and that given the fact that Tudela was so intimately connected with this culture, could certainly have been the source of Wolfram's information in one way or another.

Another clue is that Wolfram refers to God as "he who shines," which matches the interpretation of the inscription on the base of the cup, as given by Dr. Antonio Beltrán: "*li-Izahirati.*" Is it just coincidence, or did Wolfram have news of the existence of the Holy Chalice that was guarded in the secluded Monastery of San Juan de la Peña? Is is possible that he had knowledge from someone involved with adding the base to the cup? This is not at all unlikely, and it is clear that some pilgrims did manage to visit the monastery and spread the news of the Holy Grail to the multitudes that were travelling along the route to Santiago de Compostela. This certainly seems to indicate that the base was added at some point before the relic was taken to San Juan, very possibly before the Cathedral of Jaca became its custodian in 1035. It would have already been embellished with gold and jewels, therefore, for the inauguration of the Roman rite in Aragón, on the occasion of the coming of Cardinal Hugh Cándido, as the legate of Pope Alexander II, in 1071 AD. The Cardinal celebrated Mass with the holy relic, which most likely already appeared as it does today in Valencia, in this momentous event that firmly established San Juan de la Peña as its guardian.

The name *Guiot* also denotes the author of a French or Anglo-Norman account of the Grail legend, believed to contain two vital elements: the conception of a line of hereditary guardians, most likely a line of kings, and the idea of an order of knights dedicated to the Grail's defence and service, identified historically with the Order of the Knights Templar. His work may have also contained, among other Oriental wonders, a fascinating streak of alchemistic lore making mention of the *lapis eliksir* or philosopher's stone, which could partly explain why Wolfram fused the idea of *grail* with that of *lapis*, endowing the relic with magical powers, capable of providing food and drink for the guests at the grail castle. The other reason, of course, would be that he was well aware that the cup of the Holy Chalice was made of a precious stone, agate, and that the magical powers were symbolic of the relic's significance as that of the Last Supper. The concept of a line of kings as hereditary guardians is certainly historically accurate as far as the Holy Chalice is concerned, as well as that of knights and monks dedicated to its defense and service.

Other elements found in Wolfram's *Parzival* are also attributed to Guiot, such as the idea that the Grail had formerly been kept by a band of angels, and that the realm of the Grail was at one time overrun by the enemy. The latter concept is easy to explain in terms of Spanish history, because when the Moors invaded Spain in 711 there was an exodus of Christians and relics to the north. The first is a bit more complicated, but interesting. Although Wolfram speaks of "neutral" angels who left it on earth, meaning those who took neither side when Lucifer rebelled against God, and were punished for their indifference with a place midway between Hell and Heaven, the account nevertheless is strikingly similar to the ancient legendary idea that the Grail was made from a stone that fell from the crown of Lucifer, and that he who manages to serve the Grail was invested with supernatural power. Bizén d'o Río Martínez relates the tradition that the diabolical precious stone was already transformed into the Grail long before the birth of Christ, and according to this belief it was in Babel, and then in the possession of Melchizedek, Abraham, Moses (who carried it in the Ark), David and Solomon, until it was finally placed by Solomon in the Temple, where attempts were made to melt it. Later a priest stole it, who sold it to a receiver of stolen goods, until it reappeared in Jerusalem, where it is said that it was purchased by Veronica.[19]

Graham Hancock identifies the Grail with the Ark itself, an idea that may have been in Wolfram's mind also, but that has nothing to do with the reality of the Holy Chalice. It was believed that the Ark frequently served as an oracle, dispensing advice in the same manner that Wolfram describes in *Parzival*: written messages mysteriously appeared on it. Wolfram relates that "the Gral is so heavy that sinful mortals could not lift it from its place," which Hancock connects to an ancient Jewish legend that describes the moment when Moses descended Mount Sinai carrying the Stone Tablets that had just been inscribed with the laws of God. When he found the Israelites worshipping the golden calf, "he saw the writing vanish from the tablets, and at the same time became aware of their enormous weight.[20]" According to Wolfram, Flegetanis was "descended from Solomon, begotten of Israelitish kin all the way down from ancient times" and wrote of the marvels of the Gral. Being a heathen, he "worshiped a calf as though it were his god," hinting at a desire to bestow ark-like qualities on the relic. The angel legend is related by Flegetanis, who declared that he read the name of the Gral in the

[19] Revista *Argensola*, number 95, 1983.

[20] This is credited to Louis Ginzberg, *The Legends of the Jews*, The Jewish Publication Society of America, Philadelphia, 1911, vol. III, pp.128-9.

stars. Hancock interprets *lapsit exillis* as being derived from *lapis ex caelis* ("stone from heaven"), *lapsit ex caelis* ("it fell from heaven"), or even *lapis, lapsus ex caelis*, ("stone fallen from heaven"). He then suggests that Wolfram may have intended a deliberate and cryptic pun, because the words are also close to *lapis betilis*, a name with Semitic origins that was used by the late Greeks and Romans for sacred stones that had a divine life or soul, used for superstitions, magic, and fortune telling. They were thought to be meteoric stones fallen from the sky. Hancock believes that the Ark and the Grail both had a "light-generating quality" derived from a "fiery celestial energy," quoting Chrétien de Troyes who wrote that the Grail sent out a radiance "so great…that…candles lost their brilliance just as the stars do at the rising of the sun or moon."[21]

For Hancock, the Grail is the Ark, and he takes great pains to connect the two by using fantastic quotes from works of medieval fiction that are based largely on other legendary sources, although they do contain a kernel of truth. He even suggests that Wolfram's *Terre Salvaesche* might be Ethiopia, the land of the Grail, and therefore the land of the Ark. *Terre Salvaesche* also corresponds perfectly, however, with the wild, rugged terrain surrounding the Monastery of San Juan de la Peña, nestled in a cave under the large rock that conceals it so well from the eyes of the curious, and *lapis exilis* can also describe the humble agate cup that contained the divine blood of the Savior. It is not necessary to endow the relic with supernatural powers, except for the purpose of captivating the naïve with tales of the fantastic, which Hancock does as well as Wolfram did nearly one thousand years ago.

Stripped of the discourse of the fantastic, in which exaggeration leads to the supernatural, the Holy Chalice is still left with a remarkable history that not only points to authenticity, but also manifests its transcendental importance for Christians as the relic that contained the divine blood of the Savior as He held it in his hands and said the words of consecration. The only light and energy that has ever emanated from it is imperceptible to the human eye, but perhaps suggested by the fiery-colored bands of the agate. It is not difficult to see how and why the human imagination feels compelled to make the supernatural palpable, but the Holy Grail as described in medieval legendary fiction will never be found, simply because it does not exist. It is little more than a figment of the imagination.

---

[21] *The Sign and the Seal* (New York: Crown Publishers, Inc., 1992), p.68-70.

There are other similarities, however, between Wolfram's fantastic legend and the history of the Holy Chalice of Valencia. Perhaps the most notable is the story of the man that Parzival saw lying in front of the Gral, all gray yet with a clear skin. When Parzival visited *Munsalvaesche*, as the procession passed out of the hall, he saw in an inner room a beautiful old man lying on a bed, grayer even than mist. His name was Titurel, the head of the caretakers of the Grail, who was being kept alive miraculously by being in continuous sight of the Gral. Although bedridden and crippled by gout, he kept his fair complexion and continued to give counsel. This element of Wolfram's story seems to draw upon the legend of Juan de Atarés, the holy monk whose incorrupt body was found by Voto in the cave of San Juan de la Peña, indirectly responsible for the foundation of the Monastery on the site, and therefore "father" of the dynasty of monks who came to live there and later care for the Holy Grail. Although also a legend, it is the type of material that would have captivated Wolfram, and suggests familiarity with this site where the Grail was hidden at the time he wrote *Parzival*.

Another would be the fact that the kings were raised in Wolfram's Grail castle, suggesting that he was aware that the Spanish kings of Aragón were sent to the monasteries of the Pyrenees as children in the hope that they would grow to be rugged and strong, as was the case with Sancho Ramírez who was brought up in San Pedro de Siresa, one of the first sanctuaries of the Holy Chalice, high in the mountains of the Pyrenees. And finally, many heathens and Christians were imprisoned in Wolfram's famous castle, not far from the reality in Spain after the Moorish invasion, when the mountains became a refuge for those fleeing from the enemy. It is also interesting that the names of cities of Provence, Toledo, Seville, and Galicia appear frequently in the work.

Parzival's journey to the Grail of the temple is a journey towards himself, towards others, towards God, and ultimately also towards God's kingdom, as James F. Poag explains, goals that can only be reached through the Biblical virtues of love, purity, and humility, the very virtues that characterized those at *Munsalvaesche* and that are necessary for salvation. Parzival's struggle, then, symbolizes the way of salvation, the journey toward holiness that is the Christian way of achieving healing, restoration, consolation, and fullness of life.

Wolfram's Grail story can be seen, therefore, as a fantastic allegory of Christianity's quest for salvation, found in the supernatural, divine powers of the Eucharist that provide nourishment, peace, consolation and healing for the sick, and eternal life for those who seek it with purity of heart, humility, and love. The

plus qe li neurus mr trop aen un me
venart zeuos. Oves puis qe qe uos qe
feir licouient si me retozuere.

Arthur rides out with his knights as they set out on the quest.

Holy Grail is a concrete expression of the infinite, and the relic par excellence of Christianity. Only baptized Christians can see it, and only those called to the Messianic banquet are nourished by it. Through the sacramental presence of Jesus in the Eucharist it is possible to communicate with God, and by keeping Him constantly in sight, one can achieve eternal life. It is protected by the bishops, or knights, to whom it has been entrusted, in a castle that represents the Church, in the possession of a line of kings, or popes. By defending it, the Christian also becomes a "knight" who atones for any sins he may have committed. Adultery, pride, and other sin prevents one from "seeing" or understanding the mystery, which remains shrouded as if covered with a fine cloth, but those who succeed in the quest become its caretakers, or human "sanctuaries." A great light emanates from it, but it is neither magic nor cosmic energy, but rather a brilliance that cannot be seen by the naked eye, that of the glorified Christ. The allegory is simple, yet elusive for many, and the quest is the symbol for the path of salvation, beset with difficulties and dangers, but necessary for those who believe □

Galahad is presented to Arthur and his knights at the Round Table.

The Latin/Old French text between the two illustrations:

D aomm efpeo et haut et le
D euant le feignenr font ale
C il qui li amaument fon hoite
S ique chaftuns li feu encofte
E tendront deuife comment perceual
v mit chief le roy pefcheour et il unit
J uallet alaporte qui aporta vne ef
pee z le roy ta tendi aperceual

f et li uallee le uous aift
o que il parloient amfi
f uar leo entre par la porte
D ela mefon et fi aporte
E t apres deuife comment il fiftret
a table encontre z biau feu et con
ment leualler unit qui aporta latatce
qui famme z lef pucelet le famt graal

Gawain leaves Arthur and Guenever, rides on his quest, and arrives at a monastery. In the castle of the Holy Grail, the Grail is carried to a table while Percival is presented with a sword by the Maimed King.

186

5

THE AGE OF DOCUMENTATION

"The blood of martyrs is the seed of Christians."
In these few well-known words that we hear
in our childhood are enshrined the depth and
the weight of the problem we have to clarify.
We have to ask first what is a seed. A seed,
we say, is that whose essence is to reproduce
that which is closely similar to itself. Thus
"the blood of martyrs is the seed of Christians,"
hence the Christians are martyrs. There is
a second and comprehensive question:
Are we in fact Christians?

Fray Justo Pérez de Urbel

Providence is the first and principal cause
of historic events, which rules the destiny
of the world, bringing everything to the
glory of God and the good of men.

St. Augustine, de Civitate Dei

Chapter 13

THE GRAIL IS DESTINED
FOR VALENCIA

September 26, 1399, is the moment in time in which the Holy Grail enters definitively into recorded history, beginning with the previously mentioned document of King Martín el Humano, who asked for the relic from the monks of San Juan de la Peña in exchange for another golden and jewel-encrusted chalice of inestimable worth, which has unfortunately not survived the ravages of time. Martín el Humano was crowned king on April 13 in the Cathedral of Zaragoza, and was immediately forced to confront the political conflicts of the time. He managed to consolidate the dominion of Aragón in Corsica, Sardinia and Sicily, on whose battlefields he was accustomed to conquer under his slogan, which proclaimed the spirit of his actions: *Haec est Victoria quae vicit mundum: fides nostra* – this is the victory that has conquered the world: our faith.

Martín was a man of extraordinary devotion and spirituality that did not prevent him from ruling with prudence, and was a staunch defender of the dogma of the Immaculate Conception. Motivated by his great piety and devotion to relics, as soon as he found out shortly after being crowned that the Holy Cup of the Last Supper of the Lord was kept in the Monastery of San Juan de la Peña, he desired to possess the holy relic. On August 29 he sent the following letter to the Prior, asking them to bring him the stone relic:

El Rey.-«Prior: rogamos vos muyt affectuossament que luego encontinent vengades a nos e nos aportedes el calzer de piedra con el qual celebrades e trayet la carta del rey qui el dito caliz die al vuestro monasterio. E esto per res no mudedes ni dilatades como nos lo queramos veyer e ensenyas ad algunos etrangers qui son aquí con nos. Dada en Caragoca dius nuestro siello secreto a XXIX dias Agosto del anyo de nuestro Senyo MCCC.XC.VIII.-Rey Martinus.-Dirigitur priori Sancti Johannis de la penya.-Dominus Rex mandavit mihi Berengario Sarta.»[1]

The king was aided in his efforts by the Spanish antipope Benedict XIII (Pedro de Luna of Aragón), who was residing in Avignon, France; the abbot of San Juan de la Peña, the Pope's confessor and private advisor who was also living in the palace-jail of Avignon; and St. Vincent Ferrer, still devoted to the king, in spite of the fact that the monarch had been excommunicated by the Roman Pope Boniface IX for supporting Benedict XIII. They all resolved to satisfy his desire, which they accomplished with the document that appears in full in the chapter about San Juan de la Peña.

To summarize it again, the document narrates how the king desired very much to possess the Holy Chalice that was kept in the monastery of the cloistered Benedictines of San Juan de la Peña, situated in the mountains of Jaca. The king sent the Archbishop to the monastery and he returned to Zaragoza on September 26, 1399, accompanied by the monastery's Prior, Fr. Bernardo, who told the king that a meeting of all the priors and monks had been held, and that after deliberation on the royal petition they agreed unanimously to surrender to him the stone Cup of the Last Supper. The king, motivated by his desire to thank the community for its extraordinary generosity, gave the Prior a gift to be used only in the monastery: an extremely valuable golden chalice from his royal chapel. This was given under the condition that it could never be sold or pawned, and that the priors would have to swear to that stipulation.

The Holy Chalice was immediately transferred to the Chapel of the Royal Palace of the Aljafería in Zaragoza, where it was venerated among the treasures and relics of the royal chapel, as the property of the monarchs of the Crown of Aragón. The king liked to personally attend the rituals whenever his duties permitted, and established official veneration to the relic.

Twenty-three years later King Martín transferred his Court to Barcelona, where he unfortunately buried his son, also named Martín, who had died prematurely without a legitimate descendent, making his father the inheritor of

---

[1] Archives of the Crown of Aragón. Registro 2.242, fol. 171. Translated from Catalan by Mark Guscin, this reads: *The King: Prior, we request with all good will that you come to us and bring us the stone chalice you use at Mass together with the letter from the king who gave the chalice to your monastery. Do not delay or alter my request in any way as we wish to see it and to show it to some visitors who are here with us. In Zaragoza, with our secret seal, 19th August AD 1398. King Martín to the prior of San Juan de la Peña.*

the crown of Sicily. As the king did not have any more children, his advisors urged him to designate a successor. Martín, however, refused, declaring that when he died, whoever had the greatest right would rise to the throne. He passed away in that Mediterranean city on May 31, 1410, having taken with him to Barcelona his precious relics, including the Holy Grail, which appears in the inventory of goods that was drawn up a short time before his death:

> *Item I. Calix de vincle e calcedonia lo qual, segons se diu fo aquell ab que Jhesu Christ consegrá la sua Sancta e preciosa sanch lo dijous sant de la Cena encastat en aur ab dites nances e canó d'aur e lo peu del qual ha dos grenats e dos meracdes e XXVIII perles conservat en I stoix de cuyr quasi blanch empremtat e lavorat de si mateix.*[2]

The death of Martín el Humano, who died without a descendent or successor, led to the confrontation of six aspirants to the throne: Fadrique, the count of Luna; Juan, count of Prades; Jaime, count of Urgel; the dukes Alfonso de Gandía and Luis of Calabria; and Fernando de Antequera, Infante of Castilla. The dispute lasted for two years, but finally, on June 28, 1412, the Compromise of Caspe was signed and sealed, by which the Kingdom of Aragón recognized as their king Fernando, the Infante of Castilla, Martín's nephew. King Fernando was a young and great king who lacked the time to accomplish much. During the four years of his reign he was given the titles of "the Honest" and "the Just," dedicating himself to finding an acceptable way out of the Great Schism that occurred when three popes fought for control of the Church. For this reason he travelled to Perpignan to meet with Benedict XIII and the Holy Roman Emperor, Sigismund of Luxembourg, who proposed a universal council of the Church to be held on November 1, 1414 at Constance. In spite of the ties obligating him to the service of the antipope Benedict XIII, including the fact that he had won the Crown of Aragón, Fernando gave his support to the Council. Benedict XIII was subsequently deposed and expelled from the castle of the Popes in Avignon, forced to take refuge in the fortress of Peñíscola until his death in 1423.

---

[2] J. Masso Torrents, "Inventari dels bens mobles del Rey Martí d'Aragó," Revue Hispanique, XII (1905), p. 569. Translated from Catalan by Mark Guscin, this reads: Chalice made of chalcedony and gold, and which according to tradition was the one used by Jesus Christ to sanctify his sacred and precious blood during the Last Supper of Holy Thursday, whose golden base is encrusted with jewels, including two rubies and two emeralds, and is kept in white leather.

King Fernando, who was never welcomed in Cataluña, was succeeded at his death on April 2, 1416, by his son Alfonso V el Magnánimo (the Magnanimous). Although not of Valencia, those from that Mediterranean city believed that King Alfonso V always respected it as his own homeland, and they in turn, responded with support, fondness, and arms. While he was still Infante, he celebrated his marriage to María de Castilla in Valencia, who was loved and admired for her exemplary virtues and to whom Valencia owes the foundation of two monasteries. It has been said that Alfonso was the most distinguished monarch of his time, given the title *Magnánimo* not only for his military campaigns in Italy, his love for knowledge, and his Renaissance spirit of letters and arts, but also for his virtues that included courage, prudence, generosity, discretion, and wisdom.

Alfonso moved his Court to Valencia, which he visited several times, bestowing upon the people such improvements, gifts, favors, and distinctions that it has been said that he was the most "Valencian" king of all the monarchs of Aragón. Many restoration projects were undertaken due to his generosity, as well as the renovation and embellishment of the rooms and gardens of the Royal Palace that were converted into a charming residence with gardens, pools, forests, and an interesting zoological collection to which magnificent works of art were added. The king brought his relics with him to Valencia, which he kept in the Chapel of the Royal Palace that no longer exists. Among them was the Holy Cup of the Last Supper, which occupied a preferential place and was the major attraction for the most illustrious visitors of the Palace, which the king delighted in showing off, as recorded in a manuscript that still exists in the archives of the Cathedral, dated Monday, August 2, 1428, describing how the king showed the Infante of Portugal all of the relics in his Chapel.

The king, however, was continually absent from his Court, due to the military campaigns he had undertaken in the Mediterranean in the interests of Aragón. On one of these occasions, when he was involved in the war of Naples, urgently in need of money for his war expenses, he gave instructions to his brother in Valencia, Juan of Navarra, to ask for a loan from the Cathedral and the City Council. They agreed to provide the necessary funds, and as a pledge and guarantee, the king's relics were deposited in the Cathedral, in the custody of Antonio Sanz, canon and ecclesiastical superior of the Cathedral of Valencia and head chaplain of the Chapel of the Royal Palace. On March 18, 1437, as Antonio Sanz was dying, King Juan of Navarra, representing his brother, King Alfonso V of Valencia, surrendered in deposit and custody to the Chapter of the Cathedral, among other relics, the Cup in which Jesus Christ consecrated his blood at the Last Supper, *"made with two golden handles, whose base, of the same color as aforementioned Cup, is embellished around in gold with two rubies and two emeralds on the base, and with twenty-eight pearls, compared to the thickness of a pea, around the base of the Cup; the scholar Francisco Ferrer says that the rubies are garnets."* This precious relic was in a pine box covered with red cloth, trimmed with white ribbon bearing the shields of Aragón and Sicily. The donation was recorded with a summary of its contents, signed by Pedro de Anglesola, on behalf of the king, and Jaime de Monfort, on behalf on the Chapter, both notary publics. From that moment on, that agate cup, mounted on its jewel-encrusted, golden base, has been kept in the Cathedral of Valencia. The king and his successors recovered some of the pawned relics, but as they never finished paying the loan, they never managed to recuperate the Holy Chalice, and thus it became the possession of the Cathedral.

The relic has been in the Cathedral of Valencia ever since, with only three brief interruptions. The first took place on March 18, 1809, when due to the French invasion and consequent outbreak of the War of Independence, the Holy Chalice was taken on a pilgrimage in the custody of a canon delegated by the Cathedral's Chapter, in order to save it from the outrages of the Napoleonic troops. It was first transferred to Alicante, returning to Valencia at the end of January, 1810. In March of the same year it went from Ibiza to Palma de Mallorca, and in September of 1813 it returned from that city to the Cathedral of Valencia where it was venerated without interruption, first in the Chapel of the Relics, in the apse of the Chapter Room, and after 1916 in the old Chapter Room, which is the current Chapel of the Holy Grail. This absence is described by Peregrín-Luis Llorens Raga as one beset with particular dangers from the very start: sixty-one boxes were loaded into two ships that had to remain in the port for four days because of the strong sea swell, a situation that nonetheless allowed the Chapter of the Cathedral of Valencia to complete several essential things that had been forgotten: that of sealing the crates, and taking an inventory of the cargo.

The vessel departed on March 19, feast of St. Joseph, with the Holy Chalice protected in a small silver chest, wrapped in cloth of gold lamé and guarded by only one person, Dr. Calbo, the priest sent by the Cathedral, while another prelate, Dr. Alcedo, went immediately to Alicante, its destination. The relic had hardly arrived in Alicante when Dr. Alcedo died from an illness that had progressed very rapidly. Dr. Calbo wrote to the Chapter of the Cathedral and was informed that as they soon expected the return of the Holy Chalice to Valencia, they would not be sending a replacement. Although they had planned the return trip before the end of September, due to the frequent storms in the latter part of the year, dangers from the continuing war, and rumors that the enemy was lying in wait for the departure of the reliquaries, their hopes were delayed considerably. An armed vessel finally set out in January of the following year, but was forced to take refuge in Benidorm by the rough conditions at sea, arriving at last in Valencia in the middle of February to the jubilant welcome of the Chapter of the Cathedral.

Their joy didn't last long. The chests had hardly arrived after so many months of worry and uncertainty, and in fact, the relics were still being unloaded, when the news hit Valencia that the invading French army was not only approaching the city, but had already reached its walls, creating confusion and disorder. The Holy Chalice and other relics were repacked and immediately sent to the island of Ibiza on March 4, 1810, with twenty large boxes set to depart in one ship and another twenty-two distributed among three other vessels. The rest remained in the Cathedral. The box containing the monstrance, however, was so large that the launch was not able to transport it to the ship, and departure had to be delayed until a larger boat was found the following afternoon. The crate was still being loaded when gunfire was heard from the French troops that were already in sight of the port. Llorens Raga describes the sailors as being visibly aided by Divine Providence as they quickly finished the difficult operation and jumped unto the ship. When the French assaulted the wharf, the four ships were already out of reach of their gunfire, headed for Denia.

Not all of the ships that arrived in Denia set off for Ibiza, because the three smaller vessels that lagged behind because they were not as diligent in taking advantage of the favorable wind were unexpectedly ordered to remain in the port of that city by the Chapter of the Cathedral, as something totally unexpected had occurred: The French General Suchet had suddenly withdrawn his troops, finding it impossible to conquer the city. The twenty large crates that left on the larger ship, however, were unloaded on the island of Ibiza and deposited in the basement of the house of a lawyer where they remained until the end of July, 1811. At that time Dr. Calbo arrived and found a room that would be adequate to guard the sacred treasure, and began to conduct an inventory that was interrupted when Mallorca unexpectedly decreed on December 22 of the same year that the treasure must be sent to their island, insisting that the reliquaries could attract the attention and greed of the enemies, with Ibiza being defenseless against their brutality. Protests and arguments ensued, with the Chapter of the Cathedral suspecting their true motives, believing that Mallorca would only take possession of the silver and anything else of value for their own selfish purposes.

In the meantime, Suchet was trying to force Valencia to surrender by tightening a circle around the city. During several days of sieges and bombings, many lives were lost, as well as countless treasures, including libraries. The Chapter of the Cathedral was dispersed, with the canons from Valencia arriving in Ibiza as fugitives on January 28, 1812. Dr. Calbo rejoiced, believing that he could now avoid what he had considered to be inevitable. Without losing a minute, the canons protested the decree before the governor and announced what recourses they would pursue if they were not satisfied. The governor responded with many excuses, and repeated his order, to be effected during the first hours of the night. The canons petitioned a delay, alleging that the chests were not in good condition, and finally the governor acceded to a four-day time limit, warning that if the chests were not ready by that date he would make them be loaded unto the ship, no matter what their condition. After five days, the governor summoned up all his military gumption, questioning the legitimacy of the fugitive canons from a Cathedral that was now in enemy territory. A final appeal, totally ineffective, was made by the canons to the King, and the treasure was now in the hands of Mallorca.

Dr. Calbo left on a ship destined for Mallorca with nineteen crates that included the Holy Chalice of Valencia on February 15, 1812, a fateful night. A tempestuous north wind necessitated lowering the sails, and Dr. Calbo wrote in his memoirs that the gusts of wind were so violent that the schooner would tip to one side so that the mouths of the cannons were hidden at times under the water and the sea beat down on the deck. Llorens Raga comments that it was thanks to Divine Providence that the Holy Chalice was not buried forever under the sea on that uncertain and anguished night. Before nightfall of the next day, however, when the sea had already calmed, the schooner landed at the port of Palma, now faced with new problems as the governing body immediately demanded the cargo, and inquired about the whereabouts of the other crates that they erroneously believed had arrived in Ibiza.

The chests were under the control of an ecstatic Governor for three days, whose euphoria ended when a Royal Order suddenly demanded the entire sacred deposit for the purpose of melting all the silver to make coins. Without any possible recourse against this outrage, the custodian of the treasure, Dr. Calbo, began to conduct an inventory in the Chapter Room of the Cathedral where the cargo had already been transported, attracting crowds of people that wanted to see the Holy Chalice, some even going so far as to handle it without concern for its safety. After several days, with the inventory completed, Dr. Calbo watched helplessly as the first reliquaries and sacred objects were surrendered to the authorities to be melted down after the holy relics had been carefully removed to avoid profanation. Valuable reliquaries, tabernacles, sacred objects, and even an extremely finely crafted altarpiece were destroyed, with the authorities inattentive to pleas to halt the process. By the beginning of May, when it finally seemed that the danger of a second melting had been warded off, a new and even worse storm threatened to break out, this time when Dr. Calbo received an official letter from the Commander General, the marquis of Conpigni, who informed him that he must turn over the remaining silver and gold treasures from the Cathedral of Valencia to Manuel Zizur, the war commissioner in charge of reclaiming precious metal from the Church.

Dr. Calbo expressed his indignation and pleaded with him to respect the historical and sacred nature of the reliquaries, but the commissioner replied with an ultimatum that he appear at the Cathedral where the treasures were kept, in order to comply with the command. Zizur came in person to the Cathedral on May 15, the following day, where he personally carried out a profanation of the religious objects, inconceivable behavior for anyone who was not either insane or godless, as Llorens Raga comments. In seconds he completely destroyed the precious tabernacle, work of the goldsmith Juan Castellnou, with the other objects suffering the same fate. Before the horror and consternation of those who witnessed this iniquitous plundering, he took the reliquaries containing the craniums of Santo Tomás de Villanueva and San Luis, bishop, and placed them between his feet in order to be able to better extract the relics from the silver pedestals on which they had been placed. In the midst of the horrified silence that ensued, one voice suddenly rang out, that of Dr. Calbo, who had taken a reliquary into his hands. Facing Zizur head on, he told him that if he would only reflect on the contents of the reliquaries that he was destroying, he would treat them with greater respect, explaining that the one he was holding was an authentic thorn from the crown of the Lord, given to the Cathedral of Valencia by King Louis of France. Llorens Raga reports that Zizur raised his head with a diabolical grin and answered him insolently, "I will kiss the relic and take the reliquary. You can keep the bone and I will take the meat." That same afternoon all the relics were violently stripped from the reliquaries, and these were transported to the foundry to be melted down and converted into coins, in all, 8,630 ounces of silver and 238 ounces of gold.

Finally on July 5, 1813, Valencia was liberated from the French yoke, although the castles of Denia, Sagunto, Morella and Peñíscola remained in the hands of the enemy. On July 8, at the request of the Chapter of the Cathedral, Dr. Calbo left Mallorca for Valencia, taking with him the Holy Grail and whatever else he had managed to save from the terrible plundering. He arrived on September 25, and the relics were identified and restored to the Cathedral, including the Holy Chalice that had once again survived a very difficult chapter in its history.

The second absence of the Holy Chalice took place during the Spanish Civil War, and will be described in detail in the next chapter; in many ways, St. Laurence's heroic act of salvation is reflected in that of a young Spanish woman of the twentieth century. The relic was providentially saved from the fire and sacking of the Cathedral by several priests and Miss Suey, who only three hours before the turbulence erupted in the Cathedral, took charge of the relic, managing to hide it in various private residences until March 30, 1939, when, with the conflict over, it could be returned to Valencia in the care of the Recovery Committee of the Artistic National Treasury. It was officially turned over on April 9, Holy Thursday, in the Palace of La Lonja, where the services of Holy Week were being celebrated due to the desecration and severe deterioration of the Cathedral. The Holy Chalice was officially reintegrated into the Cathedral on July 9, until then its official feast.

The final departure of the Sacred Cup was triumphal, when on the occasion of the commemorative celebrations of the 17th Centennial of the martyrdom of St. Laurence and the arrival in Spain of the sacred relic, it was taken in pilgrimage in 1959 to the monasteries that had given it refuge during its historical odyssey: Huesca, Bailo, Siresa, Sasabe, Jaca, San Juan de la Peña and Zaragoza. This story, as inspirational as that of the Civil War, will also be described in greater detail in the following chapter as the modern parallel of the Daroca Eucharistic procession, which was accompanied by the population of Aragón en masse, who filled the streets and plazas in the desire to contemplate and venerate the relic that the Spaniards report appeared to be presided over by the image of its savior, the deacon martyr St. Laurence □

Chapter 14

TIME OF TRIAL:
THE SPANISH CIVIL WAR

There is no perhaps no account of danger, courage and the power of providence more inspiring than that of Elias Olmos Canalda[3], who describes the events that took place in Valencia during the Spanish Civil War with the emotion of an eyewitness, causing the reader to experience the same fear that drove the individuals responsible for the safety of the relic to heroic actions in the footsteps of the illustrious St. Laurence, potential martyrs who risked their lives rather than surrender the Holy Grail. Just as in the days of old, when Spain suffered persecution at the hands of the Romans in the early fourth century, this time religious hatred arose from oblivion with the face of Marxism, manifesting itself with the burning of convents, the expropriation of Church property, the suppression of religious rights of the clergy, and restraints imposed on the activities of the religious orders and manifestations of worship in Catholic churches. The priests, religious, and laity of the Church in Spain were the victims of the bloodiest persecution the Church has experienced since that of the Roman Emperor Diocletian: in all, 6,549 priests and 283 nuns were martyred, many in the most classic circumstances of martyrdom, offered life if they renounced their faith and death if they upheld it, in the words of Dr. Warren H. Carroll[4]. The survival of the Holy Grail through the tribulation is a testimony of the power of providence and a profile in courage that makes us aware of our human frailty, as well as of the futility of our own pretenses and disguises, as Robert A. Herrera, Ph.D. proclaims when he questions whether we find ourselves unknowingly in the enemies' camp

---

[3] *Como fue salvado el Santo Cáliz de la Cena.* (Valencia: Imp. J. Nácher, 1959).

[4] *70 Years of the Communist Revolution*, (Trinity Communications, 1989), p.184-185, and 188-189.

by not taking an uncompromising stand against the evils of the moment masquerading as the wave of the future.[5]

Dr. Carroll gives one of the best concise summaries of the causes of the Spanish Civil War, which many today do not understand because they erroneously believe that the war was merely a political struggle between the traditional Carlists and the revolutionary Marxists who established the peoples' republic under Prime Minister Manuel Azaña. As he believes, "The newly established republican government lacked legitimacy in the eyes of many of the people and had become widely discredited by the confusion and near-anarchy that had been its only enduring characteristic since its establishment....Vicious attacks on Catholic churches, monasteries, convents, schools and libraries all over Spain in May and June 1931 had been allowed to proceed unhampered by the government of vehemently anti-Catholic Prime Minister Manuel Azaña; the constitution of the republic, adopted that same year, rejected Catholicism as the official religion of Spain, banned religious orders, and legalized divorce....The chief target of the revolutionaries was not wealthy capitalists nor even persons known or thought to be associated with the military rising, but the Catholic Church." It was a religious war of Reconquest that claimed the lives of thousands of priests, bishops and religious, eighty percent of whom died between July 19 and October 1. In Carroll's estimation, Spain was rescued only in part by her top military officers; it was at least equally the fruit of Christian martyrdom and of the crusading spirit of the almost forgotten movement known in Spanish history as the Carlists.

A foolish leader of the Republic, as Olmos Canalda has written, arrogantly affirmed that *Spain is not Catholic*, and based on these words the leaders of the pernicious regime attacked and tried to erase every sign of Catholicism in Spain. In the process, however, they came up against the Spanish soul, igniting the civil war from which the Catholic spirit of Spain emerged triumphant, contradicting the affirmation of those who believed that it was political, but were ignorant of Spanish character and history. The phobia of those republican leaders who sought to drown the religious sentiment of the country prepared the reaction of the honorable conscience of the people, which was awakened in order to end the "stupid antics" of those who believed they were supporting the new regime by

---

[5] Dr. Robert A. Herrera, Ph.D., Professor of Philosophy, Seton Hall University. Forward, *Catholic Martyrs of the Spanish Civil War: 1936-1939*. By Fray Justo Perez de Urbel. (Kansas City, MO: Angelus Press, 1993).

prohibiting processions and Catholic burials, prohibiting the tolling of bells, and persecuting the priests.

According to Olmos Canalda, the Popular Front took power in February of 1936, initiating a wave of terrorism in which, during only four months, close to a thousand churches were assaulted and burned, and several hundred priests were expelled from their parishes before the passivity of the Civil Guard, who had orders to protect the outlaws, and with whom the government shared its authority and functions. General Franco swore to defend the homeland from the new barbarians, who burned works of culture and art only for the thrill of destroying, not stopping even before the archives of unpublished historical information, such as those of the Ecclesiastical Curia of the Archbishopric of Valencia, with its thirteen thousand files that contained all of the most important information concerning the region and kingdom, from the fourteenth century to the present day. They did not respect sacred relics either, not even the Holy Cup of the Last Supper.

It was during the second wave of violence, beginning on July 19, that the assault on the Cathedral of Valencia took place. As Olmos Canalda relates, on that very day the mobs had assaulted and sacked the College of St. Thomas of Villanueva and burned the Parish of the St. Johns, without concern for its famous and unique paintings by Palomino, and profaned and ransacked the Church and Convent of the Dominicans. Those involved with the Cathedral were harboring a small hope that the authorities would respect that sacred edifice, convinced that a half dozen guards, set aside for the custody of these places, would be sufficient.

On July 20 the Chapter of the Cathedral officially contacted the Governor of Valencia, explaining the danger that was threatening the city. They pleaded with him to send public agents to defend it, convinced that no matter how few they were, they would be more than sufficient to save the Cathedral from the assault of the enraged masses. They asked for this help especially for the Cathedral, citing the innumerable works of art that it contained, whose loss would be irreplaceable for Spain's artistic heritage.

The Governor did not even answer the letter. When those of the Cathedral learned of his attitude the next day, they were convinced that they could expect nothing from the authorities, who had become the accomplices of the outlaws. From that moment on, they were obsessed by one idea: to save the Holy Cup of the Last Supper, the most important of all the relics of exceptional merit possessed by the Cathedral. With that in mind, they celebrated Mass at 9:00 a.m. on the altar of the Most Holy Trinity. At the moment of the Consecration, the hordes were passing in front of the Door of the Apostles in a tumultuous manifestation, singing the International. Fearful that they would burst in, one of the sacristans closed and locked the doors. That was the last Mass celebrated in the Cathedral before the revolution. There were only four people involved with the Cathedral present at the Mass, and two of them communicated to the other two their plan, which was extremely dangerous. Aware of their immense obligations to Valencia and the entire Christian world, they felt certain that their resolution could avoid the loss of the most precious relic of Christianity, the Holy Grail, which proved to be true by the events of the next three hours.

Olmos Canalda, Archivist Canon of the Cathedral, the prebendary Juan Senchermés, the chaplain Juan Colomina, and the sacristan José Folch, took charge of the holy relic, wrapping it in silk paper and concealing it in a newspaper. The greatest difficulty would be to get it out of the Cathedral, because the hordes were camping throughout all of Valencia, and at that very hour they were assaulting and burning the parish churches of San Valero, San Martín, San Bartolomé, San Agustín, and others. Everything would be lost if one of them were recognized by one of the thousands of individuals who made up the masses: their lives, first of all, which they considered to be the least important, and the Holy Chalice, for whose salvation they would gladly die.

It so happened that among the faithful present at that Mass was an unmarried woman named María Sabina Suey Vanaclocha, who was entrusted with the dangerous mission of hiding the Holy Grail. The four people who had conceived the plan gave her instructions to bring the relic to her home, which they thought would be a safer refuge than theirs. Miss Suey, with the Holy Chalice concealed in the newspaper, left the Cathedral at ten o'clock in the morning, followed at a prudent distance by Olmos Canalda and the sacristan Folch, who were determined to protect the precious relic from any unfavorable event. She lived on the Calle de las Avellanas, not a great distance from the Cathedral, but a walk that nonetheless caused them moments of great distress because one of the streets they had to pass, the Calle del Mar, was completely filled with Marxists, armed with pistols and rifles, singing the International. Later they found out that the Communist headquarters were located there.

Less than three hours went by before the Marxist masses broke into the Cathedral, and entering the Chapel where the Holy Chalice was venerated, they burned pews, confessionals, and even the *sacrarium*, or tabernacle. The fire was so intense that it reduced to ashes extremely valuable sixteenth-century tapestries from Valencia, the artistic images and silverwork of the Cathedral, the magnificent silver chest that was used during Holy Week, and the chasuble with which Pope Calixtus II canonized St. Vincent Ferrer, among many other objects of great historic, artistic, and religious value. The Holy Chalice, if it had not been broken by the masses, would have been reduced to ashes by the flames. To make matters worse, when the fire was finally extinguished, a prestigious Freemason of Valencia zealously searched for the Holy Chalice. After several days had transpired, he discovered a clue, and made it known that he had information concerning who had saved it. He announced that he knew that it was being kept near the Cathedral, and that if the relic was not presented immediately to the Marxist authorities, the family who had it would be condemned to death and executed.

In order to better defend the Holy Chalice, Olmos Canalda, along with the priest Plebán de Oliva, Salvador Campos Pons, moved into the Suey residence where the relic was being hidden, but he was only able to remain there from July 22 until August 2, because his house had already been searched, as well as those of some of his friends. He relates that the Marxists were searching for him feverishly, and that it was expected that they would also search the residence of the Suey family, as they were among his friends. This happened on August 8, only days after Fr. Plebán had left because of the imminent danger. This first visit of the Marxists upset the residents so much that these visitors, sympathetically and perhaps even miraculously, decided to postpone the search until another day. At that moment the Holy Chalice was in a drawer of a clothes wardrobe, and would certainly have been discovered if they had conducted a search on that particular day, leaving the residents unable to explain its presence, and consequently subject to the death penalty. From that moment on, the family became concerned with hiding it properly, and for that purpose they concealed the lower space of the wardrobe with some boards painted the same color as the furniture. José Cortés Díaz did the work, helped by the Suey's son, Salvador, who was martyred a few weeks later.

Still determined to find the relic at any cost, twelve armed Marxists arrived once again at the apartment of Miss Suey on August 28. This time they carried out a thorough search, not missing a single compartment or box. They circled around the wardrobe twice, where the Holy Chalice was hidden in the secret compartment they had devised. Miss Suey, with a serenity that surprised even her, aided them in the search and saw their sacrilegious hands only three centimeters from the relics. When the search was finished, they insisted on taking Miss Suey, who asked the assassins to kill her right there. They pushed her violently to the landing of the stairway, and then one of the attackers, moved to compassion before the heartbreaking scene, picked up the young woman and threw her into the room, quickly closing the door. He severely reprimanded his companions for the criminal forces that were driving them, and they responded by calling him a fascist, but descended the stairs nonetheless. Of this man, who had managed to save the life of the caretaker of the relic, the Suey family only knew that his name was Pepe. He left the house that day so moved that four days later he returned to visit the young woman, who asked him why he was in the company of those evil men. He answered, "To satisfy the hunger; for some time I have not had work, and they offered me wages to feed my little daughters."

Fearful because of news of more searches, Miss Suey took the Holy Chalice and moved to the apartment of her brother Adolfo, where they hid the relic in the cushions of a sofa. Although two searches were carried out there, the Marxists did not even approach the place where the Holy Chalice was hidden. Miss Suey, however, felt obligated to move back to her home for greater safety, which she did on January 20, 1937. They moved the relic to another hiding place, in the rubbish cabinet under the kitchen sink, in a specially made niche that they covered with a tiled partition. This mission was confided to Bernardo Primo Alufre, although he never knew what was being hidden there, thinking only that it was some jewels.

At this point the family felt relatively tranquil from their good luck up to this point. One day, however, some construction workers arrived at the door, alleging that they had orders to carry out work in the kitchen, for better hygiene. The family, overcome with terror, decided to take the Holy Chalice to Carlet, a village about 25 kilometers from Valencia. This was the farmhouse where Bernardo Primo was living with his wife Lidia Navasquillo and other relatives, owned by the Suey family. Bernardo, still ignorant of what it was, since the Holy Chalice was wrapped in cotton in a zinc box that was properly closed and sealed, hid the relic in a niche inside a tiled wall made of stone.

There the Holy Chalice remained for the duration of the Civil War. On March 30, 1939, the day after the liberation of Valencia, Olmos Canalda found the box containing the Holy Chalice in the niche, just as it had been deposited. He turned it over to the Reclamation Committee of the National Artistic Treasury, and with the committee members, brought it to Valencia where it was taken to the artist Jesús Sugrañes so that he could clean the agate stone of some marks formed by the humidity, which he did with diligence and skill.

On April 9 of that same year, the feast of Holy Thursday, the Holy Chalice was officially turned over to the Chapter of the Cathedral of Valencia by the commander-in-chief of the army of Galicia, the liberator of Valencia, in the presence of the civil and military authorities of the capital and a crowd of faithful who were present at La Lonja. The services of Holy Week were being celebrated there because the Cathedral had been profaned and destroyed by the Marxists. The Holy Chalice remained exposed to the veneration of the faithful at La Lonja until it was temporarily taken to the private oratory of the Archbishop Prudencio Melo y Alcarde, from where the Archbishop himself moved it to the Cathedral on July 9, 1939, and placed it on the Main Altar, celebrating the annual feast that the Cathedral dedicated to the relic on this day. In the afternoon it was taken in procession to its own chapel, where it remained exposed for the veneration of the faithful.

Olmos Canalda mentions that part of the cotton with which the Holy Chalice was wrapped was divided among several young men who were marching in the front lines. They were told to have faith in what was being given to them, because it had covered a relic. Not one suffered the least mishap; in fact, a plane bomb exploded next to one of these men in Barcelona without anything happening to him.

Olmos Canalda relates one final event that is quite remarkable. In August of 1937 a friend of his by the name of Salvador Simó Fort, was going about camouflaged among the Leftists and would visit the author and his friends monthly in their refuge, although taking great precautions, because their friendship was well known. On this occasion Simó communicated to them that he had overheard a conversation in his presence, no doubt intentional, in which they were being offered 200,000 pesetas and passports for France for the sale of the Holy Chalice. Those who made the offer knew that Mr. Simó knew where they were living and would be able to persuade them to consent to the sale. At that time, some Jews of Amsterdam, residents of Paris, were offering seven million pesetas in gold for the Holy Chalice. They were involved with a Dutch company that bought treasures and valuable objects from Spain.

Mr. Simó, fearing for their lives, because they had been searched for with such determination that a nephew was assassinated for not revealing their refuge, assured the men that his friends were abroad. He then warned them that if they were found, they would be martyred slowly until they revealed the whereabouts of the relic. Olmos Canalda responded with the promise that he would never surrender the Chalice. He had already offered his life to God for the salvation of the relic on the very first day, and believed that his greatest glory would be to suffer martyrdom to save it. Mr. Simó, with tears in his eyes, hugged him, as if apologizing for having hinted at the plan of the Marxists. When he saw those people again, he lied to them, making them believe that his friends were not in Valencia. They stopped looking with so much determination, but after several months went by there was another close call. After reading an article in a newspaper of San Sebastián that affirmed that the Holy Chalice was kept in a field in the area of Valencia, the Marxists pressed Mr. Simó once again to reveal their whereabouts. He refused.

Olmos Canalda believes that it is providential that Valencia has become the reliquary of the venerated treasure, and it would be impossible to argue his point. From all indications – the events of the Valerian persecution and the decision of St. Laurence, the manner in which it was pawned by King Alfonso V el Magnánimo to the Cathedral, its nearly miraculous and providential return to Valencia after the War of Independence, and the incredible courage of those who saved it from the destruction of the Civil War – the Holy Cup of the Last Supper was destined for Valencia, the birthplace of Laurence, its first savior □

Chapter 15

MOMENTS OF GLORY:
THE LAURENTINE CENTENNIAL
AND POPE JOHN PAUL II

The personal sacrifices of those who procured to save the Holy Cup from the terrorists of the Spanish Civil War became manifest in a very special way in two moments of glory: the triumphal procession of the relic through Aragón, in celebration of the commemorative festivals of the 17th Centennial of the martyrdom of St. Laurence and the arrival in Spain of the Holy Grail, and the memorable event of 1982 when Pope John Paul II celebrated Mass with the famous relic in the Cathedral of Valencia, the first Pontiff to do so since Sixtus II, 1,724 years ago in Rome.

The first is described by many of those who were present for this historical odyssey of the Holy Grail to its sanctuaries of the past: Huesca, Bailo, Siresa, Sasabe, Jaca, San Juan de la Peña…, all of those "tough towns and legendary places whose men, in those far off times, knew how to overcome and make flesh and blood reality out of what might otherwise have seemed fabulous illusions," according to José María Lacasa.[6] The following is an eyewitness account given by Manuel Sánchez Navarrete, one of the organizers of the event, with an attempt to preserve the flavor of the original words and his emotional description of this unique event in Christianity.

At the request of some of the towns of Aragón that had once possessed the Holy Chalice, who desired that the relic be allowed to visit those places once again, the Archbishop of Valencia, Marcelino Olaechea, designated a commission to study the possibility. Headed by the Guardian Canon of the Holy Chalice, Vicente Moreno Boria, the President of the Confraternity, Luis B. Lluch Garín,

---

[6] "El Santo Grial volverá a Aragón en el año 1959." *Boletín del Instituto Cultural Hispánico de Aragón*, no. 5.

and the Secretary of the Commission, Manuel Sánchez Navarrete, the commission decided to visit not only Huesca, but also Zaragoza and the other ancient sees of the Holy Chalice, in order to personally determine the extent of love and devotion for the relic that still existed in Aragón. Considering the petitions formally made by the authorities of the towns of Aragón, and the guarantees of security, veneration, and splendor that were offered, the Chapter of the Cathedral, as custodian of the Holy Relic, agreed that it was not fitting to object to the proposals for the pilgrimage. As affirmed in the speech made by José María Lacasa, President of the Centennial Committee, as introduction to the celebration of the Laurentine Centennial, St. Laurence had made it possible by means of the Archbishop of Valencia, who immediately after proclaimed the good news about the spiritual event becoming reality.

It was a festive celebration that nevertheless required long and careful preparation, rather than being a mere outburst of faith and enthusiasm. It occurred in the final days of June, beginning on Monday, June 29, when on a placid and sunny afternoon, the Holy Grail of medieval legend returned to Aragón and made its entrance into the legendary Osca, birthplace of Laurence's parents. It is reported as a moment of indescribable emotion as the population en masse, filling streets and plazas in reverent and expectant silence, pressed together in the desire to contemplate and venerate the beloved relic. Uncontrollable emotion burst forth in a vibrant manifestation of enthusiasm and reverence as the Holy Chalice was carried by the prelate of Valencia, who appeared to be presided over by the image of its savior, the deacon martyr St. Laurence. The military forces paid their honors with shots of canons, as the bands played the National Anthem, whose notes were confused with the voices of the chorus singing Eucharistic melodies, the applause and cheers of the crowd, and the tolling of the bells, all forming a symphony of devotion, faith and love.

First in the Cathedral and then in the Church of San Pedro el Viejo, the ancient Cathedral of Huesca, that same Cup sent to Spain by Laurence, who become the martyr and holy patron of his native land, could be contemplated and venerated by the faithful for several hours. But as the crowning stage of the trip, in which all of Spain was represented by pilgrims who had arrived from the most diverse Spanish provinces, the procession quickly moved into the Monastery of San Juan de la Peña, the Covadonga of the Pyrenees, the place in which the Holy Grail came to be guarded and venerated by the highest authorities of the religious orders of Spain and the ancient Kingdoms of Aragón and Valencia. On this occasion, the pilgrims who had come from all parts, united, knelt down, and paid their homage of veneration in the old and mysterious refuge of the Holy Grail.

The procession into the Upper Monastery, composed of dignitaries and well-known personalities, was headed by the Chief of State General Franco, accompanied by his wife and two ministers; followed by the generals and captains of the Armed Forces, the governors of Huesca, Zaragoza, Valencia and Teruel, and the archbishops of Valencia and Zaragoza, who were accompanied by many bishops; many municipal and provincial mayors and presidents of Valencia, Zaragoza, Teruel, and Jaca; representatives of the courts and universities of Zaragoza, Valencia, and Huesca; the Chapter of the Cathedral of Valencia, accompanied by the Guardian of the Holy Grail, Vicente Moreno Boria; the Board of Trustees of San Juan de la Peña, the Brotherhood of Knights of San Juan de la Peña, the Confraternity of the Holy Chalice of Valencia, and so many other delegations, pilgrims, and faithful that they filled the large church to overflowing, spilling out and almost completely filling the wide area of level ground of San Ildefonso.

As the Holy Grail entered the Monastery, the ecstatic echoes of Handel's *Alleluia* resounded in the air, intoned by hundreds of voices from various choral societies. During the celebration of the Eucharistic sacrifice, officiated by the Bishop of Jaca, when the celebrant arrived at the moment of the ritual in which he slowly repeats the same sacramental words that Christ pronounced: *"Take and drink ye all of this, for this is the Cup of my blood…"*, a tremor of emotion shook those present, who before the real presence of the Cup of the Last Supper, felt themselves transported back in time to the Cenacle on that remote night, laden in mystery.

When the religious ceremony was finished, the procession transported the Sacred Relic to the Old Monastery. There, through the green field, the retinue began to slowly pass: Priests, seminarians, and choir members, intoning Eucharistic hymns; prelates in their choral habits; the messenger of Pope John Paul II carrying the Holy Chalice, with its reliquary now transformed into the custodian of the Most Holy Sacrament; and closing the procession, the municipalities and authorities, all presided over by the highest hierarchy of the State.

The spectacle was impressive and inexpressible. The procession twisted along the steep and sinuous path that descends to the cave that offered refuge to the

Holy Grail, nestled among pines and fir trees, while the children's choral group of Valencia "Juan Bautista Comes," embalmed the setting with their most beautiful melodies. José María Lacasa describes it with these words: "It is Valencia, who, bringing the perfume and fragrance of its flowers, sings through the mouth of those children dressed in white, like doves without gall…"[7]. The procession penetrated into the quiet chapel of the austere enclosure of the historic monastery, and the messenger of His Holiness reverently deposited the Holy Chalice on the same altar table on which it was given silent and hidden veneration for many centuries. The vibrant and majestic chords of *Parsifal*, interpreted by the Municipal Orchestra and the choral societies, then began to resound, as in a fantastic dream, among the unfriendly crags and the thick undergrowth of a scene so extraordinary that only nature itself is capable of creating it. At this moment the testimony of Lacasa derived its greatest meaning and force, as he later reported, *"The souls of the dead of San Juan de la Peña shivered yesterday; even the Kings of Aragón awoke from their eternal sleep and the icons of the capitals opened disproportionately their eye-sockets…"*

At 5:00 in the afternoon of that same day the Holy Chalice left for Jaca, in whose Cathedral of San Pedro the memory of that time in which it was given protective shelter was evoked. Later, as milestones of the road back to Valencia, the procession passed through the Canal of Berdún, Santa Cilia, Javierregay, Hecho, Siresa, Bailo, Salinas de Jaca, Huesca once again, and after various acts of devotion, overflowing with emotion, the final goodbye was given at the provincial border, as the Holy Chalice arrived in Zaragoza.

The relic remained in the capital of Aragón for another memorable day, with acts of inexpressible popular fervor and solemnities of unusual grandeur, and then left for its departure to the capital of Valencia. There were new milestones on the road back, and in each place the same enthusiasm that transformed the trip into a permanent rosary of alleluias was manifest, with the ringing of bells, music, Eucharistic hymns, cheers and applauses; and as a backdrop for all of that, emotion in the souls, and tears in the eyes.

On Sunday, July 5, the Holy Chalice made its return entrance into Valencia, and one of the most joyful pages written in the annals of its religious history and one of the most transcendent of the nation was closed, with the public testimony

---

[7] "El Santo Grial volvió a Aragón en 1959," in the cited bulletin, no.6.

of faith and veneration that was paid to the Sacred Relic.

For this memorable occasion, Francisco Tito, organist of the Cathedral of Valencia, composed the "Himno de las peregrinaciones al Santo Cáliz de la Cena," translated here into English:

> *Let's walk as pilgrims*
> *With faith and burning love*
> *To venerate the Cup*
> *Of our Redeemer.*
> *Jesus used this Cup on the night of the Last Supper,*
> *Night of the sublime mysteries of love,*
> *Night in which He became flesh, divine and Nazarene, in*
> *The bread that the Savior offered to his disciples.*
> *In the blessed Cup, the consecrated wine*
> *Was his precious blood that to the world was being offered*
> *With this Holy Cup the Divine Master,*
> *Instituted that night the Holy Eucharist.*
> *It was you, blessed Cup, sacred recipient*
> *Of the divine blood that redeemed the world,*
> *Today you belong to the Church, the preeminent relic*
> *That proud Valencia preserved in its Cathedral.*
> *From the Marxist invasion, ungodly sacrilege,*
> *The Cup was saved by a prudent hand.*
> *We adore in it the Holy Eucharist,*
> *The God of all love, Jesus in the Blessed Sacrament.*

Pope John Paul II and the Holy Grail

The visit made by Pope John Paul II to Valencia, on the occasion of his memorable trip to Spain in 1982, was singular in nature and of extraordinary importance in its meaning. On November 8 the successor of St. Peter once again took in his hands the same Cup used by Jesus to consecrate his blood, becoming the first to do so since Pope Sixtus II, just before he entrusted it to his deacon St. Laurence 1,724 years earlier. On this memorable occasion more than one hundred new priests were ordained on the esplanade of the Alameda of Valencia.

As Sanchez Navarrete reports, "if these were for His Holiness moments of intense emotion, when it was possible for him, continuing in the line of his most remote predecessors, to officiate once again with this venerable relic and repeat again over it those words that Peter initiated and that have been established in the Canon of the Mass: *This is the Cup...*, they were even more so for the faithful of Valencia, when in the great esplanade we were able to contemplate in his hand how the Holy Cup of the Lord was raised. Already moments before, in his brief passage through the Cathedral, John Paul II had shown his emotion when contemplating and holding in his hands the Sacred Relic, at the same time that he was listening to the explanations that were being given to him by the Archbishop of Valencia, Miguel Roca Cabanellas, and the Canon Director of the Confraternity of the Holy Chalice of Valencia, Vicente Moreno Boria, and above all, when kissing the Sacred Cup twice with devote unction."

As a historical endorsement of his visit, John Paul II deigned to accept the insignia of Knight of Perpetual Honor of the Holy Chalice, granted by the Confraternity, and recorded his signature on the sheet of parchment, that embellished with its coat of arms and legend, is an eternal testimony of that event in the *Libro de Oro* of the Confraternity. As a gift of the diocese to the Holy Father, he received an exact reproduction of the Holy Chalice, done by the goldsmith of Valencia Francisco Pajarón Andreu, who is also responsible for the monstrance that is taken in the processional entourage on the Feast of Corpus Christi. This duplicate of the Holy Chalice donated to John Paul II, was recreated, detail-by-detail, with stones similar to those of the original and with identical metals; the agate stone, because it is not found in Spain, had to be brought from Germany.

This transcendental event is recorded as follows:

The Governing Committee of the Confraternity of the Holy Cup of the Last Supper, established canonically in the Holy Cathedral Metropolitan Church of Valencia, wants to record in name and representation all of the Brothers, the most sincere testimony of its gratitude to the Most Excellent and Reverend Archbishop of Valencia, Dr. Miguel Roca Cabanellas, the Most Illustrious Dean, Dr. José Mengual Sendra and the Very Illustrious Vicente Moreno Boria, Canon Director of the Confraternity, for having served and directed the fervent desires of our Confraternity, in this memorable trip of His Holiness the Pope, John Paul II, to Valencia, completely achieving the realization of the following transcendental acts in the history of the Confraternity, that appropriately are enumerated here as a reliable record of the same:

FIRST. – That His Holiness Pope John Paul II has accepted the insignia of Knight of Perpetual Honor of the Holy Chalice that has been granted to him by the Confraternity.

SECOND. – That the Holy Father has stamped his signature on the sheet of parchment that, embellished with its coat of arms and legend, figures in first place in the Libro de Oro of this Confraternity.

THIRD. – That the last Pope who used this Holy Cup in the consecration was Sixtus II, in the year 258. And today, after 1,724 years, our Holy Father, John Paul II, has celebrated the solemn Eucharist of the priestly ordination, in the same Cup in which the Lord converted the wine into His Precious Blood, thus fulfilling with this act the great hope maintained for many years by the Confraternity of the Holy Cup of the Last Supper.

Valencia, November 24, 1982.

The President of the Governing Committee, Luis B. Lluch Garin

I testify: The Secretary of the Confraternity, José Ferrer Olmos

According to the author, with this act, "a milestone of transcendental importance was reached in the annals of the Holy Chalice, an affirmation of the mystery initiated almost twenty centuries ago in the Cenacle of Jerusalem that today is projected and perpetuated in the marvellous book of a history filled with the sublime Wagnerian resonance of mystical ecstasy, that in the sombre enclosure of the Chapel of the Holy Grail harmonizes completely with the pious and admirable veneration of the faithful before the most illustrious and moving Eucharistic relic ever preserved by humanity. It is a history that continues being written daily with a liturgy and veneration that have been perpetuated throughout the centuries." □

Poster of the Centennial of the Martyrdom of St. Laurence. Huesca, 1957-1958.

Part 6

ARCHAEOLOGY
SUPPORTS THE PAST

Archaeology neither proves the contrary to be true, nor censures the substance of the tradition concerning the Holy Chalice, but rather supports and confirms definitively its historical authenticity, because it can make, emphatically, the following affirmation: The Chalice of the Cathedral of Valencia – understanding as such the upper cup – could have been on the table of the Last Supper. It could have been the one that Jesus Christ used to drink, or to consecrate, or for both things. If someone were to find arguments against one of the affirmations or hypotheses of this work, the strong archaeological possibility that the Holy Chalice of the Cathedral of Valencia is the Cup of the Last Supper would nevertheless remain on firm ground.

Dr. Antonio Beltrán

213

Chapter 16

DESCRIPTION OF THE HOLY GRAIL

Mention is made of the Holy Chalice of the Last Supper in the document of its surrender to King Martín el Humano in 1399, but without describing it. This is not the case, however in the inventory of goods made in Barcelona in 1410, at the death of this king, nor in the inventory of 1437, where, when recording the surrender of the Sacred Chalice to the Chapter of Valencia, it is described with the characteristics that are repeated in later inventories by the various authors who have written about it, such as Sales, Sanchis Sivera, Sangorrín, and others. In this second document, dated as being written on Monday, March 18, 1437, the inventory of all the relics belonging to Alfonso V appears, and the Holy Chalice is described as follows:

First of all, a pine box covered with red cloth, trimmed with white ribbon, with the shields of Aragón and Sicily, within which were found jewels and following items...; Item, the Cup in which Jesus Christ consecrated his Blood on Holy Thursday of the Last Supper, made with two golden handles, whose base, of the same color as the upper Cup, is adorned all the way around with gold, with two rubies and two emeralds on the base of the Chalice and with 28 pearls, comparable to the thickness of a pea, around the base....

Confirmation of this information is owed to Dr. Antonio Beltrán, Archaeology Professor at the University of Zaragoza, who provided the exact measurements of each one of the pieces of which the Sacred Cup is composed. The first exhaustive scientific study of the Holy Grail of Valencia was carried out in 1960. The then Archbishop of Valencia, Marcelino Olaechea, petitioned Dr. Beltrán to proceed with the analysis *as if it were the matter of an object found in an excavation.* Keeping in mind all of the aspects of the problem, Beltrán proceeded with a detailed archaeological study that allowed him to dismantle everything and examine in detail all of the parts of this historic relic. The result of this work, which is the first and only scientific study carried out on the sacred relic, was subsequently published[1] and concludes that the Holy Chalice of Valencia is formed by three distinct parts, all from different epochs.

At first sight those who are sceptical of relics might very likely make the error of believing that the Holy Grail of Valencia could not be authentic because of its rich adornment with jewels. According to Beltrán, it has been true throughout the centuries that popular devotion tends to enrich and adorn religious objects of veneration, and in his expert opinion, it is only the upper cup, made of stone, that could have been on the table of the Last Supper.

1. The upper cup

The upper cup, according to Beltrán, was made from chalcedony, which is a conglomerate of submicroscopic crystals of quartz, in a variety called cornelian, of a cherry red color, also known by the names of carnelian or oriental cornelian. It could also be sardonyx, which has a blood red or reddish brown color, and even shows on one of its sides a wide grayish vein very similar to that of agate. As all of these classifications have a very close relationship, it would be impossible to determine the stone exactly without destroying the integrity of the cup. A system, described by Pliny, was also in use at that time, which consisted of submerging cups made of native agate in oil, so that each one absorbed it unpredictably; later they were boiled in sulphuric acid that attacked and modified in a unique way the organic material that impregnated them, thus converting the stone into colored material. This process would explain the diverse colorations of the bands or veins that appear on the cup.

The upper cup is approximately semispherical in shape, and is completely smooth, in the interior as well as on the exterior, without any adornment, with the exception of a very simple engraved line, very regular, which runs parallel to the border and a short distance from the edge. It was originally done with extremely careful workmanship, without any defects or irregularities, but now there is an obvious break, approximately through the middle that divides the cup

---

[1] Antonio Beltrán, *El Santo Cáliz de la Catedral de Valencia.* (1st edition, Valencia, 1960; 2nd revised edition, 1984).

in two parts; next to the edge these two halves show broken lines produced on the same occasion, with a minuscule portion missing today. It measures 9.5 cm average diameter at the mouth, 5.5 cm of interior depth, and 7 cm from the base to the edge. The thickness is approximately 3 mm, because it is slightly irregular. It is finished with a small base or foot that serves to keep it erect on the table. This base is now covered by the gold that forms the upper part of the center, but is easily visible in the spaces that are left by its irregular form. This circumstance is owed to the restoration of the break suffered in the eighteenth century; when gluing the bottom of the cup to the upper part of the center piece, the centers did not line up exactly. The accident occurred during the services on Good Friday, April 3, 1744, when the Holy Chalice slipped from the hand of the priest as he was taking it from its chest, breaking into two halves, with two small pieces breaking from each half. The pieces were glued together and the cup was then strongly glued to the golden center; only a small chip is missing today.

The variation of colors in the upper cup is quite remarkable, described as a "live coal" in the description given by Agustín Sales in 1736:

> The cup of the Lord, the Holy Cup of the Last Supper, is of oriental agate cornelian stone, which is agreed upon by the most renowned lapidaries who have investigated its substance with complete diligence; and it is found with this name in the Inventories of the Sacred Relics of the Metropolitan Church of Valencia. I know well that many authors affirm that it is chalcedony, but they are not correct… for not having consulted the archives of the previously mentioned Metropolitan Holy Church. The color of this Sacred Cup is so strange and extraordinary that, when turning it, different bands are being formed… and if it is indeed appears at first sight like a live coal, nevertheless, as it is such a beautiful stone, tinted with different colors, no one has been able to explore the nature of its principal color, not due to the intervention of the miracle, as the common people think, but because of the natural virtue of agate stone. The sacred cup is the size of half of a large orange, with a capacity for ten to twelve ounces of wine, four fingers tall, and it lacks any external adornment.

2. The Base

The base is formed by an oval basin, inverted in the shape of an incense burner, which is of the same color and similar material as the cup, although very distinct and inferior to it, as much in the quality of the workmanship as in the stone itself. It is not made of shell, as Agustín Sales believed, but rather of chalcedony, with a brilliant color and very translucent to light. It is, however, in need of a careful cleaning so that its beauty would be more apparent, as it is now darker and more opaque than it should be. The axis of the base measures 14.5 cm in the major axis and 9.7 cm in the minor central axis, and has an almost rectangular base with the sides rounded, set in the interior, with 4 and 3 cm of major and minor axis respectively, and a height of 5 mm. It has an openwork adornment of pure gold, with a very Gothic appearance, on which are mounted 27 pearls, two rubies, and two emeralds of great value.

Beltrán suggests two hypotheses: either a worship incense holder was used as the base of the cup, which was already embellished with a golden ornamental line along the border, or this adornment was added when the Cup was mounted so that it would be the part in contact with the supporting surface. In this case, the second golden border that surrounds the edge of the incense holder would have been added later, perhaps for reasons of safety. There is no doubt that the braces that support the stones and pearls and the base that supports them are a later addition, judging by the tiny steel plates that fasten the pins, clearly superimposed and of a different gold color.

On one of the principal slopes of the base, on its left side, an Arabic inscription is engraved, discovered, studied, and translated for the first time by Dr. Beltrán, and later by the Canon Lector of the Cathedral, Juan Angel Oñate, who contributed new studies and interpretations in his book *El Santo Grial*. No one has yet been able to decipher exactly the meaning of the ancient Arabic letters

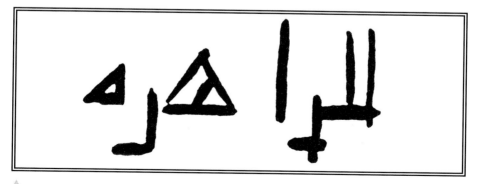

Arabic inscription on the base of the Holy Chalice. Dr. Antonio Beltrán.

in the mysterious inscription of the base, although there are several possibilities.

Beltrán believes there are two possible interpretations of its meaning: *1)* If *li-lzahirati* is transcribed, the text would have to be translated "for he who shines" or "for he who gives radiance," meaning "for God," which would be in agreement with his opinion that the vessel could have been used as an incense burner. *2)* If *lilzáhira* is transcribed, the text would have to be translated as "for the most prosperous," understanding that it is referring to the *alcázar* that Almanzor ordered built in Córdoba, being one of its expensive vessels, *made in Córdoba and not imported from the East.* According to Beltrán, this discovery is important, since normally this type of piece with precious stones is assumed to be from commerce with Egypt or Syria. It does not exclude the possibility, however, that when this vessel arrived in the West, it was used as an incense burner and that it was then carefully chosen to adorn the Cup as a base worthy of such a marvellous object.

If it is not the case that the base was imported from the East and marked later, which he does not believe to be true, one of the most important consequences of the discovery of the Arabic inscription is to connect it with the name of the place of Almanzor as the product of a workshop of Córdoba. The palace was the *Al-Madina al-Zahira*, the "flourishing city," that received the name in imitation of Medina al-Zahra that began to be built in the year 368 of Hégira, or in the years 978-979 AD. This building consisted of a great mosque and a renowned *alcázar*, or royal palace, that was marvellous. The construction was finished in the years 980-981 AD and was governed by the powerful Almanzor while the caliph Hixem II in residence; new work was done until the year 997, and at his death Almanzor passed the power on to his son, Abdelmlic the Muzzafar, who built a new palace, "Al-Hayibiyya," where he celebrated great feasts until his death in 1008, with Abd-al-Rahman Sanchol occupying the palace at that time. Mohammed ben Hisam, who later would be caliph, rebelled in 1009 with the title of Al Mahdi, making his prime minister Al-Mujira attack Al-Zahira, which was taken, sacked, and destroyed on February 9 of that year. Nothing remained of the splendor of those buildings, which were all razed to the ground. According to Torres Balbás, there is nothing left other than the trough of the "Arabic Patio" that is in the National Archaeological Museum of Madrid, and Levi Provençal adds to that three boxes of marble, one of doubtful authenticity.

Oñate, however, disagrees with Beltrán's conclusions, considering unlikely the reading of the Arabic inscription as *li-lzahirti*, or *lilzáhira*, the origin and dating of the chalice as from Córdoba, between the tenth and twelfth centuries, that the different parts of the chalice were put together in San Juan de la Peña, or that the upper cup was free-standing until the fourteenth century. He considers it most probable that the four gold strips that join the agate base to the rest of the chalice could have been added in Zaragoza from 1399 to 1410, because they are the most imperfect and even the color of the gold is different, and thinks that the pearls and precious stones would have been placed on the base at that time, although they could possibly be older. He doesn't believe that the inscription, that is said to be Arabic, has been correctly read or interpreted.

To ease his doubts concerning the interpretation of the inscription, Oñate consulted with an Arabic scholar, Dr. Youssef Al-Farkh, who testified that it must be read *ALMAGD LIMARIUM: GLORIA A MARIA.* He added that the inscription was made on the chalice much later by someone who did not know Arabic well, because the lettering is very crude, Mozarabic without doubt, explaining that an Arab of the lowest class writes better than that and with a more elegant style. Another expert in Arabic told him that these words could mean "Glory to the son of Mary."

In view of that interpretation, Oñate does not consider the conclusion valid that the base of the Holy Grail is the product of a workshop in Córdoba, dated between the tenth and twelfth centuries, with no other foundation than that of the reading and interpretation of *lilzáhira.* He personally believes that the knot is earlier than that, and the same for the handles, as well as the supports that join the Grail to the base. The knot does not appear to be Gothic to him, nor does its ornamentation.

He believes that the following are indications that the upper cup was not free-standing, or without any ornamentation until the fourteenth century: *1)* There is a rim or groove that runs around the edge of the cup that he thinks indicates that it was made to support a piece of precious metal. *2)* The entire border of the agate base is covered with a very fine and narrow strip of gold, and it seems likely that this gold engraving, and probably the handles as well, were part of the decoration of the cup before it was incorporated into the current chalice. *3)* There are cups of this type that have preserved their original decoration or framework, like that of the Museum of Copenhagen, from the third century at least.

Oñate has developed his own hypothesis concerning the origin of the gold work and jewels that were added to the upper cup. The Reliquary of the Crown of Aragón was extremely important in the time of King Martín el Humano, and among his relics there is believed to have been a chalice that was said to be that in which Jesus Christ consecrated at the Last Supper. King Jaime II had petitioned the sultan of Egypt, Abulfat Mahomet, son of King Almanzor, for this relic by means of an embassy in September of 1322. As it was well known that the Holy Grail in which the Lord consecrated at the Last Supper, that according to the tradition of Aragón, St. Laurence had sent from Rome, was in the old Monastery of San Juan de la Peña, it is logical to assume that the ecclesiastical advisors of the king induced King Martín el Humano to ask for that Holy Grail from the monks of the Monastery, for his chapel. When the Holy Cup arrived in the Aljafería of Zaragoza, the chalice petitioned from the sultan in 1322 would have been added to it as a base, since it was believed that both were from the Last Supper of the Lord.

Oñate believes that this hypothesis would resolve various problems, such as the Arabic inscription of the base, perhaps engraved when it came to Spain, the separate dating of the gold work of the Chalice that was in San Juan de la Peña, and the later dating of the gold supports that fasten the base to the rest of the Chalice, which were modified for that purpose.

There are various problems with this theory, however, according to Dr. Beltrán's analysis of the letter in question. First of all, the presence of the Holy Chalice at the Monastery of San Juan de la Peña was not well known, and it is quite possible that King Jaime was unaware of that fact. There is no documentation indicating that the sultan ever surrendered to the King another chalice reputed to be that of the Last Supper, and therefore, Oñate is merely making an assumption not based on factual evidence. The same letter also requests a large piece of the True Cross, which was already in Rome at the time, and the remains of St. Barbara. There is another letter from King Jaime to the same sultan, dated July 3, 1327, in which another request is made for the body of St. Barbara, but there is no longer any mention of the Holy Chalice or the True Cross. The sultan sent his answer to the king of Aragón after King Jaime II was already dead, promising to send him the body of St. Barbara, which never arrived, and did not name any of the other petitions of the king. It is a bit farfetched to assume that the sultan actually sent another chalice from the Last Supper, which now forms the base of the present relic, as there is no evidence that this was ever in his possession, and much less that it was ever given to the king of Spain. Beltrán gives the letter little importance, noting that according to the mentality of the epoch, innumerable petitions were made to the Turks, and merchants going to the Orient, especially those involved in trade with the Muslims, which reached its peak during the time of Almanzor and his son. These sultans began to import, for the women of their palace, planks of the wood from Noah's ark and hooves from the donkey of Uzayr; in fact, the women of the harem of Hixem II ended up with eight hooves from this mythical animal in their possession.

Oñate always believed that as the reading and interpretation of the inscription has never been definitive, it might possibly be ancient Hebrew rather than Arabic. He travelled to Jerusalem and consulted with several scholars, some of whom said it was Arabic and others that it was not. In L'Ecole Biblique they thought that it was Hebrew, but they could only distinguish letters rather than words, and could not interpret them. P. Piccirillo of the "Studium Franciscanum" studied it and according to him, it should be read as *Al-Zāhirah*, or the "rich or opulent one," an interpretation still far from conclusive. Oñate is also inclined to believe that the word *grail (graal, grail)* is not derived from the Latin *gradalis* or *gradale*, but rather from the Hebrew *goral*, meaning "stone of luck," and that is why one would say that the Grail is *lapis exilis*, meaning "fine or precious stone," from which is derived *lapis ex caelis*, or "stone from heaven."

From all of this, one might deduce that Oñate is leaning toward a possible Palestinian origin of most of the chalice as it appears today, with the exception of the jewels and some of the gold work, which certainly seems possible according to his theory. I sent the inscription to Yael Yisraeli of the Israel Museum, however, who is in charge of archaeological display units. She responded that the inscription is "clearly Arabic," not Hebrew, and supports Dr. Antonio Beltrán's interpretation of its meaning. Oñate's arguments that the upper cup could not have been freestanding, or without ornamentation, until the fourteenth century, do not hold up well under examination. The fact that there is a rim or groove along the upper edge of the cup does not necessarily indicate that it was placed there to support a piece of precious metal, because as Beltrán believes, it could be purely ornamental. This style of cup, not the traditional Christian chalice, was the normal drinking vessel in the first century for meals such as the Last Supper, which was clearly not a Jewish religious ritual in Beltrán's opinion. At the same time, a cup made of precious stone was definitely that of a rich house (Mk 14:13–15; Lk 22:10–12), and the Gospels agree that Jesus used a cup for the consecration, in Latin, *calix*. The engraving on the gold work appears to be Gothic, and the agate base is of an inferior quality and clearly not as old as the upper cup. As there does not seem to be any solid evidence to support this possibility, it seems likely that Beltrán's dating of the three components is fairly accurate. Exactly when they were joined together might be impossible to determine, but it does appear certain that this occurred at some moment during the Middle Ages, possibly before the relic went to San Juan de la Peña.

According to Beltrán, documents of the Palestinian region indicate that there is a type of cup without handles in the Judaic cycles, with the semispherical cup having a wide base that is joined to it by a narrow cylindrical stem, without a knot. This type of cup was used for the offerings of wine resulting from the *minschah*. It is said that this goblet or cup is the so-called "cup of Salvation" alluded to in Psalm 116:13-14, and is depicted on coins. It happens that this type of cup was known and relatively abundant among the upper Jewish classes, especially among the priests who used them for religious rituals, but it was not for common usage. In any case, Beltrán is convinced that the base, knot, gold work and jewels are not nearly as old as the upper agate cup, the only part of the Holy Chalice that can be dated to the first century, in his expert opinion.

3. The knot, the gold work and the stones and pearls.

The central stem with its knot, with a total length of 7cm, serves as the element that joins the cup and the base, with the addition of the handles and gold adornment, finely engraved, that supports the setting of pearls and stones on its base. The description of Sales is quite vague, which says that "The stem with its knot measures three fingers, and the two handles are of extremely pure gold with different and exquisite engravings that denote its great antiquity. Finally, the entire Sacred Cup, that is almost a palm from the top of the cup to the base, is neither so large that there would be leftover, nor so small that it would lack suitable drink for all those who drank of it."

The *knot* is a flattened drop joined by two stems of hexagonal cut, whose upper part ends in a recipient in the form of a cylindrical trunk of something more than 1 cm in height, in whose interior the base of the cup has been glued. *Two handles* in the shape of half of the letter "S" join the upper and lower extremes of the centerpiece. The gold is finely engraved with intertwined knots with a background of vermicular motives and an enamelwork appearance. The entire central stem and each one of the sides of the polygonal stem have quadrifoil rosettes with a striped center, and in each one of the four angles there is a punched vegetal motif. On the two lateral exterior facets of the handles there is a very beautiful gothic vegetal motif, of small leaves combined at both sides of the central nerve. Beltrán describes the knot and handles as a "medieval jewel," and insists that it would be completely impossible to defend a common date for the chalice in its entirety.

The pearls have always been described as the "thickness of a pea" and are most likely from two epochs, but old for the most part; only one is modern, and

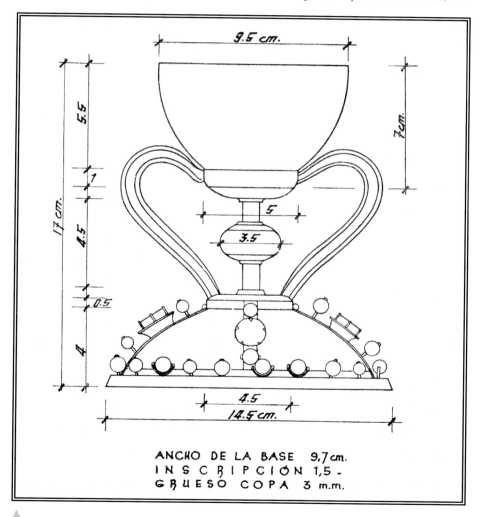

ANCHO DE LA BASE 9,7 cm.
INSCRIPCIÓN 1,5 -
GRUESO COPA 3 m.m.

Measurements of the Holy Chalice. Dr. Antonio Beltrán.

some are dirty and in poor condition. One of the emeralds is from the thirteenth or fourteenth century, and another was placed in June of 1959. The authentic one measures 1.5 x 1.5 cm and is extremely thin, of a pale green color. The beryls, similar to rubies, but of a darker color, are arranged on both sides of the center of the minor axis. The lack of faceting was already noticed in 1812 by silversmiths of the Casa de la Moneda in Palma; they show a practice that was common in the twelfth to the fourteenth centuries, which was the hollowing of hard stones in their interior, until they were reduced to a type of lens or concave crystal of very little thickness, which made them shine in the light, even though they didn't have cut edges.

After objectively examining these three parts, Beltrán concluded: *1)* That two of them are autonomous and that in a determined moment they were joined together by the third, meaning that the two cups were joined by the stem with its knot. *2)* That the only part that continues to fulfill its original purpose is the cup, while the base was once an extremely valuable piece, demonstrated by the gold trim that borders it. The gold work, apart from its functional value of serving to unite the cup and base, was added to adorn the simple cup as a sign of the esteem in which it was held.

With respect to its historical authenticity, Beltrán made the following affirmations: *1)* That the upper cup dates to the epoch between the fourth century BC and the first of the present era, and more specifically, in the second century BC to the first century AD, made in an oriental workshop of Egypt, Syria, or Palestine itself. For this reason it could have been on the table of the Last Supper, used by Jesus Christ to drink, consecrate or for both purposes. *2)* That the basin of the base, possibly from a workshop in Córdoba, is dated to between the tenth to the twelfth centuries AD, and was added to the cup around the fourteenth century as a sign of its exceptional importance. *3)* That the handles, knot, and gold work, as well as the stones and pearls that adorn it, are later, from the twelfth to the fourteenth centuries, and could be the work of a Gothic goldsmith, knowledgeable in the oriental and Mediterranean techniques and even possibly Moorish, done when the relic was being venerated in San Juan de la Peña, since in 1399 it already appeared as we see it today and thus it was recorded in the inventory of 1410, done upon the death of King Martín el Humano. The Chalice as we see it today was not modified at all in the Cathedral of Valencia, except for the restoration of 1744 and the substitution of some of the pearls, and of a stone in 1959. The rest is intact at least since the fourteenth century.

Based on his archaeological study, Dr. Beltrán has said: "Archaeology neither proves the contrary to be true, not censures the substance of the tradition concerning the Holy Chalice, but rather supports and confirms definitively its historical authenticity, because it can make, emphatically the following affirmations:

1) The Holy Chalice of the Cathedral of Valencia – understanding as such the upper cup – could have been on the table of the Last Supper. It could have been the one that Jesus Christ used to drink, or to consecrate, or for both purposes.

2) That being of a date prior to the celebration of the Last Supper and of oriental workmanship, the Holy Chalice that left San Juan de la Peña in 1399 had to have arrived at said monastery before this date, with it being of no importance for the question of its authenticity as Cup of the Last Supper the way and the moment in which it arrived there.

3) The base is an Egyptian basin or caliphal from the tenth or eleventh century and was added, with rich gold work, to the cup around the fourteenth century, because it was firmly believed at that time that it was an exceptional piece. And not being because of its material, manufacture or adornment, one must think that its importance resided in the contact that it had with the hands and the lips of the Lord.

4) If someone were to find arguments against one of the affirmations or hypotheses of this work, the strong archaeological possibility that the upper cup of the Holy Chalice of the Cathedral of Valencia is that of the Last Supper would nevertheless remain on firm ground."

After studying these conclusions, the Archbishop of Valencia, Marcelino Olaechea, wrote the following words in the prologue of Dr. Beltrán's work:

Before beginning the study, (Beltrán) nobly warned us that if he arrived at the conclusion that this cup is not authentic, the presumed Cup of the Last Supper of the Lord, he would say so with complete frankness. We encouraged him to do it, coming straight to the point, because we only wanted the truth, be what it may. And the truth, concerning Archaeology alone, here you have it, reader. If you believe in the pious tradition that has never been denied, tradition that is taken into account even today, and almost six centuries of history, you will feel reinforced in your belief. Take and read. If you don't believe, take also and read, because as an honest man, you will stop laughing at those who believe. Archaeology not only doesn't prove the contrary, nor censures the substance of the tradition, but supports it… The Cup of the Cathedral of Valencia could have been on the table of the Last Supper… □

Chapter 17

ARCHAEOLOGY OF
THE HOLY GRAIL

U ntil the archaeological investigation of Dr. Antonio Beltrán in 1960, the Holy Cup had never been treated from that point of view with the attention it deserves, perhaps because it had never been observed in a detailed manner due to emotion and reverence for the relic. It has always been described in a nebulous, inaccurate, or even contradictory manner, even by individuals renowned in the world of art history, like Elías Tormo, who gave two different descriptions, both inaccurate, saying first that the base, knot, handles, and decoration are a splendid example of Byzantine gold work, dating back to the first millennium of the Church, and only a few years later wrote that the gold work might be Romanesque, and more probably German than Byzantine, and that the technique of mounting the stones was perhaps French, thirteenth century.

Already in 1945 Beltrán was convinced that the parts of the Holy Cup were from different epochs, but as he was also limited to a superficial observation of the relic, the description he made at that time is also rather vague, and mistakes the base as being made of "shell":

The Holy Cup, the most notable relic of the Cathedral, is one of the most renowned in the world. It is the one that, according to tradition, Jesus Christ used in the Eucharistic Meal. It was taken by St. Peter to Rome, was sent by St. Laurence to Huesca during the persecution of Valerian, and in 713 went to San Juan de la Peña, from where Martín el Humano transferred it to Zaragoza (1399) and Alfonso V to Valencia, with Juan II surrendering it to the Cathedral (1437). The semispherical cup is of oriental cornelian, fine stone of a dark red color, from the Roman or Alexandrian epoch, and the shell base with a gold mounting and applications of stone and pearls (done later), links the Holy Cup with the medieval Eucharistic tradition and the modern Wagnerian ones. San Juan de la Peña and the Cup of Valencia could be Montsalvat and the Holy Grail of the legends of the Middle Ages.

Beltrán emphatically affirms that it cannot be maintained that the cup and the rest of the chalice are of the same epoch. When referring to the jewels and the mounting, a dating in the fourteenth century or a little before is certain, with a previous date, perhaps toward the tenth century, for the incense burner that serves as a base. The problem of the authenticity of the Cup depends exclusively on the cup itself, with the epoch in which the base and the gold work were added being relatively unimportant.

He affirms that one of the problems has been that the majority of the writers who are concerned with the Holy Chalice try to find a basis for their arguments in the liturgical form that the ancient consecration vessels took in the fourth century, but these chalices were composed of a cup with a base, normally concave, and of a stem that united both parts, with a central knot. At the Paschal Meal, however, there were no Christian chalices on the table, but cups of common usage. Jesus drank and consecrated in a cup or vessel of those that were used for the table service, in the shape of a bowl with a small base to support it. Beltrán oriented his investigation by searching for the cups that could have been kept in the cupboards of a rich house of Jerusalem in the first quarter of the first century, especially one that would have been used by a wealthy host to honor an exceptional guest on an occasion of ritual importance. He believes that it is logical and understandable that a cup of this kind would have been later embellished and completed with a rich base, along with gold and precious stones, so that it would fit the ritual form of the Christian cup, because there are a notable number of similar cases in Europe from the thirteenth to fifteenth centuries.

The word *cáliz* originally comes from the Greek *kylix* and is a ceramic type of drinking cup, with a wide and circular mouth and shallow, a cup with a base and handles disposed horizontally at the level of the mouth. These clay vessels were soon copied in other, more expensive, materials, especially in metal, and gems and adornments were added to them until they became, at the end of classical antiquity, deep goblets with handles or without, mounted on a tall stem with a wide base. The Romans called this kind of cup *calyx*, and they were of common usage in feasts and banquets in the first half of the fifth century BC.

When speaking of table vessels and drinking cups, Beltrán notes that there are examples of vessels in the Near East of extraordinary antiquity, done in stone, that may date back to prehistoric times. Ancient Egyptian workshops sold their products throughout the entire eastern Mediterranean, with their vessels being especially popular in Crete and Syria. They used hard stones, as well as soft ones like alabaster. It is not surprising, therefore, that stone cups were found in Palestine from the second century BC, with excavations of the near East revealing a millennium style, in these Syrian lands, of stone vessels. It can be added that in Palestine, in all of the levels of the ancient Biblical cities that have been excavated, a type of goblet or cup with a stem has also been found, often done in stone. When found associated with ritual objects they are classified as a cup of libations.

In Egypt, Syria, and the lands of the Eastern Mediterranean, the fabrication of stone vessels, at times rather large and with ornamentation, but normally of small sizes and frequently used on luxurious tables, was common in Greek and Roman times. They were used prior to the end of the first century AD, because at that time they were almost completely replaced by glass cups, beautiful and inexpensive, which definitively banished stone cups from the marketplace, because these were so costly and difficult to make.

Pliny tells us that the ancient civilizations prided themselves on making cups of expensive or precious stones to drink *(potoria)*, and transmitted to us the system that the classical artisans used to achieve greater shine and luminosity in the agate objects by treating them with oil and sulphuric acid. It is evident that in the Eastern workshops located in Egypt and Syria, from Alexandria to Antioch, many vessels were made from fine, hard stone, such as jasper, chalcedony, agate and sardonyx.

While these cups were expensive, they were not unusual in the first half of the first century. In fact, there are two examples in the British Museum in London that are almost identical in size and shape to the agate cup preserved in Valencia. Both are dated 1-50 AD, one made of chalcedony and the other of sardonyx, stones closely related to agate and carnelian. The chalcedony cup is translucent light tan with some darker brown streaking, while that of sardonyx, a variety of chalcedony, has bands of dark-brown sard and lighter chalcedony. Carnelian, or cornelian, is a translucent, semiprecious variety of chalcedony that owes its reddish-brown color to iron oxide, highly valued by the Greeks and Romans who used it in rings and signets. Agate, another variety of chalcedony, occurs in bands of varying color and transparency, occurring in cavities in eruptive rocks or ancient lavas.

228

Sard and sardonyx are historically two of the most widely used semiprecious stones, having been used in engraved jewelry for centuries, and came from Sardis, the ancient capital of Lydia. Sard, agate, and carnelian are all mentioned as adorning the breastplate or *hoshen* of Yahweh's high priests in Ex. 28:17; 39:10. Four rows of precious stones were mounted in gold filigree work on this embroidered breastplate, three in each row. The twelve different stones matched the names of the sons of Israel, and each was engraved like a seal with the name of one of the twelve tribes. It is also quite interesting that agate was used in antiquity by fishermen who submerged it in the sea hanging from a string when they looked for pearls. For that reason this stone has been compared to St. John the Baptist, who pointed out the spiritual pearl with his words, "Here is the Lamb of God."

The word *grail* itself supports the authenticity of the Holy Chalice of Valencia, believed by many scholars to have originated from the old Spanish word *graal* or *grial*, meaning drinking vessel or cup, as in the writings of Cervantes, the Archipreste de Hita or Amadís de Gaula. Most scholars believe that the word is derived from the Latin *gradale*, *gradalis* or *grasale*, which Helinandus informs us means a wide and somewhat deep dish, in which "costly viands are wont to be served to the rich successively, one morsel after another." Spanish is the only language in which the word evolved to mean cup; in the other European languages the original Latin *gradale* acquired variations more in harmony with the meaning of a wide dish. For example, in old Languedoc and Provençal *grazal* or *grasal* was a large earthen dish, and the Norse *gryta* was a pot. This suggests that the meaning was taken from the Spanish rather than the original Latin and its derivatives in other Romance languages, with the word *seynt* or *san* added in the Middle Ages to signify the Holy Chalice used by Jesus at the Last Supper. *Seynt Graal* was used in early French verse to signify the Last Supper cup, indicating that the French word *graal* was borrowed from Spanish rather than derived directly from the Latin. This supports the presence of the relic in San Juan de la Peña because it is only in medieval times when the word begins to appear in French and English as *graal* or *grail*. Skeat indicates that the two words *san graal* or *san grail*, or *holy grail*, were turned into *sang real*, or *sangre real*, meaning *royal blood*, closely related to its significance as the cup used by Jesus during the first Consecration. The explanation of *san grial* as *sang real* was not current until the later Middle Ages when the legends of the Holy Grail were circulating.

229

Oñate is inclined to believe that the word *grail* (graal, grail) is not derived from the Latin *gradale* or *gradalis*, but rather from the Hebrew *goral*, meaning stone of destiny. From this came the Latin expression for the Grail, *lapis exilis*, or insignificant stone, and *lapis ex caelis*, stone from Heaven. Wolfram von Eschenbach seems to agree with this interpretation, as his grail is a stone rather than a cup, and it is possible that his word *gral* was derived from both sources, as the words are so similar.

As Beltrán points out, between the first and fourth centuries we have very little graphic or concrete information with respect to cups in general and the Holy Cup of the Last Supper in particular. But there is nothing that might be opposed to the relic of Valencia being the Holy Cup of the Last Supper, because, although its tradition can never be proven, there is not even one testimony or argument against it being true. Also, if the Cup had still been in Rome after Constantine's Edict of Milan in 313 AD, it is strange that it would not have been mentioned in fourth-century references, and it is therefore logical to assume that it was no longer in the Eternal City. When persecutions ended in the first part of the fourth century, the peaceful period of the Church was accompanied by splendid donations to the churches, carried out by Constantine. The notice of Pope Silvester I (314-335) in the *Liber Pontificalis* (I, p.170), includes a complete catalogue, which records fabulous riches in chalices of gold and silver, including the *scyphi* or small Episcopal chalices, and the *amae*, of a larger size, used to receive the oblations of the faithful. From then on, chalices were a fundamental part of the ecclesiastical treasures.

Relics and their veneration played a fundamental role in the religious beliefs of medieval man, and as a consequence, monasteries were preoccupied with possessing a good number of them, because they gave prestige and were a source of revenue, due to the fact that pilgrims came from far off places, soliciting petitions and giving thanks for the favors received with many pious donations. It is perhaps for this reason that the medieval literature fueled by the Holy Grail reached such importance, giving impetus to the fact that many monasteries came to be attributed with the distinction of being in possession of the precious cup. When the sixteenth century arrived, the number of cups that claimed the honor of being the authentic one used by Jesus at the Last Supper had risen to at least twenty. But, little by little, in a long process of verification, one after another of the claims fell, so that in the eighteenth century there were only eight cups being considered in the dispute: four of them in France (Lyon, Reims, Albi and

Brionda), one in Flanders, another in Genoa, that of Jerusalem – which had disappeared – and that of Valencia. Added to these is the cup of Antioch that was found later, in 1910. Today, none of these can be considered authentic, with two exceptions: the Holy Chalice of Valencia and the silver cup of Antioch, which as will be explained, may be the second cup from the Last Supper, used at the Passover meal rather than the consecration.

The cup of *Lyon*, France, made of emeralds, turned out to be a gift from Charlemagne to the Cathedral of Lyon, without any information about it given when it was donated.

The cup of *Reims*, France, of silver, is shown with an inscription engraved in its base that accredits it as having been donated to that Cathedral by its Archbishop St. Remigio in the year 545.

The cup of *Albi*, France, lacks documentation or any tradition that would support its authenticity, and the same can be said of that of Brionda, in lower Auverne.

The cup of *Flanders* was a lie propagated by an annotator from Valencia. There is no documentation of any kind, nor any tradition that alludes to it.

The cup of *Genoa*, known as *Sacro Catino*, is not really a cup but a plate, and not of emerald, as it is said to be, but of vitreous paste and an irregular shape, with six points, which because of its shallow depth and perimeter of 1.20 m, could not have served as a vessel for the wine of the consecration, but could certainly have been used to offer the Paschal lamb. The people of Genoa have never called the *Sacro Catino* the Holy Grail, nor have they ever venerated it as such. According to the beautiful legend that surrounds it, the Queen of Sava, so renowned for her magnificence and beauty, when she arrived in Tyre from Jerusalem, acquired among other riches this *catino*, which was found in the Temple of Hercules, entrusted later to Solomon, who at that time was constructing the magnificent temple that bore his name. The years passed and after the destruction of the temple, the precious plate was saved, which ended up in the hands of a descendent of the owner of the house in which the Lord celebrated the Last Supper, and on whose table was among the best objects that the owner possessed, who put to the service of the Divine Master the beautiful plate that he had inherited from his elders, along with the cup that is venerated in the Cathedral of Valencia.

In 1103, after the sacking of Caesaria, the relic was snatched by the Spaniards from the Arabs, who kept it for some time in Almería, until the city was conquered by Alfonso VIII, in 1147, in an alliance with the people of Aragón and

Genoa, who were satisfied when they were in possession of the precious plate as booty and a prize for their help. This legend, taken from the Spanish chronicles, is rejected by the people of Genoa, who affirm that the famous *catino* was conquered by the Crusaders under the command of Guillermo Embriago, in Palestine, who gave it to his Cathedral. Another writer, Rev. Walter K. Skeat, reports that it was shown in Genoa as a relic until Napoleon I transported it to Paris. In 1815 it was sent back to Genoa, but was cracked during the journey. When Oñate visited the treasury of the Cathedral of St. Laurence in Genoa in August of 1950 he was told that the people of Genoa had never believed that it was the Cup of the Last Supper, but something, perhaps a plate, that the Master had used on that occasion, and that had no support other than tradition.

The cup of *Jerusalem*, recorded by the Venerable Bede, probably disappeared due to the entry of the Arabs in the city, in the time of the Calif Omar. It was a silver cup that would have been seen in a small chapel of Jerusalem, in the niche of a pillar, by the French Bishop Arculf around the year 720, according to the narration that the presbyter Adamnan made of the trip. Because of its wide mouth, handles, and two-liter capacity, it might very well have been the vessel that on the night of the Last Supper would have served to prepare the wine. Interestingly enough, this cup fits the description of the silver cup of Antioch, found in the twentieth century.

The famous silver cup of *Antioch* was unearthed quite recently and is today kept in the Museum of New York. The Spanish authors are skeptical of its authenticity, reporting that "not only its antiquity lies in a sea of ambiguities, because it very possibly is from the fourth or fifth century, but it also has been proposed by one scholar to be a modern falsification, without in any way being affirmed that it was the Cup of the Last Supper." Some eminent archaeological and scientific authorities believe that it is genuine, however. It was discovered in Syria during the drought of 1910 when people were forced to dig for roots to keep from starving, unearthing dry wells in the process that yielded all kinds of treasures. A number of altar vessels were found in one of these dry wells, among them a chalice that immediately attracted the attention of historians and scientists who called it the Chalice of Antioch.

This vessel has two parts: the inner cup is made of antique plain silver, with a capacity of two and a half quarts. The outer chalice is also of silver, intricately carved with more than 240 designs, including animal and botanical forms, two figures of Christ, and additional human figures arranged in two groups of five each. The depiction of ten figures instead of the usual 12 that would represent the apostles is rare, and according to Dr. William Newbold of the University of Pennsylvania, one group represents the Church of the East, and the other the Church of the West. He believes that placing two groups of five men in a position of authority and prestige could only have occurred in the period immediately following 50 AD, a time when two Christian churches existed: the Church of Jerusalem and the Church of Antioch, each governed by five men. He is also convinced that the inner cup is older than its holder, which appears to have been made to preserve and exhibit it.

Professor Gustavus Eisen, an authority on early Christian art and the former curator of the California Academy of Science, agrees with Dr. Newbold, after studying the chalice for nine years and writing two books on the subject. He believes that the inner cup is the Holy Grail used by Jesus at the Last Supper. It is speculated that the cup was brought to Antioch by Barnabas and Saul, and eventually entrusted to the care of the faithful. In *Acts of the Apostles*, it is recorded that the Church of Jerusalem sent Barnabas to Antioch. When he arrived and saw the grace of God at work there, he went to Tarsus to look for Saul, "and when he had found him he brought him to Antioch. For a whole year they met with the church and taught a large number of people, and it was in Antioch that the disciples were first called Christians" (11:22-26).

The seventeenth-century Spanish historian Gaspar Escolano may have already provided the solution for this seeming contradiction when he wrote about the silver chalice, also from the Last Supper, that is mentioned by Baronio in the twelfth century and appears in the work of the Venerable Bede. He believes that Jesus used two cups on the night of the Last Supper. According to St. Jerome, a silver cup was used for the dinner of Passover lamb, and one of stone for the institution of the Eucharist. As mentioned, the silver cup was later placed in a hollowed pillar in a plaza of Jerusalem, holding the sponge that was offered to Jesus on the cross, covered by an iron mesh through which the pilgrims would insert their fingers. With its rather large capacity, the silver cup of Antioch better fits the description of a dinner cup than one used for the consecration, and may very possibly be the second cup of the Last Supper, the cup of Jerusalem that was lost, also used by Jesus, but not the Holy Grail.

It is interesting that few seem to have made this connection between the cup of Antioch and that of Jerusalem, which is perhaps due to an overzealous interest in ruling out any cup with a competing claim to authenticity, especially one that has only recently appeared on the scene, which would make the skeptic suspect fraud. There are, nonetheless, no other possibilities with regard to the authentic Holy Grail, meaning the cup used for the consecration of the wine, than the Holy Chalice of Valencia. If we look at the history of the two cups in question, both with serious claims of authenticity, it is not difficult to see which was which. The Holy Chalice of Valencia was used by the first Popes to say the Mass, saved by the martyr St. Laurence who sent it to Spain, enveloped in mystery during the Middle Ages, nearly destroyed during the Spanish Civil War, and has been the object of continuous veneration by the faithful. The silver cup used for the Passover dinner, lacking any particular spiritual significance, was exposed for veneration but not used liturgically, and possibly brought to Antioch by Barnabas and Saul where it was cared for by the faithful and eventually lost for many centuries. Although it is at the very least a strong possibility that the silver cup of Antioch could indeed the lost cup of Jerusalem, also used at the Last Supper, it can never claim to be the Holy Grail, and it can therefore be concluded that the Holy Chalice of Valencia is the only reputed Holy Grail in the world that has a legitimate claim to be the genuine vessel used for the consecration, made of stone as described by St. Jerome □

Part 7

VENERATION OF THE HOLY GRAIL

Cup of the Holy Supper
That contained the Blood of God
First payment of pain;
Valencia feels filled
With your Eucharistic love!

Cup of Grace:- of both Testaments
fulfils the wonders – your Holy liquor.
Let your Blood fall – on this Christian
people of Valencia – bowed down
in your honor!

Divine relic – the highest glory
of all history – from faithful Valencia.
Because, dyed in your blood – rubies of light!
says our Cross – that Christ is your King.

Hymn to The Holy Cup

Chapter 18

DEVOTION TO
THE HOLY CHALICE

Valencia has always been proud of its unique role as custodian of the Holy Chalice of the Last Supper of the Lord, carrying on the tradition of veneration that was begun in apostolic times until the martyrdom of Pope Sixtus II, and continued in the sacred confines of San Juan de la Peña where with the Chalice "the Abbots, priors and presbyters of the Monastery were accustomed to consecrate," as affirmed in the document of surrender to King Martín el Humano on September 26, 1399. From the year 1437, when the Holy Chalice was deposited with other relics in the Sacristy of the Cathedral of Valencia, and until 1914 when it was transferred to the Old Chapter Room, converted from then on into the Chapel of the Holy Grail, the veneration of the Holy Relic can be summarized as follows: 1) Exposition for public adoration on certain occasions, 2) Public veneration on Holy Thursday and Good Friday, when it was used to preserve the Sacred Host in the Tabernacle, 3) Institution of an annual feast in its honor, and 4) Some sporadic processions, predating the annual feast, such as that which was celebrated for the occasion of the coming of Phillip II.

Exposition for Public Adoration

No one knows exactly when public veneration began, although it is believed that it was shortly after the Holy Chalice was surrendered to the Chapter of the Cathedral of Valencia in 1437. Nevertheless, it is known that in the fifteenth century the principal relics of the Cathedral were exposed for public veneration on Good Friday, and the Holy Chalice was not one of these.

In the sixteenth century the Exposition of the Relics was celebrated on

Easter Sunday, a date that was moved to the Monday of Easter Week on April 20, 1610. This custom lasted well into the nineteenth century.

From 1828 until 1914, it is certain that the Holy Chalice was exposed for the veneration of the faithful, along with other relics, in the Small Reliquary Chapel in the apse of the Chapter Room, every Thursday at 10:00 a.m. after Mass. The sacristan in charge of showing the relics would come out dressed in a surplice and stole, clenching a pointer in his right hand. As soon as the candles of the Altar of the Reliquary were lit, he would indicate that those present should kneel, after which he would open the door of the Reliquary, and kneeling down himself, would proceed to point out the relics one by one, while another sacristan read the name and origin of each one of them.

As he pointed to the Holy Chalice he would say: "On this silver pedestal is kept the Most Holy Cup in which Jesus Christ our Lord consecrated his most precious Blood and gave it to drink to the Apostles the night of the Last Supper in the Cenacle. It is of oriental cornelian agate stone.

"This sacrosanct relic reminds us of the great mysteries that the most sweet Jesus worked on behalf of mankind, and in particular, reminds us of the Mystery of the Institution of the adorable Sacrament of the Eucharist: food, consolation and hope of fervent souls. Let us give praise, then, with all our hearts to the Most High, for the honor that he has granted to Valencia among so many Catholic peoples and nations, and let us endeavor that this so singular treasure be a constant motive in us of admiration, love and thanksgiving toward divine goodness.

"Indeed, beloved Jesus, seal and strengthen with your grace the firm resolution that today we make of loving you, reverencing you and rendering you continuous kindnesses and tributes in the Most Holy Sacrament of the Altar, where humbly we adore your Most Sacred Heart, in which we desire to live forever and take our last breath at the moment of death. Amen."

Today the Holy Chalice is always exposed for public veneration in the special Chapel of the Holy Grail; there are no ceremonies or rites employed for its contemplation, and the visitor can approach the monstrance and admire the extraordinary relic up close during the hours when it is open to the public.

The Holy Chalice was formerly used during the services of Holy Thursday and Good Friday as the receptacle for the Sacred Host that was reserved in the Tabernacle. This beautiful custom was ended by a serious and unexpected accident that occurred during the services of Good Friday, April 3, 1744. The Archdeacon of the Cathedral, Vicente Frígola Brizuela, was officiating, assisted by the Archbishop, Andrés Mayoral, when, as the celebrant was taking the Sacred Host from the Holy Chalice, the agate cup detached itself from the golden base and fell to the floor, breaking in half, with two smaller pieces breaking off the edge of each one of the two pieces. The assistants were overcome with emotion, particularly the officiating Canon, who died some time afterwards from grief, as was recorded by his contemporaries. All of the fragments were collected with the utmost care, and enclosed with the other parts of the Holy Chalice in the small silver coffer in which it was kept in the Tabernacle; they were then carried to the Chapel of the Relics. That same afternoon the master goldsmith Luis Vicent was called, and aided by his two sons Luis and Juan, he repaired the agate cup right there, in the presence of several canons and of the notary Juan Claver, completing his work so perfectly that even today the fracture is barely noticeable, with only a tiny chip still missing as evidence of the tragedy.

So that no one could ever cast doubt on the authenticity of the Sacred Relic as a result of this event, the canons and the goldsmiths who intervened in the repair swore that all of the repaired fragments were the same ones that broke from the Cup, and they notarized the record of the occurrence. To avoid the possibility of any new accident of the same kind, the Chapter of the Cathedral agreed that the Holy Chalice would no longer be used in the services of Holy Week, and another gold chalice was donated for that purpose by Vicente Frígola, who had involuntarily caused the accident.

From then on the Holy Grail was no longer transferred during Holy Week, but in 1939, after the relic was returned to the Cathedral of Valencia after the events of the Civil War, the turnout of faithful who came to venerate the Holy Chalice on Holy Thursday was so great that the narrow access corridor that leads to the Chapel from the main part of the Cathedral became completely inadequate to accommodate the numbers. In light of that situation, the Chapter was compelled to agree that on that day the Holy Chalice would be exposed for public veneration in the Chapel of the Resurrection, located in the retro-choir in the ambulatory of the Cathedral. This was accomplished by transferring the relic to this chapel in the morning, in a devout processional entourage and under canopy, where it was illuminated profusely with fluorescent light inside a glass beacon in the middle of the altar, protected by closed grilles. A large crowd would then begin to flow through the ambulatory, and the faithful would not stop circulating for the rest of the day, anxious to contemplate the Holy Grail until the Chapter of the Cathedral would arrive in procession at 8:00 in the evening. Following the same ceremony, the relic was then transferred to the Main Altar for the celebration of a solemn Holy Hour in which each one of the Canons of the Cathedral would preach, and when the hour was over it was returned with the same pomp and circumstance to the monstrance of its Holy Chapel.

Institution of an annual festivity in its honor

Until the seventeenth century it is not known if there was any particular festivity in honor of the Holy Chalice, but an important event did take place in 1608 as the Canon of Valencia, Honorato Figuerola, was dying. This distinguished prelate, born in Valencia, was greatly devoted to the Holy Chalice, and after promoting the celebration of very solemn veneration in its honor, set out to work with great determination so that the devotion that was already being professed for the relic by so many faithful would grow from day to day. As one more proof of his dedication, for the purpose of assuring continued veneration of the Holy Relic after his death, he set up a trust so that a solemn feast could be celebrated each year in honor of the Holy Chalice and the Most Precious Blood of the Lord "with first Vespers, Mass, Sermon and second Vespers, all accompanied by the organ, as on the day of Corpus Christi"; two processions, one of the Chapter in the morning, and the other public, with the same route as that of the Corpus, in the afternoon, so that the Archbishop in charge of the Archdiocese would be petitioned that such day be declared a feast. He also left money for the construction of a glass Tabernacle so that the Holy Chalice could be seen without touching it, and worthy of carrying the Sacred Relic in the procession.

The last will and testament of Figuerola was recorded by the distinguished Archbishops San Juan de Ribera and Fray Isidoro Aliaga, who were favorably receptive to the idea. After carefully examining the documents in favor of the authenticity of the Holy Chalice, they definitively approved the proposal.

Sánchez Navarrete points out that San Juan de Ribera was a great lover of relics, but was so critical of their authenticity that he ordered that all those in his possession be scrutinized carefully, and that those that in his judgment did not satisfy the necessary conditions, be burned. Nevertheless, as far as the Holy Chalice was concerned, he not only accepted it with complete objective and moral certainty, but also did whatever was in his power to propagate its devotion and veneration. He became so intimately convinced of the authenticity of the Holy Chalice that as proof he left a written handwritten note in his Bible that is now kept in his famous Colegio del Corpus Christi. In the passage where St. Matthew (26:27) speaks of the Last Supper of the Lord, the word *calicem* is underlined, and in the lower margin of the page, written in Latin in his own handwriting, the notation proclaims his belief in authenticity, which begins by saying, "This Cup is kept to the present day in this, our Cathedral Church of Valencia."

In order to fulfill the conditions prescribed by Figuerola, the annual Feast of the Holy Chalice, which became extraordinarily popular, was celebrated on different dates throughout the years that followed: on September 14, the feast of the Exaltation of the Holy Cross; the feast of St. Matthew; the first Sunday of July, feast in Valencia of the Most Precious Blood of the Redeemer; since 1903, again on September 14, because the particular prayer of Valencia in honor of the Most Precious Blood of Christ Our Lord had been suppressed; later, on the first Sunday of July, and later still, on the second Sunday of October or November.

The solemnity of the feast declined for a time, to the point that it passed unnoticed by most of the faithful, due principally to the sale of Church property decreed by Mendizábal, when the State took possession of all administrative goods. The beautiful monstrance disappeared in 1812, work of the craftsman Jorge Cetina of Valencia, in order to be converted into coins by the Government, as described previously; later the government appropriated the belongings of the Foundation, and not having the means to finance the Feast, it was reduced to what in the Cathedral is called *dobla mayor*, or a procession through the interior of the Cathedral in the morning and the afternoon.

In 1888 the Feast of the Holy Chalice once again regained its solemnity, thanks to the Archbishop of Valencia at that time, Cardinal Antonio Monescillo, the great devotee of the Holy Chalice who set out to renew the splendor of the Feast in honor of the Sacred Relic, which became second only to Corpus Christi.

240

Up until this time the Holy Chalice was still kept in the Chapel of the Relics of the Cathedral, but in a session of the Chapter, celebrated on March 1, 1915, they agreed to accept the motion promoted by its Dean, José Navarro Darás, asking that the precious Relic be exposed for public veneration and that for that purpose a chapel be dedicated to it, as the esteemed relic merited and as the devotion of the people of Valencia demanded. Shortly after, on May 15 of the same year, the Chapter offered the prelate Valeriano Menéndez Conde the Old Chapter Room as the best place for such a precious treasure, and the Archbishop approved and blessed the initiative that very soon became reality. The Holy Chalice was solemnly transferred to this Chapel on the Feast of the Epiphany of the Lord in 1916, with a massive turnout of parishes, authorities, and faithful. It is still kept in this same room, now called the Chapel of the Holy Grail.

Veneration of the Holy Chalice in the Cathedral of Valencia

After the terrible strife of the years of the Civil War, 1936-1939, when the Holy Chalice was recovered from its hiding place in the niche of Carlet, a renewed fervor was soon displayed toward the relic, impelling the Chapter of the Cathedral to approve the regulations necessary for the constitution of a Confraternity of the Holy Chalice in their session of December 15, 1939.

The recently named Archbishop of Valencia, Dr. Marcelino Olaechea, piously converted by the Holy Chalice after his arrival, set out with enthusiasm to intensify devotion to the relic, with the solid cooperation of the authorities, clergy, and faithful of the city and diocese. An important step in the execution of this objective was given in a special session of the Chapter on September 16, 1948, presided by the Archbishop, in which he made known his desire to collaborate with them in the promotion of the knowledge and veneration of the Holy Chalice, proposing to establish a position for that purpose, called the Guardian of the Veneration of the Holy Chalice, a proposal that was immediately accepted. This was awarded to the Very Renowned Dr. Benjamín Civera Miralles, who on October 14, 1948, took over the job. He has been responsible for the following:

1) The restoration of traditional veneration.

2) The institution of the "Thursdays of the Holy Chalice," with the celebration of a Mass in the morning and a Holy Hour in the afternoon, so that every Thursday, the day when the Lord instituted the Holy Eucharist and consecrated his divine Blood in this Cup, the faithful could express their acknowledgment for such an immense gift and reiterate their thanks for the honor granted to the Cathedral when it was made the guardian of such an exceptional relic.

3) Giving new impetus to the Royal Brotherhood of the Holy Cup.

4) The foundation of the "Confraternity of the Holy Chalice," whose statutes were approved *ad experimentum* on March 25, 1952, and definitively on November 25, 1955.

5) Finally, the promotion of jubilees, pilgrimages, visits of parishes, schools and other entities, so that all the faithful would be able to collectively venerate the Holy Relic.

A new Guardian of the Holy Chalice was designated on March 3, 1957, the Most Excellent Vicente Moreno Boria, who not only continued the work begun by his predecessors, but who also, as a fervent devotee of the relic, sought to intensify veneration to the Holy Grail as he believed it deserved, being the relic in which Jesus consecrated his divine blood in ratification of the New and Eternal Covenant. The fruit of his preoccupation for increasing veneration has been, under the concession granted by the *Motu Propio de Pio XII «Sacrum communionem»*, being able to celebrate the Vespertine Mass. The Chapter of the Cathedral proposed changing the veneration on the "Thursdays of the Holy Chalice," with the celebration of the Holy Mass in the afternoon and before the Exposition of the Blessed Sacrament. The first Vespertine Mass was celebrated on April 25 by the Archbishop Marcelino Olaechea, and from 1958 on it is celebrated on the first Thursday of each month.

Additionally, the Chapter approved the celebration of special events in the Chapel of the Holy Grail, including weddings, baptisms, and First Communions, and the almost uninterrupted passage of faithful and pilgrims, who come from many foreign countries to venerate the Holy Grail, or the Holy Cup of the Last Supper of the Lord.

Two other annual acts of extraordinary solemnity were established. The first is the celebration of the "Day of the Holy Chalice" whose date was designated for Holy Thursday, and whose program of services now include a Holy Hour, Procession in the Cathedral and public act in honor of the Holy Chalice, a Prayer Vigil before the venerated Relic, and Exposition of the Holy Chalice to the faithful.

The second is commemorated on the last Thursday of October. It consists of *1)* Processional transfer of the Holy Chalice from its Chapel to the Main Altar of the Cathedral. *2)* Concelebrated Eucharist, presided by the Most Excellent and Reverend Archbishop of Valencia when possible, with the attendance of the Chapter, and representation of the clergy, Royal Brotherhood, Confraternity and faithful devotees of the Sacred Relic. *3)* Praying the regulatory supplications to the Holy Chalice. *4)* The return procession of the relic to its Chapel, during which the "Gozos al Santo Cáliz," in the version of the language of Valencia, are intoned, composed for the commemorative edition in 1959, in honor of the 17th Centennial of the relic's arrival in Spain. It appears here in Spanish and English:

AL SANTO CALIZ DE LA CENA
EN EL XVII CENTENARIO

Diecisiete Siglos ahora se cumplen desde que recibió el SANTO CALIZ la noble estirpe de los Iberos, pletórica de dicha por semejante don.	It is now seventeen centuries since the HOLY CUP received the noble stock of the Iberians, full of joy for such a gift.
El pueblo de Valencia, al festejar el honor que le cabe de poseer prenda tan excelsa, invita al pueblo cristiano a venir aquí para adorar el TROFEO sagrado.	The people of Valencia, when celebrating the honor they have of possessing such a sublime object, invite the Christian people to come here to adore the Sacred TROPHY.
Acudan los habitantes de Huesca, y el pueblo fiel de Zaragoza, y las piadosas gentes de Iberia a contemplar en nuestra catedral el Relicario de la divina Sangre.	The inhabitants of Huesca come, and the faithful people of Zaragoza, and the pious peoples of Iberia to contemplate in our cathedral the Reliquary of the Divine Blood.
Dense cita en nuestra ciudad los sacerdotes, las supremas jerarquías nacionales, los ciudadanos, las autoridades: visiten todos la Capilla	From this meeting in our city the priests, the supreme national hierarchies, the citizens, the authorities: all visit the Chapel

do se guarda la preciada RELIQUIA.	where the precious RELIC is kept.
¿Desean evocar los sacerdotes la muerte de Cristo y renovar su Pasión? Este es el CALIZ que ellos habrán de ofrecer y apurar.	Do the priests desire to evoke the death of Christ and renew his Passion? This is the CUP that they will have to offer and drink.
¿Siente el pecador ansias de purificación? Lave las manchas del alma con ese líquido del que se llenó este CALIZ santo en la cruz de Cristo.	Does the sinner feel the desire for purification? Wash the stains of the soul with that liquid from which this holy CUP was filled on the cross of Christ.
¿Quieres aprender a llevar el CALIZ de Jesús? Toma en tus manos la copa del dolor que Dios quiso escanciarte, y apura su contenido.	Do you want to learn to bear the CUP of Jesus? Take in your hands the cup of sorrow that God willed to serve you, and drink its contents.
Qué placer se experimenta, al nimbar con el incienso del amor ese VASO sagrado de Cristo, cuyo fulgor nos circunda, mientras profieren jubilosos nuestros labios estas sentidas palabras:	What pleasure is experienced, when surrounding with the incense of love that holy CUP of Christ, whose splendor surrounds us, while our joyful lips utter these meaningful words:
"¡Oh CALIZ de Cristo, recipiente que contuvo el precio de la Salvación el mundo! Los corazones de la hispana gente, siempre generosos, te ofrendan en esta ocasión el cántico de sus alabanzas."	"Oh CUP of Christ, receptacle that contained the price of the Salvation of the world! The hearts of the Hispanic people, always generous, offer you on this occasion the canticle of their praise."

Luis Casanoves Arnandis.

Catedrático del Seminario de Valencia, Canónigo de la S. I. Catedral

Chapter 19

THE HOLY CHALICE REPRESENTED IN ART

There are many relics in the world that do not offer the evidence of authenticity that the Holy Chalice of Valencia claims, and certainly not a single other grail that has any possibility of being authentic. What is most striking about this relic, however, beyond its tradition and history, is that it is not treated as an archaeological object, a beautiful chalice of agate, gold and jewels, or even as a historical piece, but rather as a living reality. Especially for the people of Valencia, it is the symbol of a presence, the icon of a Sacred Mystery and the testament of a Master, as Asunción Alejos Morán writes. In the words of poetry, it is a silent testimony of the depth, width and height of Someone who is hidden, it is quiet music in the midst of noise, graceful movement of the Spirit, refreshing drink for thirst, wine that strengthens the weak…it is the bridge that leads to the eternal. To contemplate it is to transcend it and to possess it is supreme. The Holy Chalice is not only present in art, but art is present in the Holy Chalice, because only from the aesthetic vision and poetic emotion that borders eternity, where language dissolves into the ineffable, can we approach the ultimate meaning that only reveals itself in what is small.[1]

To experience the Corpus Christi procession in Valencia, or the Feast of the Holy Grail in October is to begin to understand the meaning of the mystery. The Holy Chalice is not a thing, but a symbol of the living presence of the Risen One that permeates the enclosure of the Cathedral, and is then carried through the streets to the people in a living testimony of faith that can only be fully comprehended in a country that has suffered religious persecution and

---

[1] *Presencia del Santo Cáliz en el Arte* (Ajuntament de Valencia, 2000), p.123.

martyrdom. It embodies the full significance of the word *relic* for early Christians as a silent witness to uncompromising faith. It is the "blessing cup" of St. Paul, the "Lord's cup" of St. Athanasius, and the "mystical cup" of St. Ambrose: it is the symbol of Redemption expressed by the iconography of the Crucified One, from whose wounds flows the blood that is collected by angels in chalices, the origin of the theme of Christ as the Fountain of Life.

The Holy Chalice venerated in the Cathedral of Valencia is therefore not only a historic object, a relic, a memorial of the Passion, and a symbol of the Eucharist, but also, in a certain sense, it is a true "icon," which means that it is not merely a pure art object, but "theology in image," that announces and makes present the Gospel proclaimed by the word. Although in a strict sense the icon is an image of a sacred person, especially Christ, the Virgin or the Saints, we can consider the Holy Grail as a true icon that represents the "Cup of Salvation" through which we were redeemed by Christ.

This is explained by Leonid Ouspensky [2] as follows:

There are no words nor colors nor lines which could represent the Kingdom of God as we represent and describe our world. Both theology and iconography are faced with a problem which is absolutely insoluble – to express by means belonging to the created world that which is infinitely above the creature. On this plane there are no successes, for the subject itself is beyond comprehension and no matter how lofty in content and beautiful an icon may be, it cannot be perfect, just as no word or image can be perfect. In this sense both theology and iconography are always failures. Precisely in this failure lies the value of both alike; for this value results from the fact that both theology and iconography reach the limit of human possibilities and prove insufficient. Therefore the methods used by iconography for pointing to the Kingdom of God can only be figurative, symbolical, like the language of the parables in the Holy Scriptures.

The icon functions as a call to the contemplative faculty of the spirit, to the imagination, so that it may decipher the meaning and the message of the symbol and capture its figurative and symbolic nature, though real, of what lies beyond human knowledge. In the true sense of the word, this describes the Holy Chalice of Valencia perfectly, for it has truly transcended the status of historical and artistic object to become the Holy Grail of the legends, sought by all, recognized by few, and saved at the cost of life itself. Bearer of a message of utmost

---

[2] Ouspensky and Lossky, *The Meaning of Icons*, p.48-49.

importance, it is enthroned in the Chapel of the Holy Grail, carried with pomp and circumstance through the streets of Valencia, and celebrated in processional hymns and prayerful devotions. The transcendence of the Holy Chalice of Valencia is nowhere more apparent than in art, which manifests itself abundantly in the icon of the Holy Chalice venerated in Valencia, its presence in painting, the expression of the relic in the floral displays, floats and music of festive processions, and in the heraldry of the shields and coats of arms of the Brotherhoods and Confraternities.

Devotional Expression

The oldest reference to the veneration attributed to the Holy Chalice in the Cathedral of Valencia dates from the beginning of the sixteenth century, when the relics were taken from the chests in which they were kept, to be shown to the faithful. It was taken in procession on the occasion of the visit of Felipe II to Valencia, and in the supplications organized on behalf of the success of the Invincible Armada in 1588, when Juan de Ribera personally carried the Holy Chalice. After the feast was instituted by Honorato Figuerola, approved by the Archbishops San Juan de Ribera and Fray Isidoro Aliaga, the date was fixed for its celebration, which was to be six months after the feast of the Most Holy Sacrament, on Friday. It was also ordered that an expensive silver tabernacle be constructed, of great beauty, on which would be engraved the Arms of the Most Noble House of the Figuerolas. This first monstrance existed at least until 1812[3]; when it disappeared, along with many other liturgical objects of gold and silver, the so-called *"Anda de la Camiseta"* was used for the procession, constructed for the relic in 1691 by the Florentine artist José Seguen, also of silver and crowned with the Child Jesus embracing a cross.

The monstrance used today is a monumental tabernacle more than four meters in height, constructed of silver, gold, platinum, and a large number of precious stones, donated by all the people of Valencia, and directed by the silversmith Francisco Pajarón and other famous artists. Although it was taken in procession through the streets of the city in 1952, it was not completely finished

---

[3] The story of the destruction of this monstrance is described in Chapter Thirteen.

until 1955, and was intended to be "like a poem, constructed in silver in honor of the Holy Eucharist," following the argument of the poem *La Glorificación de Jesucristo Hostia*. In it are represented Biblical personages of the Old and New Testaments: patriarchs, prophets, kings and Apostles, along with the Doctors of the Church, those saints distinguished by their love for the Divine Sacrament, the saints and blessed of Valencia surrounding the *Virgen de los Desamparados*, and on the tower, the Risen Christ with the three archangels and the guardian angel of the Kingdom of Valencia. Several miracles are represented, and among the saints there are images of angels, heads of cherubim, flowers and fruits, wheat and vines. At the base there are twenty-eight heraldic shields of the nobility of Valencia, made of gilded silver and enamelwork, with small bells between them that announce the passage of the Tabernacle.

The part that encloses the Sacred Host is the synthesis of all the beauty and grace of this tabernacle, all light and color and a compendium of Eucharistic theology with a sun formed by polychrome rays surrounding a portico with columns of Solomon, inspired by the façade of the ancient church of San Andrés. The bottom of the monstrance, with its angels, columns, and bells, has in the center a transparent temple with the allegorical figures of Faith in the interior, with Hope and Charity on both sides. The transition to the base is done by means of a descent in a cascading spiral, among which are represented the Birth of Jesus, the Last Supper, the Descent from the Cross, and Jesus Christ reigning among the saints, which correspond to a stanza of one of the precious hymns that St. Thomas of Aquinas composed in honor of the Most Holy Sacrament. At the bottom of each one of the Baroque columns appears one of the four Evangelists.

The Last Supper differs from traditional iconography in that the figures are arranged on different levels in the form of a fan, in a typical Baroque style. The representation is of the Institution of the Eucharist, with the Lord standing consecrating the bread; the Apostles are seated reverently, with Judas positioned with his back to Christ. In the middle of the table, commanding the center of attention, is a small Grail, a representation in miniature of the Holy Chalice of the Cathedral of Valencia, which goes unnoticed by those who contemplate the Monstrance.

The Holy Grail in Painting

Although the presence of the Holy Grail in painting makes its first appearance very early in the history of Christianity, it is not until later that the Holy Chalice of Valencia is specifically depicted. The Grail generally appears in the context of the institution of the first Eucharist, inspired by the *fractio panis*[4] of the first Christians, but is nevertheless not always present at the table where there are often many utensils, bowls and plates. The number of cups and chalices also varies, often with no distinction made between the common drinking vessels and the Grail used by the Lord for the consecration, which when it appears, it is somewhat larger than the others and in closer proximity to the figure of Jesus.

The rite of the elevation of the Host was introduced in the twelfth century as a reaction to the heresy of Berengar of Tours, who attacked the dogma of the real presence of Jesus in the Eucharist, awakening fervent devotion for the contemplation of the Sacred Host. This, of course, had an enormous influence in the iconography of the Eucharistic supper that began to show Jesus with the host in his hands, adopting the gestures used by the priest at Mass, a formula that was repeated with frequency in art, especially from the fifteenth century on. In many of these, such as the *Retablo de Sigena* done by Jaime Serra and in the Museo de Arte de Catalonia, Christ is holding the chalice with a host suspended over it in his left hand, and blessing with his right, a posture that is repeated with variations, later tending to depict a solemn Christ raising the Host in his left hand, without the chalice, as in the painting by the Master of Borbotó in the fifteenth century, now in the Parochial Museum of the Church of Bocairente in Valencia.

The first references to reproductions of the icon of the Holy Chalice of Valencia are found in a document dated February 18, 1429, referring to the contract between the abbess of the Monastery of Santa Clara of Valencia, Sor Beatriz Soler, and Martín Torner, painter of the City and Kingdom of Mallorca and resident of Valencia, for whom he was to paint a Last Supper for the refectory of the Monastery in which would be represented *"davant la Maiestate de Ihuxst lo Sant Greal."* The reference is cited by Sanchis Sivera as a note taken from the archives[5], but the whereabouts of the painting are unknown.

---

[4] The breaking of the bread.

It is not until the sixteenth century, however, that the Holy Chalice becomes a true icon in the painting of the popular Juan Vicente Maçip, known as Juan de Juanes, popular for the introduction of mannerism, a subjective, rather exaggerated style that pervaded much of European art at that time. Although his father, Vicente Maçip, did a magnificent representation of the Last Supper in 1545, considered as *"una de las más felices versions del tema en la pintura española de todos los tiempos,"* the Last Supper that achieved most popularity was that of Juan de Juanes in the Museum of the Prado, from the altarpiece of the main altar of San Esteban of Valencia. In this masterpiece the Holy Chalice of Valencia appears on the table in front of Christ, who is holding the Host in his right hand. A variation of the same theme is found in his Last Supper of the Museum of the Cathedral of Valencia, with both becoming an iconographic model of great influence that would be later repeated by Ribalta and Espinosa.

In both versions Jesus holds the Host in the right hand, following the influence of the liturgy, with the figure of Judas with his back to the observer, who according to Evangelical accounts, leaves the Cenacle before the institution of the Eucharist. The table is set with a very beautiful and elegant wine vessel made of glass, with the Apostles expressing their adoration and showing their surprise for this singular occasion. It appears to have been inspired by Leonardo da Vinci, and is perhaps the most popular Last Supper scene among all Spaniards. The version of the Cathedral is more intimate, expressed by the lack of detail in the background and a shorter table, a familiarity accentuated by the posture of St. John reclining on the chest of the Master. Some of the details are original, such as the bones of the Paschal lamb reproduced on a large silver plate, but what is truly novel is the authentic recreation of the Holy Chalice of the Cathedral of Valencia, reflecting the growing interest in the Sacred Relic, to whose knowledge and veneration Juan de Juanes greatly contributed.

One of the first imitations, that of the Holy Supper of the Museum of Fine Arts of Valencia, was considered for a long time to be the sketch for the Last Supper done by Juan de Juanes for the Church of San Esteban in Valencia. This idea was later rejected by Carlos Soler, who sees in it the style of Vicente Juanes, the painter's son, based particularly on the lack of consistency between the drawing and the composition, and the more diluted chromatic tones. Apart from

---

[5] The reference is found in the Protocol of Pedro Rubiols of the Archivo Notorial of Valencia.

the differences in the architectural background of the painting, in which two arched windows substitute the single arched opening of the original, the same elements are presented, including the positions and gestures of the Apostles. As in the original, Jesus holds the Host in his right hand, with the Holy Chalice of Valencia on the table immediately in front of him.

The second theme of Juan de Juanes is that of the Eucharistic Savior with the Holy Grail, portrayed in a series of paintings that is much more prolific than those of the Last Supper, with a faithful reproduction of the Holy Chalice that had enormous repercussions, especially in popular devotion. In this iconography from medieval roots, Jesus is converted into priest, instituting the Eucharist in a scene with far greater theological and liturgical profundity than the betrayal theme of the Last Supper. The tendency was begun by his father, Vicente, with a painting of the Savior in the parish of Villatorcas (Castellón) that disappeared at the start of the Civil War in 1936. The innovation of Juan de Juanes is that once again he reproduces the details of the Holy Chalice of Valencia, at the same time softening the penetrating gaze of Christ the Savior that characterizes the work of his father. As icons of the institution of the Eucharist, it became the custom and devotion to place these paintings on the door of the tabernacle.

There are two variations of this theme: the first is that of Jesus raising the Host in his right hand and holding the chalice in his left, showing clearly the influence of his father. Of this group, two can be found in the Museum of the Prado, and two in the Museum of Fine Arts in Valencia, one with dark hair, and the other fair-haired. The first painting in the Prado is unique for two reasons. In this version, Christ is holding a Host stamped with the scene of the crucifixion, and the chalice is still Gothic rather than a representation of the Holy Chalice of Valencia. All are characterized by a similar double aureole with three rays emanating from the top and sides of the head. The halo has disappeared in the second version, which now depicts the Savior still raising the Host in the right hand, with the left resting against the chest and the Holy Chalice resting on the table. Of this group, the most notable example is the very beautiful painting found in the Museum of the Cathedral of Valencia.

No less worthy of being pointed out are two extraordinary Last Supper paintings by Francisco Ribalta, the first part of the main altarpiece of the parochial church of Algemesí, painted in 1603, and the second done in 1606 for the main altarpiece of the Church of the Colegio del Patriarca. The whereabouts of the first are unknown, which was formerly the centerpiece of the altar, depicting the Holy Chalice on a round table on which St. John reclines in front of the Savior. The first two elements prefigure the round table and Holy Chalice that are also found in the second painting of the Colegio del Patriarca, which appears to have been partly inspired by that of an anonymous painter from Genoa, preserved in the gallery underneath the cloister of the Colegio, and that can be seen on the feast of the Most Holy Sacrament during the octave of the Corpus. This second work of Ribalta has been classified as a marvel, in which the figures of the Apostles are placed around a circular table, similar to an immense wafer because of its whiteness, at the very moment in which Christ is consecrating the Host, with the Holy Chalice of Valencia placed by itself in the center of the table next to a paten. The figures in this large painting (4.785 x 2.665 m) are magnificent, full of nobility and character, all looking at Jesus with the exception of Judas, who instead gazes at the spectator.

Two other painters deserve mention for their depictions of the Holy Chalice. The first is Jerónimo Jacinto de Espinosa of Valencia, whose paintings revolve around the theme of the Eucharist and are executed with an allegorical realism that manifests love for detail. The best example is the Last Supper of the museum of the Church of Santa María de Morella (Castellón), painted in the middle of the seventeenth century. It was part of the main altarpiece of this church, and was directly inspired by the Last Supper of the Colegio de Corpus Christi, painted by Ribata in 1606. The composition is centered on the Holy Chalice, the only object on the table, but not as visible because it is placed between the hands of Jesus and the head of Judas. It was seriously damaged after the Civil War, but restored in 1967.

The second is José Segrelles, a modern painter of Valencia best known for post-Civil War watercolors and illustrations with symbolist and mysterious themes expressed by means of dream-like color schemes. One of the earliest works in which the Holy Chalice appears is an oil painting on wood, representing Christ with the bread and the Holy Grail, done in 1944 for the door of the tabernacle of the Communion Chapel of the church of San Juan and San Vicente in Valencia. The iconography is in the style of Juan de Juanes, with the Host raised and the left hand resting on the chest, with the Holy Chalice resting on the table. This new Juanes filled an endless number of tabernacle doors with the multicolor light of his paintings, more fantastic and coloristic than those of his predecessors.

The altarpiece of Albaida, done between 1947 and 1950, is perhaps one of the best examples of the Segrelles' religious painting. The work depicts the full figure of the Eucharistic Savior standing on clouds that suggest a sunset in the background, carrying the Sacred Host and the Holy Chalice of Valencia, whose coloring is closer to the original agate than many of his other golden chalices. Another work comprises five scenes from the life of St. Francis of Borgia, done for the altarpiece of the Communion Chapel of the Palace of Santo Duque de Gandía, which introduces mystical elements that transcend the physical world. All are related to the Eucharist, of which the Saint was a fervent devotee, who is represented accompanying the Viaticum, celebrating the Eucharistic Sacrifice, giving Communion to his son, praying before the Tabernacle, and conversing with St. Teresa of Jesus. In this last scene the Savior is depicted between the two saints, elevating the Sacred Host over the Holy Grail, executed in mystical white tones that form a stark contrast with the darker, more realistic colors that portray St. Teresa standing before a podium writing, conversing with St. Francis who is seated in a Spanish-style leather chair with a simple black crucifix above his head. St. Teresa mentions him in *The Way of Perfection*, when describing the Prayer of Quiet: "I know someone to whom the Lord often granted this favor; she could not understand it and asked a great contemplative[6] about it; he told her that what she described was quite possible and had happened to himself." The painting suggests the idea of the Carmelite nun consulting with Fr. Francis, and the wise advice that he would have given her through divine inspiration.

One of the last paintings of Segrelles is a large painting entitled the Death of St. Bruno, signed in 1965 and created expressly for the Cartuja de Portacoeli. The scene is situated in the interior of the cell, with a window opening to a starry sky, whose blue and violet tones inundate the room and surround the image of Our Lady, who is extending her right hand. The Virgin is carrying the Baby Jesus in

---

[6] The footnote states, "In the margin of T. the author adds, in her own hand, that this contemplative was St. Francis Gorgia, Duke of Gandía (cf. *Life*, Chapter XXIV: Vol. I, p.154, above). No doubt, then, the other person referred to was St. Teresa herself. The addition reads: 'who was a religious of the Company of Jesus, who had been Duke of Gandia,' and to this are added some words, also in St. Teresa's hand, but partially scored out and partially cut by the binder, which seem to be 'who knew it well by experience.'" St. Teresa of Avila, *The Way of Perfection* (Garden City, NY: Image Books, 1964).

José Segrelles. The death of St. Bruno. Cartuja de Porta-Coeli, Valencia.

her left arm, who holds the Holy Grail that is depicted with the gold and oranges tones of a live ember. It is an expression of the Christian vision of Parsifal, the pure knight who was given the privilege of contemplating the Sacred Cup, the culmination of the process that leads to contemplation and union with God □

a. Juan de Juanes. The Savior. Museum of Fine Arts, Valencia. ***b.*** José Segrelles. Eucharistic Savior. Parochial Church of Albaida, Valencia.

a. José Segrelles. Jesus with the Holy Chalice and the Host. Drawing. *b.* José Segrelles. St. Francis of Borja and St. Teresa. Altarpiece of the Palace of St. Duke. Gandía, Valencia.

Chapter 20

VENERATION OF ST. LAURENCE IN HUESCA

The tradition of Huesca

According to Ambrosio de Morales, Francisco Diago, Gaspar de Escolano, and the manuscript of St. Donato, it can be deduced that the tradition that Laurence was born in Huesca seems to have originated in the fact that his parents were natives of that city and the Grail was sent there after Laurence's martyrdom, as well as in similarities between the Latin name for Huesca, *Osca*, and the fact that the town where the family resided in Italy was called a hamlet of *Capua Osca*, so that when it was read that Pope Sixtus II came to *Osca*, many assumed that he came to Spain rather than a town close to Rome. As the seventeenth century historians Diago and Escolano affirm, ancient writers agreed that Laurence was indeed born in Valencia and left Spain at a very young age, which explains why his homeland is also disputed by the Italians, with many convinced that he was not a Spaniard at all. Even Prudentius, native of Zaragoza, although convinced that Laurence was a Spaniard, did not claim that Huesca was his birthplace, a significant omission for someone of the same region who would certainly not have done so if he were not certain that Laurence was born elsewhere.

Nevertheless, the tradition of Huesca is interesting as it is based on various errors such as those mentioned, as well as the belief that another relative, Orencio, who later became Bishop of Aix, France, was Laurence's brother. Damián Peñart y Peñart, a native of Huesca, explains Laurence's childhood according to this tradition, which is depicted in the art of the churches dedicated to Laurence in that city. It is imperative to explain this dispute between Huesca and Valencia over the birthplace of Laurence, because it is far more logical that he would have been born in accordance with what Donato maintains in his biography, and as other ancient writers have recorded, with the tradition originating, as Ambrosio de

Morales believes, in the next century when the people of Huesca took the veneration being given to Laurence as proof that he was born there. It might be mentioned that at the church of San Pedro el Viejo I spoke with a priest from Huesca, explaining that I was writing a book about St. Laurence and the Holy Grail. He asked me if I was familiar with Peñart's book, and immediately volunteered the information that he does not agree with the tradition that Laurence was born in Huesca, because in his opinion it would have been impossible for Sixtus to visit Spain and take Laurence back with him to Rome. He claims that Peñart had a falling out with the Bishop of Zaragoza after his book was published, and that the Spanish author "wrote from his heart," rather than his mind. This is, in fact, the essence of the dispute, which highlights the fact that Huesca's claim stems more from emotion than solid evidence and common sense. Peñart presents the tradition as follows:

In the middle of the third century there lived in Huesca a simple, just, and God-fearing man named Orencio. He had two homes: one in Huesca, on the site of the Basilica of St. Laurence, and another outside the city, in the place called Loret or Loreto, about four kilometers in distance. Orencio was a rich nobleman and married a lady called Paciencia, his equal in nobility, goodness and virtue.

Paciencia gave birth to two sons, Orencio and Laurence. The two were virtuous and God-fearing. From childhood they were educated in the Christian faith, and at the appropriate time, they began to study in a school in the town. A small monument, halfway between Huesca and Loreto, remembers the place where the mother accompanied her children and where she would go to greet them as they returned from school. With time, Orencio was ordained a priest, and Laurence, a deacon.

One day a virtuous man of Greek origin, named Sixtus, who later was bishop of Rome and was called Sixtus II. He was returning from a trip, as legate of the Pope, to visit Toledo and some Spanish churches, when he passed through Loreto, where the venerable Orencio received him and welcomed him to stay in his home.

Sixtus, captivated by the good qualities of Laurence, took a liking to him, wanting to have him accompany him to Rome. He saw that the young man of Huesca was very firm in his faith, virtuous in the customs, well prepared in his studies, wise, robust and strong for any work or mission. With convincing words, Sixtus expressed his desire to Laurence's parents, who granted his petition.

Before leaving for Rome, Sixtus had a revelation of the martyrdom of Laurence and right there, in the house of his parents, he dedicated to him a chapel, with the desire to honor his name there.

Shortly thereafter, Sixtus and Laurence set out on the trip to Rome with great enthusiasm and happiness, while Laurence's parents remained consoled with the encouraging words that Sixtus has pronounced at the time of farewell. From that day, Orencio and Paciencia, more inflamed with the Christian faith, practiced charity even more ardently with all those in need.

Sixtus and Laurence had hardly arrived in Rome when they found out that Pope Stephen had just died. Sixtus was elected to succeed him, and he made Laurence his archdeacon or first deacon. This position placed Laurence in second place in the ecclesiastical hierarchy of Rome, immediately after the Pope, who was normally succeeded by the archdeacon. The archdeacon was in charge of the administration of the ecclesiastical possessions, cemeteries, income, archives and sacred vessels, and was also the first person responsible for charitable works.

Laurence was faithfully fulfilling these jobs when the Valerian persecution broke out, during which his martyrdom took place, according to the general information left us by the Holy Fathers, Prudentius, and the Passio Polychronii.

We have left Laurence's parents and his brother Orencio in the farm or farmhouse of Loreto. The tradition of Huesca remembers that a day arrived when the Lord wanted to give the eternal reward to Paciencia. This holy woman died and her body was buried in the chapel dedicated to her son by Sixtus.

Orencio, now an old man, was then afflicted and sad. One night, while he was praying, he heard a voice that asked of him, just like Abraham, that he leave his home and family. In the company of his son Orencio, he set out on the road, and guided by a light from heaven, the two came to the fields of Labedán, in the diocese of Tarbes, in the south of France.

Orencio, father, and Orencio, son, soon won the esteem of all the inhabitants of the region and their presence was the reason for several miracles of heaven to aid them, until one day an angel indicated that he should return once again to the land of Huesca.

They were already ready to leave, when his son Orencio was elected bishop of Aix, in France. And the two were still in Labedán when the news arrived of Laurence's martyrdom in Rome, news that the father received from Laurence himself, who appeared to him in a dream and showed him that he was enjoying a reward superior to what the torments of martyrdom merited. At the same time he indicated to him that he should return to his native land of Huesca, because great hunger was being suffered on account of the drought, and he was going to grant the benefit of rain through his intercession.

With great sadness Orencio's neighbors and friends saw him depart for the land of Huesca and his home in Loreto. The inhabitants of Huesca and of the neighboring towns received the elderly Orencio with great happiness, and by his side, all united by prayer, they petitioned heaven and obtained the rain that the dry fields of valley of Huesca needed.

Finally, weary from work, and laden down with age and merits, the time arrived for Orencio to receive the reward for his long pilgrimage. With a penitent attitude and under the protection of his son Laurence, he gave up his spirit to the Lord.

The aged Orencio was buried in the same tomb as St. Paciencia. Those who had joined their lives in holy matrimony were now joined by death in the same sepulcher. Both Orencio and Paciencia later received the petitions and veneration of the town of Huesca, that considered them to be saints and came to them with confidence asking help for the fields that they themselves had worked and watered with the sweat of the brow.

Peñart concludes that, as can be seen, the story also touched on the relatives of St. Laurence according to the tradition of Huesca, whose narration of the events shares common ground with the hagiographic histories that are, without doubt, garlanded with legend. Nevertheless, the ecclesiastical history and the *Roman Martyrology* consider Sts. Orencio and Paciencia natives of Huesca, and the tradition of Huesca presents them, with a very strong conviction, as the parents of St. Laurence, and in addition, as confessors of the faith. Both the *Cronicones* of L. F. Dextro and the *Roman Martyrologies* were opposed to this classification, however, considering them martyrs. The *Roman Martyrology*, due to the posture and pressure of Huesca, later changed the classification.[7]

It is quite interesting that Laurence's parents were formerly considered martyrs of the Church until the town of Huesca forced the classification to be changed so that it would agree with their tradition, as St. Donato was certainly convinced that Orencio and Paciencia were martyred in Rome in accordance with the belief of the early Church. Furthermore, it is not difficult to see the inconsistencies and problems with the tradition of Huesca that set it apart as a legend with little credibility. For example, we know from history that Sixtus II was Pope for less than a year, elected on August 30, 257, and martyred on August 6 of the following year. According to this story, as soon as Sixtus II and Laurence arrived in Rome, Sixtus was elected Pope and Laurence became his deacon. Therefore, in less than a year, Laurence's mother died, and his father, "now an old man," set out for the south of France with his son, Orencio, where they "won the esteem of all the inhabitants of the region," and Orencio, the son, was elected

---

[7] Damián Peñart y Peñart, *San Lorenzo, santo español y oscense* (Huesca: D. Peñart, 1987), p.85-86.

bishop of Aix. All these events occurred before they heard the news of Laurence's death. It is also farfetched to think that the chapel of Loreto was founded in Laurence's honor before he left Spain, based on a revelation, not to mention the extreme unlikelihood that Sixtus II just happened to be travelling through Spain so soon before Pope Stephen's death. The Valerian persecution broke out before St. Stephen's death, not after. It is also rather significant that the French have an entirely different version of the events involving Orencio, the bishop of Aix, who Donato firmly believed was not Laurence's brother.

Damián Iguacen Borau also defends the tradition of Huesca in his book *La Basilica de San Lorenzo de Huesca*, claiming that it has been constant and that there has never been a serious argument to challenge its validity, although he admits that Huesca has no monuments that would prove their tradition, prior to the recovery of the city from the Saracens, and that the lack of documents is explained for many reasons, among them the Roman persecution, in which books and Christian documents were destroyed, the successive invasions of Visigoths and Arabs, and the two fires at San Juan de la Peña, one shortly after its foundation and the other in 1494, which destroyed many important documents belonging to the crown of Aragón.

He uses three arguments to defend the tradition: *1)* that it has been constant, *2)* that there has been uninterrupted veneration of these saints, and *3)* there is evidence in the liturgical customs of the churches, based on missals and breviaries that no longer exist.

From the year 1096 on, date of the reconquest of the city, testimonies of the constant tradition are found. Only six years later, the existence of the church in Loreto, under the protection of St. Laurence, is recorded, and a Confraternity was founded there in 1240, obligating the members to go there three times a year: In procession on May 1st, on the vigil of the feast of St. Laurence to attend the services on that day, and on the Monday after the feast of All Saints to celebrate a Mass. In addition, in the year 1283 another Confraternity of St. Laurence in Huesca was founded at the Basilica.

He explains that the special reason for the confraternities and veneration was no other than the firm belief that Loreto was either the birthplace of Laurence or the place where his parents lived, and that by the year 1316 it was commonly believed that St. Laurence had been born in Huesca, more specifically in Loreto. Clement VII, the Pope of Avignon, France, who obeyed at that time the kings of Spain, sent a Papal Bull in 1387 granting indulgences to whoever would contribute to the construction of the church, and in it said: "Thus, desiring that the Church of St. Laurence of Loreto be honored as it merits, in which it is maintained that this saint was born, and where the bodies of his parents Orencio and Paciencia were buried..."[8] He concludes that from all this "it can be deduced that the people of Huesca of the thirteenth century, at least, believed that St. Laurence had been born in this city."

Iguacen then mentions the fact that the figure of St. Laurence is carved in the capitals of the Cathedral of Jaca, and asserts that the only satisfactory explanation is to think that the sculptor placed them there because he believed that the saint had been born in the diocese, noting that during the Middle Ages the Cathedral of Jaca was intimately united with the See of Huesca and that during that time there were two Cathedrals, rather than one: Jaca and Huesca. The image of St. Laurence is sculpted next to those of the Apostles on the façade of the latter, due to Huesca being his birthplace.

Added to this is the tradition in Huesca that from time immemorial, even during the Muslim domination, St. Laurence was venerated in the same place where the Basilica is now, due to the belief that the parents of the saint had their residence here. He notes that all the historians agree that, keeping in mind the dedication of Loreto to St. Laurence, at least since the first years following the reconquest of Huesca at the end of the eleventh century, it is logical to think that the belief that this saint is native of Huesca was the legacy of the Mozarabic people of Huesca, who can be thanked for the uninterrupted Christian veneration in Huesca.

Finally, Iguacen says that the Liturgical books of the diocese of Huesca express the belief that St. Laurence was a native of Huesca and son of Orencio and Paciencia. The old Breviary manuscript, taken by the Bollandists, says that Orencio was a citizen of Huesca, that he had his residence in Loreto, and that he married Paciencia who gave birth to two sons in one pregnancy: St. Laurence and St. Orencio.

These arguments, however, are not proof that Laurence was born in Huesca, but only that his parents and relatives were natives of the city. Donato indicates that the parents had two residences, one in the city and the other on their farm

---

[8] From a copy of the Bull in the Lumen Ecclesiae, cited by Damián de Iguacen Borau, *La Basilica de S. Lorenzo de Huesca* (Huesca, 1968), p.19.

near Huesca. According to Ambrosio de Morales, the belief that Laurence was born in that city originated when veneration of the saint was later initiated at those sites, perhaps only 100 years after his martyrdom, because the people assumed that it was for that reason, and not simply due to the fact that his parents, also saints, were from the area and that Laurence, a very well-known and illustrious martyr, sent the Holy Grail to those family members who had remained in Huesca. It is certainly logical that the residences of his parents would be converted into churches, and it is believed that one of these was the first guardian of the Grail, hence the fervent devotion and veneration to St. Laurence for so many centuries. Finally, it is not surprising that the old breviaries and martyrologies would reflect this tradition, which may have originated in the fourth century, but it is also noteworthy that the *Roman Martyrology* formerly listed the parents as martyrs, until they were pressured by Huesca to change the classification to confessors.

Donato explains the error for believing that Sts. Laurence and Orencio were brothers, which is due to mistaken information. In fact, Laurence and Vincent are presented as companions in other traditions, such as the poem by Gonzalo de Berceo, in which both are trained by the Bishop of Zaragoza, which is historically impossible, and that Pope Sixtus chose Laurence instead of Vincent to come to Rome with him. It is interesting that Iguacen cites this poem as proof of Huesca's tradition that Laurence was born there, as it is a highly inaccurate literary creation, as discussed previously, which also depicts Laurence enveloped in flames. Finally, the fact that Orencio's relics were brought to Huesca from Aix is hardly proof that he was Laurence's brother, because Donato explains the error: he was the grandson of one of Orencio's brothers, named Facundo, and, therefore, another family member from Huesca.

It can be deduced from this and other clues in Donato's biography that Orencio was much older than Paciencia, who would have been quite young when she left Huesca. The nearly fifty-year difference in time between the martyrdoms of Laurence and Vincent is therefore plausible. If Laurence was born in 225 when his mother was perhaps twenty years old, the year of her birth is 205. It would have been possible for her sister Enola to be born twenty years later, more or less, or around 235. Vincent could have been born from 265 to 275, which would make him between 28 and 38 years old when he was martyred in 303, well in accordance with the belief that he was a young man when he died. With a forty-year or more difference in age, it is impossible that Laurence and

Vincent could have been companions in Huesca, both trained by the Bishop of Zaragoza as Gonzalo de Berceo writes, but no one could deny that they were cousins who never knew each other.

The relics of St. Laurence

As discussed earlier, the veneration of Christian martyrs began with that of their relics, which were given great importance because they were considered to be a genuine expression of the spirit of Christianity, and devotion to these saints was a homage of the faithful to those who gave everything for Christ, a prayer that ascends to the saint, epitomized in the litanies of the saints that repeat the petitions, "pray for us," and "make intercession for us." In the early Church the Christians gathered around the sepulcher of the martyr, especially on the date of birth in heaven, which corresponds to the date of death. In that same place churches were later built, because it was customary from the fourth century on that the altar was constructed on the tomb itself of the martyr, which was the case with the Basilica of St. Laurence Outside the Walls in Rome, the first church dedicated to the saint. Besides, the Romans believed that the sepulcher should not be profaned, and did not allow the sarcophagi to be transported from one place to another.

Peñart relates that it is historical fact that in the year 529 the Emperor Justin tried to obtain a relic of the Apostles Peter and Paul and of St. Laurence for a Basilica that he was building close to Constantinople, but the legates of the Pope refused his petition, alleging that Roman custom did not allow it. Instead, they sent part of the gridiron of St. Laurence and some pieces of cloth that had been in contact with his relics. Years later, Pope St. Gregory the Great (590-604 AD) gave the same response to the Empress Constantina, who had solicited the head of St. Paul for another church in Constantinople. The Pontiff replied, "It is not customary for the Roman Church to touch the bodies of the Saints in order to distribute their bones. It is only customary to send pieces of cloth that have touched the relics. For the Romans and the other peoples of the West it is something completely inappropriate and sacrilegious." On the other hand, Peñart writes that in the East, the bodies of the Saints were being moved and dismembered since the fourth century. The Bishop of Brescia in Italy travelled to the Orient at that time and returned laden down with relics, which he distributed among the other bishops.

Between the fifth and eighth centuries, however, with the invasion of Rome by the Barbarians, many tombs were violated. At that time many bodies of martyrs were transported to other churches in order to protect them, providing the occasion for the dismemberment of the corpses and the consequent distribution of relics throughout all of Europe. Interest in relics grew during the Middle Ages, with an increased demand, so that there was a frequent exchange and donation of relics among kings, bishops, and abbots. The trafficking led to falsifications, and already in the first part of the fifth century, St. Augustine warned against the merchants who, dressed as monks, negotiated the bones of the Saints. Later, the Council of Carthage condemned the relics that were said to have been found through "revelations in dreams." More recently, the Lutherans and Calvinists, rejecting the practice, destroyed many of them, some authentic and some not.

With respect to St. Laurence, he is one of the few saints of early Christianity whose body has never been moved to another church throughout the centuries. His body was buried by Hippolytus and Justin in the Campo Verano on the Via Tiburtina in Rome, now the location of the Basilica of St. Laurence Outside the Walls, and remained completely intact until the seventh century. However, given the veneration to St. Laurence in the entire Christian world and the growing number of churches dedicated to him, which desired to have relics of the saint in order to have a sign of his spiritual presence and protection, relics of his body began to be distributed. The majority of them, however, remain in Rome in the Basilica dedicated to his name.

The most important relic of those that were distributed is the cranium, taken to the Vatican during the pontificate of Sixtus V (1585-1590). It is kept in the Chapel of Matilda, exposed every year on August 10, the feast day of the saint, to the veneration of the faithful in the Church of St. Anne. Iguacen relates that the Bishop of Huesca, Basilio Gil y Bueno, when he was in Rome for the First Vatican Council, obtained a large photograph of the relic, which he sent to the Basilica of St. Laurence in Huesca and the Cathedral. It shows signs of Laurence's torture: the face is still covered with scorched skin, the upper lip is visibly contracted from the violence of the fire's heat, and the tip of the nose is burnt. So much for the theory of some scholars that Laurence was beheaded rather than roasted, as maintained by Patrick Healy, P. Franchi de' Cavalieri, and Delahaye, who obviously did not study the relics of the saint. The Bishop of Huesca died in Rome at 10:15 a.m. on February 12, 1870, while he was still attending the First Vatican Council.

The Basilica of St. Laurence in Huesca has several relics of St. Laurence in its treasury. One is a knuckle from one of the fingers of the martyr, given by king Jaime II to the Basilica on August 10, 1307. King Jaime had a great devotion to Laurence because he was born on his feast day, and obtained the relic from Pope Boniface VII in the year 1297 when he was in Rome. The relic is enclosed in a precious reliquary of gilded silver, exposed for the veneration of the faithful every Friday of the year, the day especially dedicated to St. Laurence. The entire city of Huesca contributed to making the reliquary, in thanksgiving for a victory they won against the Lutherans in Biescas, attributed to the special protection of St. Laurence.

Another is a bone from the head, *ex ossibus capitis*, obtained by Bishop Zacarías Martínez y Núñez in the Escorial in 1920. The relic had been in the custody of priests of the Order of St. Augustine in the Royal Monastery of San Lorenzo of the Escorial when it was donated to the Bishop of Huesca on behalf of the enthusiastic jubilation demonstrated by that city in view of the possession of the relic of that saint of Huesca, because of his faith, glorious martyrdom, and as son of Orencio and Paciencia, also venerated on their altars.

The Escorial has several in its possession: another bone from the cranium, a finger, a tooth, and a piece of clothing. Philip II petitioned Pope Gregory XIII for some relics, and obtained from Huesca some relics of Sts. Orencio and Paciencia, Laurence's parents. Zaragoza and Córdoba have also acquired several relics of Laurence.

Peñart lists relics in the possession of many churches in Rome: the Basilica of St. Laurence in Lucina has part of the gridiron, the fork used to stoke the fire, and pieces of chains, among other things. Other churches claim pieces of clothing, the gridiron, and chains. Many churches in France profess to have relics of bones and the gridiron; one has a tooth, and another, two fingers.

One of the most interesting relics in Italy is called "the miraculous blood of Amaseno," a town of Lazio, about 130 kms. from Rome, and close to Ferentino and Fromisone. It is located to the north of the valley of Ferentino, in a type of amphitheater between Mts. Lepidos and Ausonios. It is populated by farmers. Peñart relates that at the beginning of the twelfth century this region received the name of Valley of St. Laurence, and it is certainly possible that this was where his parents settled after the shipwreck in Italy. Its church, which possesses the mysterious blood, was consecrated in 1165 by Rodolfo, the bishop of Ferentino. Already in that time the church possessed a relic of St. Laurence, as recorded in a document that reads: *Delle grassencze de sanctu Laurentiu martiru, de la graseza del mártir San Lorenzo.*

The relic is a flask with the blood of martyrs, quite common in the region of Naples. Scientists have analyzed many of these since the seventeenth century and it has been proved that not all contain true blood. Chemical analyses, the microscope and the spectrometer have revealed the true nature of the composition of a good number of them, and many contain substances such as balsam, oil, and wine. The rest have turned out to be true blood, or remains of blood.

The relic of the blood of St. Laurence of Amaseno consists primarily of a bloody mass, mixed with fat, ash or dust, and a small piece of skin, with the total contents of the flask in the quantity of about 50 grams. This blood is normally in a solid state, but turns to liquid on the annual celebration of the feast of St. Laurence, beginning with the first Vespers, and turns a more vivid red color, easily distinguished from the other elements.

The manner in which the phenomenon occurs is not always the same: sometimes it liquefies suddenly and instantaneously, and at other times, more slowly and progressively. The complete liquefaction occurs only on August 10, the feast of St. Laurence. On that day, the blood shows maximum transparency and liquidity, and the dust can be easily distinguished on the bottom of the flask, while the skin floats in the middle of the blood and the fat floats on top. All of this is in agreement with the descriptions given by the first historians.

Fr. Enrico Gianetta, beginning in 1942, wrote some articles on the subject that were published in *L'Osservatore Romano* and in the *Quotidiano*, and published a book in 1965 entitled *Il Sangue miraculoso di S. Lorenzo Martire* or *The Miraculous Blood of St. Laurence Martyr*. He says that the flask is not hermetically sealed or sterilized, and that, nevertheless, the contents has remained unaltered for centuries, without evaporating, drying out, or becoming contaminated from contact with the air or microbes. Also, the volume increases considerably during the liquefaction and takes on a vivid red color on August 10 of each year, which has occurred for centuries. The phenomenon, he concludes, transcends the ordinary laws of nature and enters into the sphere of the supernatural. Msgr. Constancio Miranda, Bishop of Ferentino, in the prologue to this book written on Christmas Day, 1964, said, "The phenomenon of the blood that is preserved in the artistic reliquary of Amaseno is an incontrovertible reality. While it is preserved the entire year in a state of coagulation, on the vigil of the feast day it is gradually liquidated until it completely acquires the liquid state, a red color, on the day of the feast."

Legends about St. Laurence

There are a number of interesting legends surrounding the story of St. Laurence that appeared throughout the ages. Many are quite charming, but unlike tradition, these have little to do with historical truth, as will soon be seen. Peñart relates several related to Laurence's infancy and says that perhaps the most well known is that referring to the theft of St. Laurence by the devil, when he was only an infant. It appeared for the first time in a codex by Pomersfeld in 1394, and shortly thereafter appeared in an Italian poem entitled *Leggenda di Sant Lorenzo*. A century later it emerged in an Italian song called *Navitá di Santo Lorenzo*, and finally found its way to Spain at the end of the fifteenth century in a book written by a Sicilian who happened to be a professor at the University of Salamanca, as well as an historian. In 1670 the poet Clemente Negrete of Córdoba included it in a long poem about Laurence, insisting at the same time that the saint was born in that city, rather than Huesca or Valencia. It is now depicted in the reliquary bust of St. Laurence in the Basilica of the saint in Huesca, a sixteenth-century work, as well as in a panel of the altarpiece of the Cathedral of Coira, Switzerland, done in the same epoch.

Peñart notes that there are some variations, with Laurence portrayed as son of the kings of Spain in one, and as the offspring of Spanish dukes in another. For some he was abandoned in the current of a river, detained by a laurel, and for others, he was found in the forest, at the foot of a laurel. Despite these differences, the basic legend can be summarised as follows:

> St. Laurence was son of a Spanish military chief. When he was very small and while he was sleeping in his crib, he was taken by the devil, who abandoned him in the middle of a dense forest. St. Sixtus was at that time travelling along the roads of Spain, preaching the Gospel. And it happened one day that he heard among the trees the crying of a baby. Sixtus began to look for the child with great interest, feeling immense compassion for that child that was crying so inconsolably. Finally, he found him underneath a laurel. He took him in his arms, gave him the name of Laurence in reference to the laurel where he was found, and took him with him. Sixtus took care of his upbringing and education, and later,

when he was Pope, made him his deacon.

It is interesting to note that this legend is a copy of another from the eleventh century about the first martyr, St. Stephen.

Other curious legends adorn the popular sentiment that Laurence was a native of Huesca, according to Iguacen. The first he relates is the above legend, which this time mentions that Orencio and Paciencia are the parents. The second refers to the veneration of the saint in Huesca, and originated when the body of St. Stephen was being moved to Rome during the time of Pope Pelagius I (551–560). The event is described in the Martyrology as follows: "In Rome, the move of the body of St. Stephen, the first martyr, that in the time of the High Pontiff Palagius I, was taken from Constantinople to Rome and placed in the sepulcher of the martyr Laurence in the Campo Verano, is venerated with great devotion by the faithful." Motivated by this move, popular imagination created the following legend:

> *Entering into the church singing in a loud voice, they arrived at the sepulcher of the blessed Laurence. And while they were thinking about how to put the body in it, because the tomb was small and there was little room for both, they opened it, and in the sight of all those present, the tomb of St. Laurence widened slightly and, what an admirable thing! The face of Laurence, as in anticipation of the resurrection of the body, appeared smiling. Laurence went to one side, giving Stephen the other half of his sepulcher, and offering him the right hand. And there the body of the first martyr was placed. And those who witnessed the scene, in admiration, exclaimed, "How courteous is this Spaniard!" For this reason, from then on, they called the Holy Martyr Laurence "Hispanus civilis et urbanus," which means "the Courteous Spaniard."*

The scene is represented in the sacristy of the Basilica of St. Laurence in Huesca in a painting by Jusepe Martínez with the following description, "When to those of St. Laurence the bones of St. Stephen were united, the name of Courteous Spaniard originated."

Iguacen relates one final event, that is more strange than legendary, but related to the St. Laurence's native land of Spain:

> *His Majesty the Catholic King Philip II the Prudent, having asked His Holiness for some part of the relics of the Saint, in order to put them in the famous Royal Monastery of St. Laurence, commonly called the Escorial. His Holiness, complying with this just petition, committed the division and donation to two Cardinals, giving them a piece of paper, so that that they could cut the relic to its size. They had orders*

to make a small steel file like a saw in order to reverently cut the holy relic.

With the sepulcher open, they saw a bone, at the end of which the paper adapted itself well, and they began to cut, but the file was never able to make a dent. Surprised by this, they tried to cut farther up, so that the relic came to be notably larger, and the file had hardly touched the sacred bone when they suddenly found it parted. The notaries testified with a public record of this miracle, and when the Cardinals went to the Pontiff to tell him what had happened, he said, "St. Laurence indeed wants to return to Spain." And then he sent the King the relic, the authenticated miracle, and the file, all of which were in the possession of that holy Bishop of Tarazona, Diego de Yepes, who at that time was confessor of his Majesty, and that same bishop referred all that was said to Dr. Gaspar Ram, Professor of Theology at this illustrious University of Huesca, later confessor of Pedro de Toledo, Governor of the States of Milan and Vicar General of his Army, and now Archpriest of Daroca in the Holy Metropolitan Church of Zaragoza, and I know that many times he has been heard to talk about it and preached it in the Cathedral of Huesca on the feast day of St. Laurence in the year 1615."

Churches dedicated to St. Laurence in Huesca

The oldest of the churches in Huesca dedicated to St. Laurence is San Pedro el Viejo, which tradition maintains was the family parish of Laurence's parents and where his cousin St. Vincent was baptized. It is situated in the oldest part of the city, clearly medieval in appearance. It was first a Roman church, then Visigoth, later Mozarabic, and finally in the twelfth century the present church was constructed, which has survived to the present with a considerable amount of restoration work. It was the only church of Huesca that retained its Christian character during the Muslim domination. In 1096 it was already called San Pedro "el Viejo," a certain indication of its age nearly one thousand years ago. It was in that year when the battle of Alcoraz was won and Pedro I made a triumphal entry into Huesca; for several days the church of San Pedro was the see of the bishop.

After the conquest of the city the church was given to the abbey and monastery of San Ponce de Tomeras in France, fulfilling a promise of the king. It was converted at that time into a Benedictine monastery, and received the benefit of many donations that were used to embellish it. Not long after, in 1177, the Mozarabic church was leveled to build another, which is the same structure that exists today, although restored numerous times since then. Twenty years after it was built King Ramiro el Monje (the Monk) left his reign to his future son-in-law Ramón Berenguer, count of Barcelona, and retired to the monastery of San Pedro to continue the monastic life that he had abandoned when he took the throne at the death of his brother Alfonso I el Batallador (the Fighter). He died there and is buried in the chapel of San Bartolomé.

The monastic life ended at the end of the fifteenth century when the Catholic King Ferdinand, with ecclesiastical approval, removed the Benedictine monks and replaced them with regular priests headed by a prior, Juan Cortéz. The priory was suppressed in 1535 by Pope Paul II at the request of King Carlos I and the city of Huesca so that its income could be used by the Colegio Imperial y Mayor de Santiago that had just been founded. The church of San Pedro el Viejo rapidly declined, falling into complete ruin. Later, Felipe II petitioned Pope Pius V to once again fund the church, and this was done with one stipulation: the singing of the hours in chorus and other devotions in honor of Sts. Justus and Pastor[9], some of whose relics are preserved in the church.

The church and cloister of San Pedro el Viejo were declared a national monument on April 18, 1885. It is not difficult to find representations of Sts. Laurence and Vincent, which abound. Entering the church, the first altarpiece is found on the left, named *Nuestra Señora de la Esperanza*, dated 1584. The Virgin of Hope stands in the middle, flanked by Sts. Laurence and Vincent on each side. Beneath the statues of the saints are lower relieves depicting their martyrdoms. The main altarpiece is Renaissance in style, dedicated to St. Peter, done in 1602 by Juan de Berrueta and Juan de Allí. St. Peter is seated in the center holding the keys. Above him to each side are representations of Sts. Laurence and Vincent, patrons of Huesca, and on the third level Sts. Orencio and Paciencia are found on each side of the crucifixion scene.

---

[9] Justus and Pastor were two brothers who were martyred in the persecution of 304 under Dacian, the governor of Spain under Diocletian and Maximian (the same persecution that claimed the life of St. Vincent, Laurence's cousin). Dacian came to Alcalá de Henares and began to torture the Christians that were brought before him. Justus was thirteen years old, and Pastor, nine. Hearing of the torments that were being inflicted, the two children threw down their books, ran to the place where the interrogations were taking place, and professed their faith. They were severely whipped, and then beheaded. The remains of Justus and Pastor are enshrined at Alcalá, and they are patrons of that city and Madrid.

Another magnificent sixteenth-century altarpiece is that of the *Cristo de la Sangre*, with an anonymous painting of the crucifixion that is noteworthy for its depiction of four angels collecting blood from the wounds of Christ in chalices, one at each hand, another at the side, and the last next to the feet.

The chorus is separated from the rest of the central nave by an iron grill adorned with carvings of three saints: St. Vincent, with smaller representations of Sts. Justus and Pastor on either side, carrying symbols of martyrdom, according to Jesús Vallés Almudévar. I was told, however, that the carvings depict Orencio with his twin sons, Laurence and Orencio, who are dressed identically and are approximately the same height, in accordance with Huesca's tradition. As Orencio the father is normally portrayed as an older man, and the figure in the center is quite young, perhaps thirty years old, I would tend to agree with Almudévar. On closer examination the figure on the right is slightly taller, so the mistaken identity is most likely common, even for those intimately involved with this church.

Santa María de Loreto, the hermitage built where it was believed that Orencio and Paciencia had their farm, is located about three kilometers west of the city, and relics of the parents have been preserved there since the Middle Ages. Loreto was a small town in the thirteenth century, with a Confraternity of St. Laurence, and the church was then called St. Laurence of Loreto, changed at the end of the sixteenth century when it was converted into an Augustinian monastery under King Felipe II, who had dedicated the Monastery of the Escorial to St. Laurence. The church today is quite large, constructed in the eighteenth century, with a large statue of St. Laurence in the façade, the work of Gabriel Rubio, but suffered great damage during the Spanish Civil War.

The Basilica of St. Laurence is the finest edifice dedicated to St. Laurence in terms of its treasury of relics, paintings, statues, and other reminders of the martyr. The first church constructed at the site was probably Romanesque because there is documented word of it around 1224, but little remains of this building. Later a Gothic church was built under the patronage of King Jaime II of Aragón, who was very devoted to the saint. The neighborhood was inhabited by the Muslims who still lived in Huesca, but the Christian population grew to such an extent in this part of the city that two parishes were created in the thirteenth century: San Lorenzo and San Martín. People of both faiths lived together, but at times there were conflicts, such as in 1307 when King Jaime II had to prohibit the Islamic blacksmiths, whose workshops were close to the church, from hammering their metal during the Mass on Sundays and feast days. This Gothic church was also quite small, and was finally leveled in 1607 in order to build the church that stands today. The construction began with more popular enthusiasm than economic resources, and on many occasions it was the people of Huesca themselves who built the church with their own hands, without asking for any material compensation.

An account of what happened in the building of the church, which Iguacen says was a popular and religious event with many interesting anecdotes, was recorded by a priest who witnessed the events[10]. They concern accidents during the construction, when parts of the church fell, either when no one was present, or miraculously missing the construction workers, such as on the occasion when one of them was thrown from his horse, but returned to work completely unharmed. On another occasion a brick fell and although it appeared that it would strike the head of a worker, he inexplicably stepped a bit to the side at the moment of impact, so that the brick only touched his clothing. The priest saw these events as evidence of the providence of the Lord.

The Basilica of St. Laurence is a veritable museum dedicated to the martyr, dominated by the gridiron theme. The façade is in the form of a grill, and above the central door rises the bell tower, situated in the center of the façade, forming the "handle." The niches hold the figures of St. Laurence and his parents, St. Paciencia and St. Orencio, made of plaster: Orencio is kneeling next to a walnut tree with Paciencia to his right, while Laurence holds the gridiron in his hand as the symbol of his martyrdom. It is the work of Luis Muñoz, done in 1782. In front of the façade is the plaza of St. Laurence, an important place for the city, because on the morning of August 10, the feast of St. Laurence, the people of Huesca gather to watch the ancestral dances that are performed in honor of their patron saint, done right in front of the door of the Basilica and in the presence of the silver reliquary bust of the saint, which is taken in procession immediately after the performance. On August 15, the last day of the festivities, an enormous grill is placed on the façade of the church, where it is decorated with flowers and fruits by the people of Huesca who, wearing the typical costumes of Aragón, come to offer one last homage to their saint after a procession through the central street of the city.

---

[10] Padre Francisco Diego de Aynsa y de Iriarte, Fundación, excelencias, grandezas y cosas memorables de la antiquísima ciudad de Huesca, libro II, cap. X.

The sacristy is adorned with seventeen paintings depicting scenes from the life of the saint, done by Antonio Bisquert in 1833, and it is here where the reliquary bust of St. Laurence is kept, the most precious treasure of the Basilica. It is placed on a pedestal with twelve faces representing scenes from the life of the saint. The head is crowned with a laurel, referring not only to his name, but also the legendary moment when Pope Sixtus II found him under a laurel in the forest, took him to Rome, and made him a deacon. The altarpiece is baroque, of gilded wood, made by Sebastián de Ruesta. In the lower part is a bas-relief of St. Laurence distributing bread to the poor. In the central body, between paired columns and two large wooden sculptures of his parents, is found a large painting by Bartolomé Vicente, depicting St. Laurence on the grill. In the upper part there is a painting of the Assumption of the Virgin, by the same painter, accompanied by two sculptures of the martyrs Stephen and Vincent. A sculpture of St. Laurence is located to the right of the main altar, of polychrome wood, taken from the old Gothic altarpiece. Laurence is dressed as a deacon, and holds in his hands the book of the Gospels, a grill and a palm.

The Basilica also has a seventeenth-century altarpiece dedicated to St. Hippolytus, with a large sculpture of the saint. There are ten chapels in the interior of the church, with five dedicated to Saints Andrew, Bernard, Orencio (bishop of Aix), St. John the Baptist, and James (Santiago), and the others to Christ, the Virgin of Montserrat, the Virgin of the Pillar (Zaragoza), the Virgin of Beautiful Love, and Our Lady of Lourdes. Above each one of these chapels are ten paintings that narrate moments from the life of St. Laurence, all situated in landscapes taken from the vicinity of the city of Huesca. They were done by Bermúdez y Echevarría, and mounted in 1931. The grill motif appears on the pews, ceiling, holy water fountain, and other unexpected places.

Laurence has always been venerated in this church with very special devotion and reverence, especially on Fridays that are consecrated to the saint, following a very ancient local tradition. On these days the relic of the finger is exposed for veneration and a special Mass is celebrated. Formerly special devotions were celebrated on the first Friday of every month, but now the ten Fridays preceding the feast day of St. Laurence are solemnized. Fridays are dedicated to St. Laurence because this has been the day dedicated to the saint since the time of the early Church, because St. Gregory Turonense says that it is tradition that St. Laurence descends every Friday to mitigate with his glorious flames the purifying fires of Purgatory, besides being the day when the Most Precious

Blood of the Savior was shed and which therefore evokes the memory of a martyr who suffered exceptional circumstances of martyrdom. Ten Fridays are dedicated, not only because August 10 is the feast day of the saint, but also because it is believed that the principal torments that Laurence suffered were ten, listed as follows: *1)* He was thrown in a dark jail. *2)* He was whipped with very cruel rods. *3)* He was placed in the *catasta*, or cross, tormented with steel *escorpiones*. *4)* They applied red-hot sheets of steel to his skin. *5)* He was torn with leaded whips. *6)* They scratched his skin with iron combs. *7)* He was placed in a terrible jail, without food or drink. 8) This was the great torment of the gridiron or grill. *9)* This was of the iron claws with which they turned his body in the fire. *10)* This was of the salt that they threw on his wounds when he was on the gridiron.

Due to the torment of fire to which Laurence was subjected, and from which he was purified, according to Iguacen, this saint has been connected with Purgatory as the place of purification by fire, and for that reason he has always been considered special protector of the souls of Purgatory. The author relates a curious legend:

> *In 1062, during the Pontificate of Alexander II, a Benedictine monk was praying before the altar of St. Laurence in Rome, and saw how Sts. Peter, Laurence and Stephen were coming into the Basilica, followed by a great multitude of faithful. It seemed to the monk that St. Laurence was approaching him and asking him to communicate to the Pope his desire that he grant special aid and indulgences for the dead. In order to confirm the vision Laurence gave him a cord. The monk communicated all of this to the Pope and the Cardinals, who at the sight of the miraculous cord went in procession to the Basilica in the Campo Verano. On the way they came upon a funeral. To prove the veracity of the vision of the monk and the virtue of the strange cord, they touched the cadaver with it, and the dead man immediately came back to life and sat up.*

> *And the wonders did not stop there, according to the legend, because, when they entered in the Basilica at the time of celebrating the Mass, they saw how St. Laurence appeared above the altar, leading to Paradise, in the form of a child, a soul liberated from the flames of Purgatory.*

In Huesca it is customary to celebrate Masses on the altar of St. Laurence every Friday for those who died during the week, in accordance with what St. Gregory Turonense says, that it has always been tradition that St. Laurence descends to Purgatory every Friday to alleviate the faithful detained there □

St. Laurence. 15th-century Breviary of the Catholic Kings. Monastery Library of the Escorial.

Epilogue

I only vaguely remember the first time I saw the Holy Chalice of the Cathedral of Valencia. I surprised me very much that it was in Valencia, because I had never heard or read anything about it prior to that trip. I picked up a small brochure in poor English that didn't offer much information, and didn't think about it much after that, perhaps because I wasn't all that impressed with the agate cup that is displayed in the Chapel of the Holy Grail. I later considered writing about it, but only as part of a book about relics of Spain in general. It was not until much later that I began to comprehend its importance within the Church, especially in Spain. This appreciation has grown rather slowly, gradually increasing with each bit of information I have found, and at times laboriously translated from Spanish into English. The result is a book that in no way resembles what I expected it to be when I started the investigation.

I do remember the first time I went into the Biblioteca Nacional. I had decided to stay in Madrid for a few days by myself, after a trip with my husband, for the sole purpose of doing some research on relics in that library. Armed with a list of some Spanish sources I had found in a U.S. library, I confidently marched through the door, where I was met by security officers and metal detectors. I was immediately informed that I could not enter without a card and identification. In response to my request for a card, the person in charge replied that this is a private research library, and advised me to go to the public library, which was free and open to anyone. I have no idea where my resourcefulness and courage came from, but I said a quick prayer, and politely protested, explaining that I was writing a book and that I couldn't find my sources anywhere else. For some strange reason, in spite of the fact that I couldn't produce a business card or anything else that would prove my case, the man examined the list of sources I showed him in a desperate effort to gain entrance, and agreed to issue a temporary pass.

On the last day, as I was flipping through a manual card catalogue for information on St. Laurence, I found the manuscript translated by Fr. Buenaventura Ausina. It was located in the Cervantes Room, dedicated to older materials. I placed my request, and after a considerable amount of time the book was placed on my desk. The first thing I noticed was how small it was, a copy in fairly poor condition of an original manuscript kept in Valencia. I greatly feared that I would not be able to read it, but soon found that it was not so difficult once I had deciphered the peculiar characteristics of its early seventeenth-century Spanish. It impressed me so much that I spent three solid hours examining it, and finally decided to order copies, particularly because I had noticed the reference to the surrender of the Holy Grail and knew that it contained information I had never seen anywhere else. I soon discovered that I was the first person to do so, because the library makes film negatives of its old manuscripts before making reproductions of the pages, and none existed for this work.

The copies arrived in the U.S. six weeks later. I started translating the book, found it rather difficult, and left it for a long time. After finishing my first book about the Sudarium of Oviedo, I came back to the work, this time with greater determination, and managed to complete the job. As I could not find a single thing written about this work, I was faced with the overwhelming task of comparing it with all other accounts of Laurence's life, and finding support for St. Donato's account of Laurence's early life in the ancient histories. The second time I approached the Biblioteca Nacional was last June. This time I had a copy of my first book with me, and was issued a permanent card, without questions. I was easily able to find the references to St. Donato in Francisco Diago's *Anales*, including the detailed information concerning the location of the Servitano Monastery. It was not until this last month, however, during yet another trip to Spain, that I found Peñart's book, the story of the Holy Chalice during the War of Independence, and the other sources that completed the story of St. Laurence and the Holy Grail.

Writing this book might be compared to working on a jigsaw puzzle. I have been translating and studying bits of information, without knowing exactly how they would fit together in the end, and searching for pieces in sometimes unlikely places. It is only now that even I can see the complete picture, and I am completely in awe at the result. I set out in the beginning to prove the authenticity of the only extant document that mentions the surrender of the Holy Grail to St. Laurence, and in the process have made so many interesting discoveries that I sincerely hope will contribute to the understanding of Laurence's life, the mindset of the early Church, the nature and importance of relics and martyrdom, the difference between legend and tradition, and the history of what is perhaps the greatest relic known to Christianity: the Holy Cup used by Jesus to institute the sacrament of the Eucharist at the Last Supper.

For some reason it bothered me immensely that so many modern scholars have tried to strip Laurence of his glory, disputing every detail provided by tradition concerning his life and passion, and especially his death on the gridiron. For this reason I delved into the various traditions and legends, in order to show that the Laurentine tradition is very solid, based on logic and reason, and cannot be dismissed so easily. What I found in the end is that Laurence's death by fire is absolutely proven by the undeniable evidence of Laurence's mortal remains, untouched in their original burial place for centuries, clearly showing that the martyr was not beheaded, but burned, and demonstrating unequivocally that the tradition is founded on solid ground. It is the equivalent of finding the smoking gun in a murder trial, hard evidence that simply cannot be disputed.

One of the arguments scholars have used to cast doubt on Laurence's death has been that the traditional accounts mention that both Decius and Valerian were present at his trial and passion, impossible because Decius was already dead at the time. I am very pleased to have discovered the reason for the error, that of the scholars, that is, not of the tradition. St. Donato clearly distinguishes between the *Emperor* Decius who initiated the persecution of 250 AD, and the *Prefect* Decius who presided over the martyrdom. It is a coincidence of name, not ignorance or erroneous tradition, that was sometimes confused by the other sources.

I was quite surprised to find that Laurence's martyrdom and the terrible events of the Valerian persecution have a modern parallel in modern times, manifested in an especially dramatic way during the Spanish Civil War when the famous relic was saved from destruction in the fires that ravaged the Cathedral. The story, written by Olmos Canalda, is only found in a small book I found in the Biblioteca Nacional, mentioned but not described by the other Spanish authors. It is an account filled with emotion, epic bravery, and courage that should not only make us question whether or nor we are truly Christians, but also why a Christian would offer his life for a relic, following the example of Laurence so many years ago. It should be food for thought for all who profess to be Christians. The incredible difficulties suffered by the Holy Chalice during its history, namely the Valerian persecution, the Moorish invasion of Spain, "cleptomaniac" relic thieves, the War of Independence, Marxist barbarians from recent times, and a host of other problems, greatly underscore the authenticity of the relic: why would an insignificant agate cup – the *lapis exilis* of Wolfram's *Parzival* – encounter so much danger if it did not have transcendental significance for humanity? Why was it necessary to keep it shrouded in ignorance and oblivion for so many centuries, where it has remained to the present day?

Writing this book has truly been a learning experience, an inspiration, unbelievably difficult detective work, countless trips to Spain, long hours in the library, the tedious job of translating, and many, many weeks in front of the computer. It has been the most challenging, formidable task I have ever undertaken in my life, as well as the most rewarding. Someone recently asked me if I found it relevant to what I am personally experiencing at this time, and surprisingly, the answer is yes □

Chronology

64-67 St. Peter is martyred in Rome.

250 The Holy Grail is present in Rome, used by the first Popes to celebrate the Mass, saying the words, *"Accipiens et HUNC PRAECLARUM CALICEM in sanctas ac venerabiles manus suas…"* It is believed that the Holy Grail went to Rome with St. Peter.

258 Sixtus II, the 24th Pope of the Catholic Church, surrendered the Holy Grail to his deacon Laurence for safekeeping, two days before he was martyred by the Romans under Valerian in a cemetery. Laurence entrusted the relic to a fellow Spaniard shortly before he was also martyred, on a gridiron. It is believed that the Grail went to Huesca, along with a letter written by Laurence, today lost. It is referred to in Parchment #136 of King Martín el Humano's collection. St. Donato's manuscript also mentions the surrender of the Holy Grail to Laurence, as well as the name of the Spaniard.

553 The Holy Grail is placed in the Cathedral of Huesca when it is built in this year, leaving its former refuge in the former home of Laurence's parents where it had been for almost three centuries.

711 The Moors invade Spain, an event that presented grave dangers for Christians and their relics, who fled to enclaves in the Pyrenees. The Holy Grail is moved from its haven in Huesca to secluded monasteries in the mountains of the Pyrenees, among them the cave of Yebra, San Pedro de Siresa, San Adrián de Sasabe, and San Pedro de Jaca.

777 Charlemagne's army crosses the Pyrenees in an expedition; some believe that he introduced "Grailmania" in Europe after he heard rumors about the Holy Grail being in this region.

830 The Holy Grail is in the Monastery of San Pedro de Siresa, because the kings and counts of Aragón and Navarra made substantial contributions to "el culto a las santas reliquias" or the veneration of the sacred relics. The name of the Holy Grail is explicitly omitted.

1071 The Holy Grail is taken to San Juan de la Peña, where it will stay for almost three hundred years.

1190 Cretién de Troyes writes *Perceval, ou Le Conte du Graal*, a poem with 9,324 verses about the Holy Grail. This initiated a new trend in thirteenth-century romance literature, which began to treat the subject of the Holy Grail as the object of legendary quest.

1134 The first written reference to the Holy Grail is found at San Juan de la Peña. A document by D. Carreras Ramírez, Canon of Zaragoza, dated December 14, 1134, says: *"en un arca de márfil está el Cáliz en que Cristo N. Señor consagró su sangre, el cual envió S. Laurenzo a su patria, Huesca."* *(Vida de S. Laurenzo,* t. I, p.109).

1209 Wolfram von Eschenbach writes *Parcival*, a tale whose story is based on Spanish traditions, which later inspired Richard Wagner to write the opera *Parsifal*. It contains many historical references to the Holy Grail in Spain, including the names of people and towns.

1322 Abulfat Mahomet, sultan of Egypt, claims that he acquired from Jerusalem the cup used by Jesus at the Last Supper. Don Jaime II, the king of Valencia and Aragón, buys this chalice from the sultan and places it in the Palace of the Alfajería in Zaragoza. The Spaniard Oñate hypothesizes that this cup was converted into the base of the Holy Grail by King Martín el Humano.

1399 King Martín el Humano, King of Aragón, as well as Valencia, Majorca, Sardinia, Corsica and Sicily, demanded the Holy Grail from the Abbot of San Juan de la Peña. This is recorded in a notarized manuscript: *"Cáliz de piedra en el cual N. Sr. Jesucristo consagró su preciosa sangre."* The Holy Grail was taken to the Palace of the Aljafería, and later transferred to the king's residence in Barcelona.

1416 King Alfonso V of Aragón sends the Holy Grail to Valencia. It is placed in the Palacio Real, demolished in 1810.

1585 The procession of the Santo Cáliz is established by San Juan de Ribera.

1608 Honorato Figuerola, Canon of Valencia, dies, donating a part of his inheritance to establish an annual celebration in honor of the Santo Cáliz. The feast day is set on September 14th.

1744 During the services of Holy Week, as the Archpriest Vicente Frigola takes the Holy Grail into his hands, it slips and falls to the ground, breaking into four pieces. The repair was carried out by the master jeweler Luis Vicent, who glued the pieces together and fastened it securely to its golden base. There is still a small chip missing.

1809 The Spanish War of Independence against the French troops of Napoleon begins. The Grail is moved to Alicante, Majorca and Ibiza.

1813 After the War of Independence ends, the Holy Grail returns to the Cathedral of Valencia.

1882 Richard Wagner writes the opera *Parsifal*, locating the castle of the Holy Grail in the southern Pyrenees.

1916 The Chapel of the Holy Grail is built inside the Cathedral of Valencia. The Grail remains in this chapel to the present day.

1918 The Archbishop, Salvador Barrera, approves the *Real Hermandad del Santo Cáliz*, or the Royal Brotherhood of the Holy Chalice.

1936 At the beginning of the Spanish Civil War, a young woman named María Sabina Suey manages to move the Holy Grail to safety, in spite of the satanic efforts of the Marxists to take it. It is hidden in unlikely places, including a wardrobe, under the cushions of a sofa, and in a niche carved in a stone wall.

1939 The Civil War ends, and the Holy Grail returns to the devastated Cathedral of Valencia. It first goes to La Lonja, until the Cathedral is repaired.

1951 Marcelino Olaechea creates the *Cofradía del Santo Cáliz*, or the Confraternity of the Holy Chalice.

1959 For the occasion of the 17th Centennial of the Holy Grail, a delegation carries the *Santo Cáliz* to all of its traditional refuges, from Huesca to the monasteries of the Pyrenees.

1960 Dr. Antonio Beltrán, head of the Department of Archaeology of the University of Zaragoza, in collaboration with other European colleagues, carries out an exhaustive study of the *Santo Cáliz* of Valencia, concluding that "there is no evidence against the possibility that this Cup would have been used by Jesus Christ at the Last Supper."

1979 The *Capilla del Santo Cáliz* (Chapel of the Holy Grail) is restored for the final time.

1982 Pope John Paul II visits Valencia. He kisses the Santo Cáliz twice in the Cathedral, and then uses it to celebrate the Mass.

1994 The Holy Grail makes another pilgrimage, this time to Jaca and San Juan de la Peña.

1996 Members of the *Cofradía del Santo Cáliz* go on a pilgrimage to the Basilica of St. Laurence in Rome in thanksgiving for the sending of the Holy Grail to Spain □

Bibliography

Actas del XXII Congreso Eucarístico Internacional celebrado en… Madrid desde el 23 de Junio al 1° de Julio de 1911… Madrid: Imp. del Asilo de Huérfanos del S.C. de Jesús, 1912.

Alejos Morán, Asunción. *Presencia del Santo Cáliz en el Arte.* Valencia: Ajuntament, 2000.

Antuñano Alea, Salvador. *El Misterio del Santo Grial: Tradición y leyenda del Santo Cáliz.* Valencia: Kairos Media and Edicep C.B., 1999.

Atienza, Juan G. *Guía de la España griálica.* Barcelona: Ariel, 1988.

——. *La ruta sagrada: Historia, leyendas y enigmas del camino de Santiago, con la guía más completa del peregrino a Compostela.* Barcelona: Ediciones Robinbook, 1992.

——. *Leyendas del Camino de Santiago: La ruta Jacobea a través de sus ritos, mitos y leyendas.* Madrid: Editorial EDAF, 1998.

——. *Montes y Simas Sagrados de España.* Madrid: Edaf y Morales, S.A., 2000.

Attwater, Donald with Catherine Rachel John. *The Penguin Dictionary of Saints.* 3rd Ed. London: Penguin Books, 1995.

Bajo Álvarez, Fe. "España antigua y medieval." *Historia de España.* Madrid: Sociedad General Española de Librería, S.A., 1998.

Becker, Udo. *Encyclopedia de los símbolos.* Barcelona: Robinbook, 1996.

Beltrán, Antonio. *Estudio sobre el Santo Cáliz de la Catedral de Valencia.* Valencia: Octavio y Félez, S.A., Revised edition, 1984.

Berceo, Gonzalo de. *Obras completas.* Estudio y edición crítica por Brian Dutton. London: Tamesis Books, 1984.

Biedermann, Hans. *Dictionary of Symbolism.* New York: Meridian, 1994.

Bouchier, E.S. *Spain under the Roman Empire.* Oxford: B.H. Blackwell, 1914.

Bokenkotter, Thomas. *A Concise History of the Catholic Church.* New York: Doubleday, 1990.

Brégy, Catherine. *From Dante to Jeanne D'Arc: Adventures in Medieval Life and Letters.* Westport, CT: Greenwood Press, 1978.

Buesa Conde, Domingo J. *Monasterio de San Juan de la Peña.* León: Editorial Everest, S.A., 1996.

Carrau Leonarte, Ignacio. *El Santo Grial y el Tercer Milenio de la Era Cristiana.* Valencia: Cofradía del Santo Cáliz, 1996.

Catechism of the Catholic Church. Second edition. Ligouri, MO: Ligouri Publications, 1997.

Cirlot, J. E. *A Dictionary of Symbols.* New York: Barnes & Noble, 1995.

Collins, Roger. *Early Medieval Spain*: Unity in Diversity, 400-1000. New York: St. Martin's Press, 1983.

Comenge Gabasa, Carlos. *Rutas del Santo Cáliz de la cena del Señor: Conferencia pronunciada en el... Colegio de las Escuelas Pías de Zaragoza el día 12 de Marzo de 1959...*Zaragoza: Hermandad de Caballeros de San Juan de la Peña, 1959.

Cruz, Joan Carroll. *Relics.* Huntington, IN: Our Sunday Visitor, 1984.

Curchin, Leonard A. *Roman Spain: Conquest and assimilation.* New York: Routledge, 1991.

Dal Maso, Leonardo B. *Rome of the Caesars.* Florence: Bonechi-Edizioni «Il Turismo», 1988.

Dictionary of the Bible. James Hastings, ed. New York: Macmillan Publishing Company, 1963.

Encyclopedia Britannica. Fifteenth edition, 1982.

Encyclopedia Judaica Jerusalem. 16 vols. Jerusalem, Israel: Keter Publishing House Ltd., 1971.

Diago, Francisco. *Anales del Reyno de Valencia.* Tomo I (único publicado). Valencia: Pedro Patricio Mey, 1613.

Elpuente Torrente, Lucio. *El Santo Grial, fuera y dentro de la corona de Aragón.* Huesca: Lucio Elpuente Torrente, D.L. 1991.

Eschenbach, Wolfram von. *Parzival.* Translated into English verse from the original German by Jessie L. Weston. London: David Nutt in the Strand, 1894.

Escolano, Gaspar de. *Década primera de la Historia de la Insigne y coronada Ciudad y Reyno de Valencia.* Valencia: Pedro Patricio Mey, 1610.

Eusebius. *The Church History.* Trans. by Paul L. Maier. Grand Rapids, MI: Kregel, 1999.

Ford, Richard. *Hand-book for Spain* (1845). 3 vols. Carbondale, IL: Southern Ill. University Press, 1966.

Forest, Jim. *Praying with Icons.* Maryknoll, NY: Orbis Books, 1997.

Garcés, Carlos. *Guía Turística de la ciudad de Huesca.* Zaragoza, Prames, S.A., 1996.

Greene, Kevin. *Roman Pottery.* London: British Museum Press, 1992.

Hancock, Graham. *The Sign and the Seal: The Quest for the Lost Ark of the Covenant* New York: Crown Publishers, Inc., 1992.

285

Hayes, John W. *Handbook of Mediterranean Roman Pottery*. London: British Museum Press, 1997.

Healy, Patrick Joseph. *The Valerian persecution: A study of the relations between church and state in the third century* A.D. Boston and New York: Houghton, Mifflin and Company, 1905.

Iguacen Borau, Damián. *La Basilica de S. Lorenzo de Huesca*. Huesca: (s.n.), 1969 (Zaragoza: Tipo-Línea).

Jeremias, Joachim. *The Eucharistic Words of Jesus*. Translated by Norman Perrin from the German 3rd ed. London: SCM Press Ltd., Third impression, 1974 (First published 1966).

Johnson, Paul. *A History of Christianity*. New York: Athenium, 1979.

Johnson, Sidney. "Doing his own Thing: Wolfram's Grail." *In A Companion to Wolfram's Parzival*. Edited by Will Hasty. Columbia, SC: Camden House, 1999.

Juergens, Sylvester P. *The New Marian Missal for Daily Mass*. New York: Regina Press, 1957.

Keller, John Esten. *Gonzalo de Berceo*. New York: Twayne Publishers, Inc., 1972.

Livermore, Harold Victor. *The Origins of Spain and Portugal*. London: George Allen & Unwin Ltd., 1971.

Lapeña Paul, Ana Isabel. "Los siglos medievales en la historia del Monasterio de San Juan de la Peña." *San Juan de la Peña: Suma de estudios*, I. Zaragoza: Mira Editores, S.A., 2000.

Llorens Raga, Peregrín-Luis. *Cuando la invasión francesa: Rutas inéditas del Santo Cáliz, relicarios y tesoro de la catedral valenciana*. Valencia: [s.n.], 1964.

Loomis, Roger Sherman. *The Grail: From Celtic Myth to Christian Symbol*. New York: Columbia University Press, 1963.

Malamud, Martha A. *A Poetics of Transformation: Prudentius and Classical Mythology*. Ithaca and London: Cornell University Press, 1989.

Mancinelli, Fabrizio. *The Catacombs of Rome and the Origins of Christianity*. In collaboration with the Pontificia Commissione di Archeologia Sacra and the Vatican Museums. Florence: Scala, 1981.

Martina, Padre Sergio. *La Basilica Patriarcale di San Lorenzo Fuori le Mura*. Rome, 1997.

Mateu y Sanz, Lorenzo y Abad Donato. *Vida y martirio de el glorioso español san Lorenzo: sacados de vnos antiquísimos escritos del Abad Donato / dalos à la estampa... Fr. Buenauentura Ausina*. Salamanca: Iacinto Taberniel, 1636.

Matthews, John. *The grail: Quest for the eternal.* New York: Crossroad Pub., 1981.

McCarthy, William. "Prudentius, *Peristephanon* 2: Vapor and the Martyrdom of Lawrence." *Vigiliae Christianae* 36 (1982) 282-286: E. J. Brill, Laeiden.

McKenzie, John L., S.J. *Dictionary of the Bible.* New York: Macmillan, 1965.

McManners, John. *The Oxford Illustrated History of Christianity.* New York: Oxford University Press, 1990.

Meagher, James. L., D.D. *How Christ Said the First Mass.* Rockford, IL: Tan Books and Publishers, Inc., 1984.

Meller, Walter Clifford. *Old Times: Relics, Talismans, Forgotten Customs & Beliefs of the Past.* London: T. Werner Laurie Limited, 1925.

Merriam-Webster's Encyclopedia of Literature. Springfield, Massachusetts: Merriam-Webster, 1995.

New Catholic Encyclopedia. Washington, D.C.: The Catholic University of America, 1967.

Nigel of Canterbury. *The Passion of St. Lawrence: Epigrams and Marginal Poems.* Edited and translated by Jan M. Ziolkowski. Leiden-New York-Koln: E.J. Brill, 1994.

O'Callaghan, Joseph F. *A History of Medieval Spain.* Ithaca and London: Cornell University Press, 1975.

Olmos Canalda, Elias. *Cómo fue salvado el Santo Cáliz de la Cena: Rutas del Santo Grial desde Jerusalén a Valencia.* Valencia: Imp. J. Nácher, 1959.

Oñate Ojeda, Juan Ángel. *El Santo Grial: Su historia, su culto, sus destinos.* Valencia: Imprenta Nácher, S.L., 1990.

Orrios de la Torre, Tomás. *Compendio Sagrado de la peregrina historia de los Santísimos Corporales y Misterio de Daroca.* Con licencia de José María Magallón, Zaragoza, 1860. Séptima edición. Zaragoza: Imprenta Cometa, S.A., 1993.

Owen, D.D.R. *The Evolution of the Grail Legend.* Edinburgh and London: Oliver and Boyd, 1968.

Packer, J. I., Merrill C. Tenney and William White, Jr. *The Bible Almanac.* Nashville, Tennessee: Thomas Nelson Publishers, 1980.

Palmer, Anne-Marie. *Prudentius on the Martyrs.* Oxford: Clarendon Press, 1989.

Pedro IV, King of Aragon, 1319?-1387. *Crónica de San Juan de la Peña.* English. The chronicle of San Juan de la Peña: A fourteenth-century official history of the crown of Aragon. Translated and with an introduction and notes by Lynn H. Nelson. Philadelphia: University of Pennsylvania Press, 1991.

Peñart y Peñart, Damián. *San Lorenzo, santo español y oscense*. Huesca: D. Peñart, 1987 (Huesca: Gras. Alós).

Perez de Urbel, Fray Justo. *Catholic Martyrs of the Spanish Civil War: 1936-1939*. Kansas City, MO: Angelus Press, 1993.

Poag, James. *Wolfram von Eschenbach*. New York: Twayne Publishers, Inc., 1972.

Prudentius. *Prudentius*/with an English translation by H.J. Thomson. London: W. Heinemann; Cambridge, MA: Harvard University Press, 1949-53.

Richardson, J.S. *The Romans in Spain*. Oxford: Blackwell Publishers, 1996.

Richey, Margaret Fitzgerald. *Studies of Wolfram von Eschenbach: With translations in English verse of passages from his poetry*. Edinburgh: Oliver and Boyd, 1957.

Rodríguez, Jorge-Manuel. "En busca del Santo Grial": 1.- Lo que afirma la Tradición." *LINTEUM* 17-18 (Junio 96): 24-26.

——. "En busca del Santo Grial": 2.- Lo que relatan las leyendas, lo que refiere la Historia." *LINTEUM* 19 (Diciembre 96): 22.24.

——. "En busca del Santo Grial": 3.- Lo que afirma la Arqueología." *LINTEUM* 21 (Diciembre 97): 8-11.

Ross, Jill. "Dynamic Writing and Martyrs' Bodies in Prudentius' *Peristephanon.*" *Journal of Early Christian Studies* 3:3:325-355. John Hopkins University Press, 1995.

Russell, D.W. *La Vie de Saint Laurent: An Anglo-Norman Poem of the Twelfth Century*. London: Anglo-Norman Text Society, 1976.

Sacker, Hugh. *An Introduction to Wolfram's 'Parzival.'* Cambridge University Press, 1963.

Sánchez Navarrete, Manuel. *El Santo Cáliz de la Cena: Santo Grial Venerado en la Catedral de Valencia*. Valencia: Cofradía del Santo Cáliz de la Cena de Valencia, 1994.

Sanchis y Sivera, José. *El Santo Cáliz de la Cena (Santo Grial) Venerado en Valencia*. Valencia: Librería Suc. De Badal, 1914.

Serrano Dolader, Alberto. *Historias fantásticas del Viejo Aragón*. Zaragoza: Mira, 1994.

Schlauch, Margaret. *Medieval Narrative, a Book of Translations*. New York: Prentice-Hall, Inc., 1928.

Sierra, Javier and Jesús Callejo. *La España Extraña: Un viaje por los misterios que permanecen vivos en nuestra geografía*. Madrid: Editorial EDAF, 1997.

Sinclair, Andrew. *The Discovery of the Grail*. London: Arrow Books Limited, 1998.

Synopsis of the Four Gospels. Kurt Aland, ed. United Bible Societies, 1982.

288

The Catholic Study Bible. New American Bible. Donald Senior, General Editor. New York: Oxford University Press, 1990.

The Green Guide: The Spirit of Discovery. Clermont-Ferrand, France: Michelin Travel Publications, 2001.

The Jewish Encyclopedia. Isidore Singer, ed. 12 vols. New York: KTAV Publishing House.

The Navarre Bible: St. John. In the Revised Standard Version and New Vulgate with a commentary by members of the Faculty of Theology of the University of Navarre. Dublin: Four Courts Press, First edition 1987.

Thurston, Herbert J., S.J. and Donald Attwater. *Butler's Lives of the Saints.* Four volumes. Allen, Texas: Christian Classics, second edition published 1956.

Ubieto Arteta, Agustín. *"San Juan de la Peña es tanto realidad como leyenda."* San *Juan de la Peña: Suma de estudios,* I. Ana Isabel Lapeña Paul, Coordinación. Zaragoza: Mira Editores, S.A., 2000.

Ubodi, Flavio. *Saint Lawrence Deacon and Martyr (between history and legend).* Rome, 1999.

Vallés Almudévar, Jesús. *Guía de San Pedro el Viejo.* Huesca, 1997.

Vilaplana Zurita, David. *La Catedral de Valencia.* León: Editorial Everest, S.A., 1997.

Walsh, Michael J., ed. Lives of the Popes: *Illustrated Biographies of Every Pope from St. Peter to the Present.* New York: Salamander Books Ltd., 1998.

Wilkinson, John. *Egeria's Travels.* Warminster, England: Aris and Phillips Ltd., 1999.

Williams, Mark. *The Story of Spain.* Málaga: Ediciones Santana S.L., 2000. (1st edition published in 1990).

Wireker, Nigellus. *Passio Sancti Laurentii martyris.* English and Latin. The passion of St. Lawrence; Epigrams and marginal poems / Nigel of Canterbury; edited and translated by Jan M. Ziolkowski. New York: E.J. Brill, 1994.

Wright, Thomas. *Early Travels in Palestine.* London: Henry G. Bohn, 1848. Republished in 1968 Gregg Press Ltd., Hants, England ☐

Index

Q

R